D0984597

Biblical References
in Shakespeare's History Plays

Biblical References in Shakespeare's History Plays

Naseeb Shaheen

DELAWARE

Newark: University of Delaware Press
London and Toronto: Associated University Presses

Associated University Presses
440 Forsgate Drive
Cranbury, NJ 08512

Associated University Presses
25 Sicilian Avenue
London WC1A 2QH, England

Associated University Presses
P.O. Box 488, Port Credit
Mississauga, Ontario
Canada L5G 4M2

The paper used in this publication meets the requirements of the American National Standard for Permanence of Paper for Printed Library Materials Z39.48-1984.

Library of Congress Cataloging-in-Publication Data

Shaheen, Naseeb, 1931–
    Biblical references in Shakespeare's history plays.

    Bibliography: p.
    Includes index.
    1. Shakespeare, William, 1564–1616—Religion.
2. Bible in literature. 3. Shakespeare, William,
1564–1616—Histories. 4. Shakespeare, William,
1564–1616—Quotations. I. Title.
    PR3012.S5 1989   822.3'3   87-40703
    ISBN 0-87413-341-6 (alk. paper)

Printed in the United States of America

Contents

Introduction

This study of Shakespeare's biblical references differs from those attempted by others in that it considers Shakespeare's references in the light of his literary sources. Shakespeare's plays are often best understood when compared with the sources he used when writing those plays, and that is also true of his biblical references. In searching for the biblical and liturgical references in Shakespeare's history plays, therefore, I have read every source that Shakespeare is known to have read or consulted prior to writing each play, as well as those works that give evidence of having come to his mind as he wrote the play. Only in this way can we determine how Shakespeare reworked his sources, and which biblical references in those sources he accepted, which he rejected, and how he adapted the ones that he did borrow.

An equally important reason for checking Shakespeare's sources is to determine if the many passages in his history plays that resemble Scripture but are not clear biblical references were actually taken from Scripture. Some critics consider any passage in Shakespeare that resembles Scripture to be a biblical reference. Others are more cautious and find far fewer biblical references in Shakespeare's plays. The best way to resolve the problem would be to check Shakespeare's sources. If the passage in Shakespeare over which there is uncertainty also occurs in one of his sources, then we can reasonably conclude that Shakespeare was not making a biblical reference; instead, Shakespeare probably borrowed that passage from his source. If no parallel passage exists in any of Shakespeare's sources, then the likelihood is increased that Shakespeare may have borrowed that idea or passage from Scripture. The value of this procedure becomes apparent when we consider the great variety of opinion that exists among critics as to what constitutes a valid reference.

A few illustrations follow. When Richard of Gloucester orders Hastings's death, he shouts: "Off with his head! Now by Saint Paul I swear / I will not dine until I see the same" (*Richard III* 3.4.76–77). Is this a reference to the account in Acts 23.12? There we read that "certaine of the Iewes . . . bound them selues with an oth, saying, that they would neither eate nor drinke, till they had killed Paul." The fact that Richard swears by Saint Paul supposedly strengthens this conclusion. Shakespeare, however, borrowed Richard's oath from his sources. In Edward Hall's chronicle, *The Union of the Two Noble and Illustre Families of Lancaster and York*, first published in 1548, Richard not only swears "by sainct Poule . . . I wyll not dyne tyll I se thy head off" when he arrests Hastings, but also threatens Lord Stanley at the Battle of Bosworth that if Stanley refused to fight on his side, "he sware by Christes passion that he woulde stryke of his sonnes hedde before he dined." Both of these oaths also occur in Holinshed's life of Richard, since Holinshed borrowed freely from Hall, often word for word. Richard's oath about Hastings also occurs in the anonymous play, *The True Tragedy of Richard the Third*: "By the blessed Saint *Paule* I sweare, I will not dine till I see the traitors head," as well as in Sir Thomas More's *The History of King Richard the Third*, written about 1513, upon which both Hall and Holinshed relied heavily.

That being the case, it seems clear that Shakespeare borrowed this passage from his sources and was not making a biblical reference. Even if he was aware of the similarity between his sources and the account in Acts (and that similarity is not as close as it should be to be considered a clear reference), it is best to conclude that Shakespeare was not making a conscious reference to Scripture at 3.4.76–77.

Consider also the words of Henry to Queen Katherine in *Henry VIII:*

> Half your suit
> Never name to us; you have half our power.
> The other moi'ty ere you ask is given.
>
> (1.2.10–12)

Were these words of Henry inspired by King Herod's words to the daughter of Herodias at Mark 6:22–23? The account relates that on the occasion of Herod's birthday celebration with all of his lords and captains, Herodias's daughter danced before Herod and his guests and he was so pleased with her that he "said vnto the maide, Aske of me what thou wilt, and I will giue it thee. And he sweare vnto her, Whatsoeuer thou shalt aske of mee, I will giue it thee, euen vnto the halfe of my kingdome."

Although the spirit of Henry's words and those of Herod are the same, the comparison of Henry and Katherine to Herod and Herodias's daughter is strange, and at first glance appears to be farfetched. But a check of all of Shakespeare's sources for *Henry VIII* reveals nothing remotely parallel to Shakespeare's passage. That passage seems to have originated with Shakespeare himself. That being so, the chances that Shakespeare patterned these lines on the account in the Gospel of Mark are greatly increased. If true, this would be another example of Shakespeare borrowing Scripture as best fits the needs of his drama regardless of context, and without seeking to suggest an allegory between any of these four characters.

Finally, consider Philip the Bastard's words in *King John:* "I am amaz'd, methinks, and lose my way / Among the thorns and dangers of this world" (4.3.140–41). Are these words based on Jesus' parable of the sower in both

Matthew and Luke where Jesus said that the person who "receiueth the seede among thornes, is he that heareth the word: but the care of this worlde, and the deceitfulnes of riches choke the worde" (Matt. 13:22)? The resemblance is not readily apparent on first reading the play. If a parallel passage occurs in any of Shakespeare's sources for the play, especially in *The Troublesome Raigne of Iohn King of England* that he followed closely, then the answer would be No. The parallel passage in Shakespeare's source would be Shakespeare's inspiration for the Bastard's words, and the resemblance to Scripture would be accidental. But since none of Shakespeare's sources contain anything parallel to these words, it seems plausible that Shakespeare had in mind Jesus' parable of the sower, although the circumstances under which the Bastard speaks these words differ considerably from the context of the parable.

I have checked Shakespeare's sources repeatedly not only for passages such as these over which there is uncertainty, but for every reference listed in this volume. Even in instances where a reference to Scripture seems certain, if a similar passage also occurs in any of Shakespeare's sources, then that passage is pointed out with the words, "Closest parallel in Shakespeare's sources. . . ." This comparison will enable the reader to judge for himself to what extent Shakespeare's biblical reference may have been influenced by a similar passage in his sources, or whether that passage, although not itself a reference, may have suggested the biblical reference that Shakespeare makes in his play. If no quotation from one of Shakespeare's sources appears after a reference, it should be understood that there is no similar passage in any of Shakespeare's sources and that the reference is Shakespeare's own.

I have made every effort to find not only all of Shakespeare's biblical references, but also his references to the *Book of Common Prayer* and the *Book of Homilies*. My aim, however, has not been to present the longest list of references. Many marginal items that have been suggested by previous authorities have been excluded, since they are not *bona fide* references. On the other hand, many references that have been overlooked by previous scholars are included for the first time.

Unless indicated otherwise, quotations are made from the Geneva Bible of 1582, *Short-Title Catalogue* 2133. Whenever other versions are referred to, the following editions have been used:

Bishops' Bible	1584	*STC* 2141
Great Bible	1553	*STC* 2091
Coverdale Bible	1553	*STC* 2090
Matthew Bible	1549	*STC* 2077
Taverner Bible	1539	*STC* 2067
Tyndale's New Testament	1535	*STC* 2830

Rheim's New Testament   1582   *STC* 2884
Douay Old Testament, 2 vols.   1609–10   *STC* 2207

Quotations from the Psalms appear from the Prayer Book Psalter, the version of the Psalms that was said or sung daily in the morning and evening services of the Anglican Church, the version of the Psalms that Shakespeare heard most often. The Psalter was actually Coverdale's version of the Psalms as it appeared in the Great Bible. That version was adopted by the Prayer Books of 1549, 1552, and 1559 and became the Psalter used in all the services of the English Church. I have used the 1584 edition of the Psalter that was published in the Bishops' Bible cited above.

Sternhold and Hopkins' highly popular metrical version of the Psalms is quoted from the 1583 edition published by John Day (*STC* 2466). Tomson's New Testament is according to the edition of 1583 (*STC* 2885), and the Junius Revelation follows the edition of 1600 (*STC* 2991). Passages from the Latin Vulgate follow the edition of 1598, published in Rome on the Vatican Press.

Quotations from the *Book of Common Prayer* are from the 1605 edition, *STC* 16329ᵃ. The text for the *Book of Homilies* is that of 1623 (*STC* 13659), a Jacobean reprint of the Elizabethan Homilies, but I have also consulted *The Seconde Tome of Homelyes*, 1563 (*STC* 13663).

Except for Tyndale's New Testament and the Taverner Bible, which I have been unable to acquire, my research into Shakespeare's use of Scripture has been done in original editions of all these Bibles. Thus in attempting to determine which Bible Shakespeare used, I have not had to rely on the readings of reprints, including hexapla and octapla editions of the Bible, which are not always reliable. Although exceptionally rare, both Tyndale's New Testament and the Taverner Bible are available on microfilm. Whenever it seemed necessary, I checked the text of the Geneva Bible, the most popular version of the day, in as many editions of the Geneva Bible as was necessary, using my collection of over seventy different editions.

The text of Shakespeare's plays is that of *The Riverside Shakespeare*, edited by G. Blakemore Evans, 1974. Unless indicated otherwise, I have re-produced passages from Shakespeare exactly as they appear in *The Riverside Shakespeare*, but have often added an initial capital letter and end punctuation, even though such punctuation does not occur in the text. Shakespeare's sources are most frequently quoted from Geoffrey Bullough's *Narrative and Dramatic Sources of Shakespeare*, eight volumes, 1957–75. References to the *Short-Title Catalogue* are to the second edition, two volumes, 1976–86.

Biblical References
in Shakespeare's History Plays

1
The English Bible in Shakespeare's Day

John Wycliffe

The history of the English Bible properly begins with the Oxford theologian John Wycliffe.[1] Between 1380 and 1400, Wycliffe and his followers produced two versions of the Bible, not from the original Hebrew and Greek, but from the Latin Vulgate. This was the first complete Bible to be translated into English that Shakespeare could have consulted; only extracts of Scripture had appeared in English prior to Wycliffe's time.

The outstanding characteristic of the Wycliffe Bible is its highly Latinate diction. The Latin order of words is often retained and Latin constructions are imitated in English. So literal was the first translation that no sooner was it completed than a revision was undertaken into more idiomatic English. In spite of its shortcomings, the Wycliffe Bible continued to be circulated widely until it was superseded by printed Tudor versions of the sixteenth century.

It is unlikely that Shakespeare possessed a copy of the Wycliffe Bible or that it had any influence on him, for it was not printed until 1731, when the New Testament of the revised version was first published. The invention of printing opened up a completely new chapter of Bible history. Once English Bibles began to be printed, a variety of translations became readily available to Shakespeare.

William Tyndale

In 1526 William Tyndale printed his New Testament in English. His was the first new English translation since Wycliffe's, which by that time had become difficult to read. Tyndale translated not from the Latin Vulgate, but from the original Greek. He was forced to publish his version on the Continent, but English merchants smuggled copies into England by the hundreds, often hidden in bales of merchandise. Tyndale was unable to finish translating the entire Bible. In 1530 he published his translation of the Pentateuch and in 1535, his final revision of the New Testament. Then he was arrested, imprisoned, and burned at the stake in 1536.

It would be difficult to emphasize sufficiently the debt that the English Bible owes to Tyndale. The debt is not because he was the first to translate from the original Hebrew and Greek, but because of his matchless style that has influenced the English language so profoundly. His was a clear and direct English prose, free from needless ornament. He was also innovative and either coined or was among the first to use many words and phrases that are still current today. The fact remains that all of the later sixteenth-century English Bibles (with the exception of the Rheims New Testament with its highly Latinate diction) were but improvements on Tyndale's basic style. One-third of the text of the King James New Testament is worded exactly as Tyndale left it. In the remaining two-thirds, the underlying sentence structure follows the pattern that Tyndale laid down. The same is true of Tyndale's translation of the Old Testament.

Miles Coverdale

The work of translating the Bible that Tyndale left unfinished was completed by Miles Coverdale, an acquaintance of Tyndale whose name stands second in importance only to Tyndale's in the history of the English Bible. Coverdale's Bible was the first complete Bible to be printed in English. In 1529, Coverdale spent eight months at Hamburg helping Tyndale with his translation of the Pentateuch. Coverdale's complete English Bible appeared in 1535. Tyndale had not yet been executed when it appeared.

The Coverdale Bible was not, as is often supposed, a mere completion of Tyndale's work. Coverdale relied heavily on Tyndale in the portions of the Bible that Tyndale had already translated, yet his version was a new translation, not from the original Hebrew and Greek, but from a total of five Latin, German, and English versions. He had an ear for rhythm and balanced utterance, so that in numerous instances where he differs from Tyndale, his readings were adopted by the translators of the Authorized Version of 1611. His style is not so vigorous or terse as Tyndale's, but it is smoother and more melodious.

Coverdale is at his best in his translation of the Psalms, and the version of the Psalms that he prepared for a later translation, the Great Bible, had a profound influence on Shakespeare. The Psalter of the Anglican Church, the version of the Psalms that was said daily during Morning and Evening Prayer, was based on Coverdale's version of the Psalms that appeared in the Great Bible. Whenever it is possible to trace Shakespeare's references to the Psalms to a particular version, it is almost always to the Psalter.

Coverdale separated the Apocrypha from the rest of the Old Testament. He followed the lead of European translations and placed the Apocrypha between the Old and New Testaments. In time, the Apocrypha was dropped altogether from Protestant versions of the Bible, but it was well known to

Shakespeare, for it appeared in all complete English Bibles published during his lifetime. When the Authorized Version of 1611 appeared, it included the Apocrypha.

Thomas Matthew

While Coverdale worked on his translation, another version was being prepared. Printed in Antwerp and published in England, the new version was called "Matthew's Bible," since its compiler, John Rogers, adopted the pseudonym "Thomas Matthew," lest he meet Tyndale's fate. Before Tyndale was executed, Rogers obtained from him the portion of the Bible from Joshua to Second Chronicles that Tyndale had translated but was unable to publish. These Rogers printed for the first time along with Tyndale's 1530 edition of the Pentateuch, Coverdale's translation of the rest of the Old Testament and the Apocrypha, and Tyndale's 1535 New Testament. Thus Rogers's work involved no translation, only compilation, and was two-thirds the work of Tyndale and one-third that of Coverdale. Yet, whereas Tyndale's translation under his own name had been banned in England, Matthew's Bible, which was basically Tyndale's, was granted a royal license when it appeared in 1537. Its title page bore the words: "Set forth with the Kinges most gracyous lycence." Thus it came about that Tyndale's work greatly influenced subsequent versions of the Bible.

Richard Taverner

Before we come to the well-known Great Bible of 1539, Taverner's Bible, also published in 1539, must be mentioned. The Taverner Bible was a revision of Matthew's Bible made at the request of the printers. It was the first English Bible to be printed entirely in England. Richard Taverner was a lawyer known to be an outstanding Greek scholar. He knew no Hebrew and thus used the Vulgate to revise the Old Testament portion of Matthew's Bible. A prominent feature of his version is its terse, vigorous style, even more Anglo-Saxon than Tyndale's. Although some of the phrases he coined were adopted by later versions, his influence on later versions was minimal. It is unfortunate that his Bible had to compete with the Great Bible, which had royal sanction and thus eclipsed his version.

The Great Bible

Coverdale played the principal part in the production of the Great Bible. In 1538, Cromwell commissioned him to prepare another English Bible.

Coverdale revised Matthew's Bible, rather than his own version. The Apocrypha was left almost as it had been in Matthew's Bible. The new revision lacked Tyndale's vitality, but it made many minor improvements.

The Great Bible, so called because of its large size, was the first authorized version of the English Bible, and a copy was ordered to be placed in every church. Previous Bibles had only been given royal license, that is, they were allowed to circulate. The first edition of the Great Bible appeared in April of 1539, and by December of 1541 seven editions had been published. An impressive preface by Cranmer appeared in the second and all five subsequent editions, and thus the Great Bible is often called "Cranmer's Bible," although Cranmer had nothing to do with the translating work. The second edition of April 1540, thoroughly revised, became the standard text, and bore the words, "This is the Byble apoynted to the vse of the churches."

The novelty of making an English Bible freely available to the people led to a variety of interpretations and many disorders, and Henry's government reversed its position and took steps to restrict circulation of the Bible. An act of 1543 prohibited the use of the Tyndale or any other annotated Bible in English. Soon the Great Bible alone remained unforbidden and a great destruction of earlier Bibles and Testaments took place.

Considering the reaction against and destruction of Bibles in the latter part of Henry's reign, the chances that Shakespeare possessed a Bible published prior to 1547, with the possible exception of the Great Bible, are slight. Sir Thomas More and Bishop Tunstall succeeded in destroying most of the Tyndale Bibles that had been smuggled into England earlier, and by 1547 most English Bibles, except for the seven editions of the Great Bible, had been destroyed.

With the accession of Edward VI in 1547, many editions of the Bible followed each other in rapid succession. These included eleven editions of the complete Bible, twenty-nine editions of the New Testament, besides metrical versions of the Psalms, and other select books of the Bible. The first two Books of Common Prayer, which provided for extensive Bible reading in the churches, also appeared during Edward's reign. But when Mary came to the throne in 1553, public use of the Bible was banned and Bible burnings were held in which hundreds of Bibles in the vernacular were publicly destroyed.

The Geneva Bible

Indirectly, however, Mary was responsible for what would become the most popular and scholarly sixteenth-century translation of the English Bible, produced by the Marian exiles at Geneva. William Whittingham was the principal (perhaps sole) translator of a new version of the New Testament in 1557. That New Testament was thoroughly revised, and in 1560 appeared as the New Testament of the popular Geneva Bible. The reasons for the popularity of the Geneva Bible were obvious. For the first time an English Bible was printed in Roman type. Although the first edition was a large quarto, most editions were published as compact, handy-sized quarto volumes. The Geneva Bible was obviously meant to be quoted, for it followed the Whittingham New Testament practice of dividing the text into both chapters and verses, rather than just chapters, and each verse was made a separate paragraph. The marginal comments in the Geneva Bible made it all the more popular, for there was great demand by the public for explanatory notes.

From 1576, when the Geneva Bible first began to be printed in England, until 1611, when Shakespeare's dramatic career was almost over and the King James Bible appeared, ninety-two editions of the complete Bible were published in England. Eighty-one of these were Geneva Bibles, and eleven were Bishops' Bibles. These statistics indicate the relative availability of the various versions of the Bible during most of Shakespeare's lifetime.

The last Geneva Bibles to be published in England appeared in 1616. Shortly after the Authorized Version appeared, King James would not allow the Geneva Bible to be published in England, since he took exception to its notes. But after production ceased in England, many editions of the Geneva Bible continued to be published on the Continent and exported to England, often bearing the imprint of an English publisher. The last edition of the Geneva Bible was published in 1644 in Amsterdam, eighty-four years after the translation first appeared. It is the Geneva Bible that is often called "The Breeches Bible," since at Genesis 3.7 it says that Adam and Eve sewed fig leaves together and made themselves "breeches," whereas other contemporary versions have "aprons."

The Bishops' Bible

When Elizabeth ascended the throne in 1558, the Great Bible was allowed to retain its place as the official version of the English Church. But the Geneva Bible made the defects of the Great Bible apparent. In 1561, therefore, Archbishop Parker took steps to bring out a new version. He divided the Bible into several parts, and sent each part to a bishop or some other learned person for revision. The revisers then returned their revisions to the Archbishop, who published the new version. Since most of the revisers were bishops, the version became known as the Bishops' Bible.

The Bishops' Bible appeared in 1568 in a magnificent folio volume. More than 140 woodcuts appeared throughout the volume. It displaced the Great Bible as the official Bible of the English Church. The principal defect of the new version was the difference in quality in its various parts, since the revisers did not consult each other to ensure uniformity. The New Testament, for example, was considerably superior to the Old since the Greek scholarship of the revisers was superior to their Hebrew scholarship. Moreover, the superior New Testament was carefully revised in 1572, while the revisions in the Old Testament were minor. That 1572 edition of the Bishops' Bible with the revised New Testament became the standard text.

Were it not for the Geneva Bible, the Bishops' would have been the best English Bible to appear in the sixteenth century. But the scholarship of the Geneva Bible was superior to that of the Bishops'. Moreover, the Bishops' Bible was primarily designed for use in the churches. The average person could hardly afford to buy a heavy, expensive folio edition, yet the last handy quarto edition of the complete Bishops' Bible was that of 1584. The New Testament, however, continued to be published in handy octavo editions until 1617, but that was not sufficient to enable it to compete with the Geneva.

Tomson's New Testament

An important version of the New Testament appeared in 1576, when Laurence Tomson published his revision of the Geneva New Testament. The importance of Tomson's New Testament lay not in the text, but in the notes that accompanied the text. The distinguishing feature of the text is that Tomson followed Beza in emphasizing the Greek definite article. Thus we have, "I am that good shepherd: that good shepherd giueth his life for his sheepe," at John 10.11, and "Syr, we would see that Iesus," at John 12.21. Occasionally the results of emphasizing the Greek article are extreme, as at 1 John 5.12:

He that hath that Sonne, hath that life: and he that hath not that Sonne of God, hath not that life.

Except for this peculiarity, Tomson's New Testament is much like the Geneva's.

The extensive notes in Tomson's text, however, created a great demand for his New Testament. So much so, that it often displaced the Geneva New Testament. Starting in 1587, the Tomson New Testament began to be bound with the Geneva Old Testament and Apocrypha to form a Geneva-Tomson Bible. Most quarto Geneva Bibles printed in Roman type after 1587 contained the Tomson New Testament; black letter quartos and most folio editions contained the standard Geneva New Testament.

Shakespeare appears to have had either a copy of Tomson's New Testament or else a Geneva-Tomson version of the Bible. Several of Shakespeare's plays appear to reflect information contained in Tomson's notes, which made his New Testament so popular.

Franciscus Junius

In 1592, Richard Field published a volume entitled *Apocalypsis. A briefe and learned commentarie vpon the Reuelation of Saint Iohn the Apostle and Euangelist. . . . Written in Latine by M. Francis Iunius, Doctor of Diuinitie . . . And translated into English.* The work consisted of a new translation of the book of Revelation and of the commentary on it by Franciscus Junius, a Huguenot professor of divinity at the University of Heidelberg. Almost every verse in the book of Revelation is accompanied by Junius's extended comments on it, so that the Junius Revelation contains more commentary than text.

The demand for more extensive notes on Revelation in a Geneva Bible was filled when the Junius notes on Revelation were substituted for Tomson's in Geneva Bibles with a Tomson New Testament. The first Geneva-Tomson-Junius Bible appeared in 1602 (*STC* 2902). In these editions, the Junius text of Revelation was generally not used; instead, Junius's notes were substituted for Tomson's in Tomson's text of Revelation. This "Junius" Revelation appears in most folio Geneva Bibles published after 1602 and in most of the Roman letter quartos.

Shakespeare was acquainted with the book of Revelation. Although only three chapters of Revelation were appointed to be said during Morning and Evening Prayer in the Anglican Church (chapter 19 on 1 November, All Saints' Day, and chapters 1 and 22 on 27 December, the Feast of Saint John), Shakespeare refers to Revelation in several of his plays. But no trace of Junius's notes on Revelation is evident in the plays.

The Rheims New Testament

Just as the Protestant Marian exiles produced the Geneva Bible, so also the Catholic Elizabethan exiles sought to bring out a vernacular translation of their own. Of the several schools and seminaries that were founded on the Continent by Catholic exiles, that at Douay in northern France, proved to be the most important. Permission was obtained from the Pope to undertake an English translation of the Bible, and in 1582, the New Testament was published in Rheims, where the college was located from 1578 to 1593. The Old Testament was published in two volumes in 1609–10, after the college had returned to Douay.

The new version was based on the Latin Vulgate and not on the original

Hebrew and Greek. The translators sensed that this was a shortcoming that would bring much criticism, and they devoted many pages of their preface to justifying their use of the Latin. Theirs was a scholarly and conscientious work, published carefully in an attractive format. But it was so pedantic and literal that many passages were altogether unintelligible. Its highly Latinate diction, especially in the Epistles, often resulted in passages that could be understood only by those proficient in Latin. A few of the many words of Latin origin employed by the Rheims New Testament are *supererogate* for *spend more*, *prefinition of worlds* for *eternal purpose*, *exinanited* for *made himself of no reputation*, *depositum* for *that which is committed*, *neophyte* for *novice*, and *prescience* for *foreknowledge*. Even the Lord's Prayer has "Giue vs to day our supersubstantial bread."

Although the readings of the Rheims New Testament are taken into consideration throughout this volume, it is most unlikely that Shakespeare possessed a copy or that he was acquainted with its readings. Arguments by a few Catholic scholars that Shakespeare was an adherent of the Old Faith and was acquainted with the Rheims are too farfetched and contrived to be taken seriously. Whenever a biblical reference in Shakespeare appears to be closest to both the Rheims and the Geneva versions and least like the authorized versions of the day, it is not because Shakespeare possessed a copy of the Rheims as a few scholars claim, but because the translators of the Rheims frequently borrowed Geneva readings in their translation, although at the same time they attacked all Protestant translations. Possession of a Rheims New Testament in Elizabeth's day was suspect. Priests found with copies of it were imprisoned; those who circulated it were often tortured.

Which Version Shakespeare Used

Which of these versions did Shakespeare use? The vast majority of Shakespeare's biblical references cannot be traced to any one version, since the many Tudor Bibles are often too similar to be differentiated. But of the four hundred or so references that are listed in this volume (excluding references to the Psalms, which will be discussed separately), there are at least twenty instances in which Shakespeare is closer to one version, or to several versions, than to others.

Shakespeare referred to the Geneva Bible more often than to any other version. It was the most popular version of the day, and it is only natural to assume that he owned a copy. There are at least ten passages in the history plays in which Shakespeare seems to have the Geneva Bible in mind, or in which he is closer to that version than to others:

1. *Richard II* 1.1.174–75: "Lions make leopards tame. / . . . Yea, but not change his spots." A clear reference to the Geneva Bible. All other

English versions of Shakespeare's day have "catte of the mountaine" instead of "leopard" at Jer. 13.23.

2. *1 Henry IV* 4.2.34–35: "A hundred and fifty totter'd prodigals lately come from swine-keeping, from eating draff and husks." A clear reference to the Geneva Bible at Luke 15.16. All other versions except the Rheims New Testament have "cods" rather than "huskes." The Rheims followed the Geneva, as did the Authorized King James Bible.

3. *2 Henry IV* 2.4.57–59: "You cannot one bear with another's confirmities. . . . one must bear, and that must be you." Only the Geneva has "beare the infirmities" at Rom. 15.1. Most other Bibles have "beare the frailenes." Taverner has "beare the fraylite." The Rheims has "susteine the infirmities." (Shakespeare facetiously has the Hostess say "confirmities" rather than "infirmities.")

4. *1 Henry VI* 2.1.26: "God is our fortress." Shakespeare had the Geneva Bible in mind. At 2 Sam. 22.2 the Geneva reads: "The Lord is my rocke and my fortresse." All other versions have "castle" rather than "fortresse."

   If Shakespeare had the Psalms in mind in this passage, then he is even closer to the Geneva Psalms than to the Psalter:
   Ps. 31.3, Geneva: "For thou art my rocke and my fortresse."
   Psalter (31.4): "For thou art my strong rocke, and my castell."
   Ps. 18.2, Geneva: "The Lord is my rocke, and my fortresse."
   Psalter (18.1): "The Lorde is my stonie rocke and my defence."

5. *2 Henry IV* 4.2.27: "Under the counterfeited zeal of God." The Geneva was the first version to use the expression "zeale of God" at Rom. 10.2, to be followed by the Bishops' Bible, the Rheims New Testament, and the Authorized King James Bible. Earlier versions had "a feruent minde to god warde" (Tyndale, Matthew, Great); "are zelous Gods cause" (Coverdale); or "a feruent mynde towardes God" (Taverner). Shakespeare is most likely indebted to the Geneva.

6. *Henry V* 4.7.61–62: "As swift as stones / Enforced from the old Assyrian slings." At Judith 9.7 the Geneva reads: "Behold, the Assyrians. . . . they trust in shield, speare and bow, and sling." All other versions of the day differ substantially from the Geneva, and contain no reference to slings.

Other passages in which Shakespeare seems to have the Geneva Bible in mind, although these are not as certain as the preceding references, are *2 Henry IV* 5.3.111–12; *Richard II* 1.2.20; *1 Henry VI* 3.3.42; and *2 Henry VI* 2.3.24–25 ("my stay").

In addition to the foregoing passages, there are others in which Shakespeare would be referring to the Geneva Bible if he had a certain text in mind. But since the same thought occurs in another Scripture text, if Shakespeare had the alternate text in mind, his reference could be to a version other than the Geneva, since at the latter text the other version has the same reading as the Geneva. Thus we cannot be sure that Shakespeare was referring to the Geneva.

Consider *Richard III* 5.3.12, for example: "The King's name is a tower of strength." If Shakespeare had Prov. 18.10 in mind, which is likely, then his reference is to the Geneva Bible, since only the Geneva has "The Name of the Lorde is a strong tower" at that text. All other versions have, "The name of the Lord is a strong castle." But at Ps. 61.3, the Psalter has, "For thou hast bene my hope, and a strong towre for me against the enemie." The Geneva has, "For thou hast bene mine hope, and a strong tower against the enemie." Since it is possible that Shakespeare had the Psalter in mind, we cannot count this passage as a reference to the Geneva Bible and to no other version.

A similar situation exists at *Richard II* 1.3.101–2; *1 Henry VI* 1.6.16; *1 Henry IV* 1.2.102; *2 Henry IV* 1.1.47, and elsewhere. It is likely that in at least some of these passages, Shakespeare was referring to the Geneva.

But the Geneva was not the only version to which Shakespeare referred. There are two passages in the history plays where Shakespeare refers to the Bishops' Bible:

1. *Richard II* 1.3.202: "My name be blotted from the book of life." Only the Bishops' Bible has "blot out" at Rev. 3.5: "I will not blot out his name out of the booke of life." All other versions have "put out." Richard's words at 4.1.236, "Mark'd with a blot, damn'd in the book of heaven," are probably another reference to the Bishops' Bible at Rev. 3.5.
2. *Henry V* 2.2.42: "It was excess of wine that set him on." At 1 Peter 4.3, the Bishops' and Great Bibles have, "In excesse of wines." The Rheims has "excesse of wine." All other versions have "drunkennes." Shakespeare most likely had the Bishops' Bible in mind since that was the authorized Bible of the Anglican Church during most of his lifetime. The Bishops' followed the Great Bible, the first authorized Bible in England. It is highly unlikely that Shakespeare's reference was to the Rheims New Testament.

Besides these two references to the Bishops' Bible, there are several passages in Shakespeare's history plays where Shakespeare is *least* like the Geneva Bible and closer to most of the other versions of the day:

1. *2 Henry IV* 5.5.53–54: "The grave doth gape / For thee." At Isa. 5.14, all versions except the Geneva have "therefore gapeth hell." The Geneva has "hell hath inlarged it selfe." Shakespeare is least like the Geneva in this passage and closer to the other versions of the day.

The same point applies to the parallel passage at *Henry V* 2.1.61: "The grave doth gape, and doting death is near."

2. *Henry V* 4.1.137: "Shall join together at the latter day." All versions except the Geneva have, "I shall rise out of the earth in the latter day," at Job 19.25. The Geneva has, "he shall stand the last on the earth."

3. *Henry V* 4.1.180: "And dying so, death is to him advantage." At Phil. 1.21, all versions except the Geneva and the Rheims have, "For Christ is to mee life, and death is to me aduauntage." The Geneva has, "For Christ is to me both in life, and in death aduantage." The Rheims has "to die is gaine." Shakespeare is closest to the standard Bibles of his day in the Tyndale tradition (Tyndale, Coverdale, Matthew, Taverner, Great, Bishops'), all of which have identical readings. He is less like the Geneva, and least like the Rheims.

4. *Henry V* 3.2.22: "Be merciful, great duke, to men of mould." At Job 33.6, all versions except the Geneva have, "I am fashioned and made euen of the same moulde." The Geneva has, "I am also formed of the clay." At Tobit 8.8, all versions but the Geneva have, "Thou madest Adam of the moulde of the earth." The Geneva (8.6 in the Geneva) has, "Thou madest Adam," and omits "of the moulde of the earth."

Other passages where Shakespeare seems to be least like the Geneva Bible are *1 Henry IV* 1.2.88–89; *King John* 3.3.61; *Henry V* 2.2.79–81; and *1 Henry VI* 1.5.9.

These examples make it clear that although there is a definite influence of the popular Geneva Bible in Shakespeare's history plays, there is also a clear influence of versions other than the Geneva. Thus, in addition to a copy of the Geneva, Shakespeare may have owned another version of the Bible, most likely the Bishops', the authorized Bible of his day. These were available not only in large folio editions for use in the churches, but also in handy-sized quarto editions. Seven editions of the complete Bishops' Bible were published in quarto editions between 1569 and 1584 (*STC* 2105, 2108, 2114, 2115, 2121, 2122, and 2142).

When we consider the Psalms, the problem is less complex since the choice is principally between the Psalter and the Geneva version of the Psalms. Shakespeare must have been well acquainted with the Psalter since it was the version of the Psalms that was said or sung daily in church in Morning and Evening Prayer. The Psalter frequently appeared in copies of the Geneva Bible as part of the Prayer Book that was often bound in at the beginning of many Geneva Bibles. There is little likelihood that Shakespeare had the Bishops' Psalms in mind, for its version of the Psalms was published in the Bishops' Bible only four times, in 1568, 1569, 1572 (when it appeared in parallel columns with the Psalter), and 1585. In all other editions of the Bishops' Bible, the Psalter was printed rather than the Bishops' Psalms. Moreover, the Psalter and the Great Bible edition of the Psalms are almost identical, since the Great Bible Psalms became the Psalter. And the Matthew and Coverdale Psalms, which are identical (the Matthew Bible was a compilation of earlier translations), are generally so close to the Psalter that they cannot be differentiated from it. Thus, the two principal choices, when considering which version of the Psalms Shakespeare refers to, are the Psalter and the Geneva Psalms.

In the histories, Shakespeare refers more often to the Psalms than to any other book of the Bible, and whenever his references resemble a particular version of the Psalms, it is almost always the Psalter rather than the Geneva:

1. *Richard III* 5.3.110: "Put in their hands thy bruising irons of wrath."
   Ps. 2.9, Psalter: "Thou shalt bruise them with a rod of iron."
   Geneva: "Thou shalt krush them with a scepter of yron."
2. *Richard II* 1.2.43: "To God, the widow's champion and defense."
   Ps. 68.5, Psalter: "He . . . defendeth the cause of the widowes."
   Ps. 146.9, Psalter: "The Lord . . . defendeth the fatherlesse and widow."
   Shakespeare is closer to the Psalter in both Psalms. Instead of "defendeth," the Geneva has "a Iudge of the widowes" in the former text, and "relieueth the fatherles and widowe" at Ps. 146.9.
3. *Richard II* 3.1.34: "The pains of hell."
   Ps. 18.4, Psalter: "The paines of hell came about me."
   Ps. 116.3, Psalter: "The paynes of hell gat holde vpon me."
   The Geneva has "sorowes of the graue" in the former passage (18.5 in the Geneva), and "griefes of the graue" at Ps. 116.3.
4. *King John* 4.3.138: "Let hell want pains enough to torture me."
   As in the preceding reference, Shakespeare again refers to the Psalter rather than the Geneva in both Ps. 18.4 and 116.3
5. *2 Henry IV* 4.1.213–214: "The King hath wasted all his rods / On late offenders."
   Ps. 89.32, Psalter: "I will visite their offences with the rod."
   The Geneva has "transgression" rather than "offences" in this Psalm.
6. *Henry VIII* 1.1.223: "My life is spann'd already."
   Ps. 39.6, Psalter: "Thou hast made my dayes as it were a span long."
   The Geneva (39.5) has "hand breadth" instead of "span": "Thou hast made my dayes as an hand breadth."
7. *Henry VIII* 2.1.128–30: "They . . . fall away / Like water from ye."
   Ps. 58.6, Psalter: "Let them fall away like water."
   Geneva (58.7): "Let them melt like the waters."

It is apparent, therefore, that no one version can be referred to as "Shakespeare's Bible." Shakespeare was well acquainted with the Geneva and the Psalter. But in a significant number of other passages, his references are least like the Geneva and closer to the other versions of the day, particularly the Bishops' Bible, the authorized Bible of the day.

NOTE

1. For a more detailed account of the English Bibles of Shakespeare's day, as well as an account of the influence of the Anglican liturgy on Shakespeare, see chapters 1 and 2 in the companion volume, *Biblical References in Shakespeare's Tragedies.*

2

Biblical and Liturgical References in Shakespeare's History Plays

The following system has been employed to indicate whether a reference is certain, probable, or possible:

(1) Whenever a passage in Shakespeare is a certain or a highly probable biblical reference, the Bible text on which it is based is quoted without qualifications. References to Pilate, Judas, or to a leopard changing his spots come under this category. (2) If a passage is either a probable or possible reference, the Scripture that it seems to refer to is preceded by "Compare. . . ." Many of these passages are reasonably clear biblical references, but "Compare . . ." is used to indicate a degree of uncertainty. (3) For passages in which the possibility that Shakespeare echoed Scripture is remote, or in which only a resemblance or a parallel idea may be involved, the biblical text is also preceded by "Compare . . . ," but for these entries the comment is made that most likely an analogy rather than a reference is involved. (4) Finally, there are those instances where only a common idea or phrase occurs in both Shakespeare and Scripture. These items appear only in small type enclosed in brackets, where they are cited rather than quoted.

A large number of supposed biblical references suggested by others have been omitted. Thus, comparisons such as, "The killing of the princes in *Richard III* is a massacre of the innocents, and their mother is like Rachel weeping for her children," are not included, these comparisons being too farfetched and general to be considered valid references.

Although I have made every effort to find all the biblical and liturgical references in Shakespeare's plays, I have also been careful not to read into Shakespeare something that is not there, and find references where there are none. And although the decisions on which passages should be included in this volume have been mine, the decisions have been tempered, I hope, by a thorough knowledge of Shakespeare, Shakespeare's sources, Scripture, and the Anglican liturgy, as well as the spirit in which all the relevant passages are used.

1 Henry VI

Although *The First Part of Henry the Sixth* was not a popular play after Shakespeare's death, it seems to have been one of the most popular plays when it first appeared. Henslowe's *Diary* records that it netted a handsome profit at its first performance on 3 March 1592, and that it was repeated fourteen times by 19 June, when the theaters were about to be closed on account of the plague. In *Pierce Penilesse*, published later in 1592, Nashe tells us that the heroic death of Lord Talbot brought tears to the eyes of "ten thousand spectators at least" when they beheld Talbot "fresh bleeding" on the stage. And although we cannot be certain whether Henslowe's reference to a *harey the vj* play is to *1 Henry VI* as printed in the First Folio or to some other play, it is quite likely that Nashe's 1592 reference to "braue *Talbot*" applies to the *1 Henry VI* that we know, in which Talbot plays a leading part.

The authorship of *1 Henry VI* presents more problems than any other Shakespeare play. Some scholars would dissect the play into scenes written by Nashe, Greene, Peele, and Shakespeare himself, or to any combination of these and even other writers. But it is probably best to conclude, as most scholars now do, that the play as we have it in the First Folio is substantially and perhaps entirely Shakespeare's.

Shakespeare's primary source for the play was Edward Hall's chronicle, *The Union of the Two Noble and Illustre Families of Lancaster and York*, first published in 1548 (*STC* 12721–12723ᵃ). Shakespeare also consulted the second edition of Holinshed's *Chronicles* (1587), Richard Grafton's *A Chronicle at Large* (1569; *STC* 12147), and Robert Fabyan's *Chronicle* which first appeared in 1516 (last edition 1559; *STC* 10664). But since Holinshed and Grafton often copied Hall, Grafton being almost a reprint of Hall, it is often impossible to tell which chronicle is being used. The chief importance of Fabyan's account is that it was used for the details of the brawls in 1.3.57–79 and 3.1.76–111.

Shakespeare found relatively few biblical references in these works. The portions of Hall's chronicle that are relevant to part one of the play have some six or seven references. Holinshed's entire life of Henry VI, which covers the material in all three parts of the play, contains approximately fourteen biblical references. The outstanding reference that Shakespeare borrowed from Holinshed is the comparison of Joan of Arc to Deborah at

1.2.104–5. Quite surprising, however, is a reference in Holinshed about Joan of Arc that Shakespeare did not borrow. Holinshed mentions that Joan's holy words, fasting, and prayers were deceptions, "sith satan (after S. Paule) can change himselfe into an angell of light" (3/605). Holinshed's application of 2 Corinthians 11.14 to Joan of Arc is most apt, and that reference is one that Shakespeare used several times in other plays. But for some reason he chose not to borrow it in *1 Henry VI*, although it would have lent itself well to his portrayal of Joan as a sorceress. Thus, most of Shakespeare's biblical references in the play are his own; the few that were borrowed from or suggested by his sources are indicated below.

In the list that follows, page numbers for Hall, Holinshed, and Fabyan that are preceded by the number 3, as in (3.56), refer to volume 3 of Bullough. References to passages from Holinshed's *Chronicles* that are not included in Bullough, are to the second edition of 1587, volume 3 (*STC* 13569, variant 2). These are also indicated by the number 3, but are followed by a slash, as (3/485), to distinguish them from references to volume 3 of Bullough. The reference to Hall's chronicle at 4.1.191–92 for a passage from Hall not in Bullough is to the 1550 edition, *STC* 12723.

1.1.28:   He was a king blest of the King of kings.

Rev. 19.16: "THE KING OF KINGS, AND LORDE OF LORDES."
Rev. 17.14: "He is Lord of Lordes, and King of Kings."
1 Tim. 6.15: "The King of Kings, and Lord of Lords."

1.1.29–30:   Unto the French the dreadful Judgment Day
            So dreadful will not be as was his sight.

A general reference to the biblical Day of Judgment, one description of which occurs at Rev. 6.14–17: "And heauen departed away, . . . and euery mountaine and yle were moued out of their places. And the Kings of the earth, and the great men, . . . and euerie bondman, and euery free man, hid them selues in dennes, and among the rockes of the mountaines. And said to the mountaines and rocks, Fal on vs, and hide vs from the presence of him that sitteth on the throne, and from the wrath of the Lambe. For the great day of his wrath is come, and who can stand?"
Compare also Rev. 20.11–15.

1.1.31:   The battles of the Lord of hosts he fought.

The Bishop of Winchester seems to be comparing Henry V to David. In 1 Sam. 25.28, David was said to fight "the battels of the Lorde."

See also 1 Sam. 18.17, where Saul tells David: "Bee a valiant sonne vnto me, and fight the Lordes battels."

1.1.31:   The Lord of hosts.

An expression that occurs frequently in the Old Testament from 1 Samuel 1.3 and on; a title that designates God as a commander of mighty armies.

1 Sam. 1.3: "To sacrifice vnto the Lord of hostes in Shiloh."

2 Sam. 5.10: "And Dauid prospered and grewe: for the Lord God of hostes was with him."

Ps. 24.10: "Who is the King of glory: euen the Lorde of hostes, he is the King of glory."

1 Chron. 17.24: "The Lorde of hostes, God of Israel, is the God of Israel."

The expression is especially frequent in Isaiah and Jeremiah, as at Isa. 1.24; 2.12; 6.3, 5; 13.13; 23.9 and Jer. 10.16; 31.35; 46.18; 48.15.

[1.1.41: 1 John 2.15–16.]

[1.1.43: a clear antithesis to Matt. 5.44; Luke 6.27–28.]

[1.1.67: Gen. 35.18; Matt. 27.50; Acts 5.10; compare also Gen. 49.33.]

1.2.26:   He fighteth as one weary of his life.

Compare Gen. 27.46: "I am weary of my life."

Compare Eccles. 2.17, all versions except Geneva (Coverdale, Matthew, Taverner, Great, Bishops'): "Thus began I to be weary of my life."

Geneva: "Therefore I hated life."

To "become weary" or to "wax weary" was probably a common expression in Shakespeare's day. Compare Holinshed's comment about the Duke of Gloucester's unwise marriage to Lady Jacquet (Jacqueline): "At length . . . he began to wax wearie of his wife" (3/590). Nonetheless, Shakespeare may have had Scripture in mind when he used this expression. Neither Tilley nor Dent record "weary of life."

1.2.27–28:   The other lords, like lions wanting food,
                      Do rush upon us as their hungry prey.

Compare Ps. 17.12: "Like as a Lion that is greedie of his pray."
Compare also Ezek. 22.25: "Like a roaring lyon, rauening the pray."
If Shakespeare is referring to Scripture in this passage, he is more likely to
have had Psalm 17 in mind than the passage in Ezekiel.

1.2.33:   None but Samsons and Goliases.

A reference to Samson and Goliath, two outstanding Old Testament
warriors. Samson's exploits are recorded in Judges 14 to 16. Goliath was the
Philistine champion whose "height was six cubites and an hand breadth,"
and continually taunted the Israelites, "I defie the hoste of Israel" (1 Sam.
17.4, 10).

Shakespeare's spelling "Golias" is strange. All sixteenth-century Bibles
have "Goliath." The Vulgate and the Douay Old Testament (1609) likewise
have "Goliath." Both fourteenth-century Wycliffe versions of the Bible, still
not printed in Shakespeare's day, also have "Goliath." The form "Golias"
occurs in Chaucer's "Man of Law's Tale" (934). Chaucer was a contemporary
of Wycliffe, but his "Golias" follows neither Wycliffe nor the Vulgate. In
Have with You to Saffron-Walden, Thomas Nashe likewise has "Golias"
(Nashe 3.85). Why Shakespeare chose that spelling rather than the spelling in
all English Bibles is not clear, although some would see this as evidence of
Nashe's hand in the writing of this scene.

1.2.55:   The spirit of deep prophecy.

A similar expression occurs in Revelation 19.10: "The Spirit of prophesie."
Compare also 1 Cor. 12.9–10.
Compare gloss "c" at Judges 4.4: "At that time Deborah a Prophetesse the
wife of Lapidoth ᶜiudged Israel." Gloss "c" in the Geneva Bible reads: "By
the spirite of prophecie." Shakespeare refers to Deborah a few lines later. See
1.2.104–5, below. But "spirit of prophecy" seems to have been a common
religious expression in the sixteenth century.

1.2.77, 84:   And to sun's parching heat display'd my cheeks,

            . . . .

            And whereas I was black and swart before. . . .

Compare these words of Joan of Arc to those of the beloved maiden in the
Song of Solomon 1.4–5 (1.5–6, AV): "I am blacke . . . but comely. . . .

Regard ye mee not because I am blacke: for the sunne hath looked vpon mee."

In Hall, Joan of Arc is depicted as being ugly: "Because of her foule face, that no man would desire it" (3.56). In Holinshed, she is fair: "Of favour was she counted likesome" (3.75). Shakespeare may be reconciling these two accounts by having Joan of Arc claim that when the virgin Mary appeared to her, she miraculously became beautiful. But the thought that Joan of Arc was once dark because she had been exposed to the sun as a child, seems to be borrowed from Scripture.

1.2.104–5:   Stay, stay thy hands! Thou art an Amazon,
             And fightest with the sword of Deborah.

A reference to the prophetess Deborah, judge of Israel, who united all Israel to defeat the Canaanite king Jabin and his captain, Sisera. Judges, chapters 4 and 5. At Judges 4.4, the Geneva gloss says that Deborah judged Israel "by the spirite of prophecie," an expression that Shakespeare uses at 1.2.55, above. Shakespeare's metaphor comparing Joan of Arc with Deborah was probably suggested by Holinshed, although Holinshed places the comparison in a completely different context. Holinshed says that in order to clear himself of the charge of dealing in "diuelish practises with misbeleeuers and witches" after Joan had been burned at the stake, the Dauphin arranged with the pope and other churchmen for a hearing to annul the charge of witchcraft against her. The verdict, handed down in July of 1456, proclaimed Joan "a damsell diuine," and "likened to Debora, Iahell [Jael], and Iudith" (3/605).

1.2.143:   Nor yet Saint Philip's daughters, were like thee.

Acts 21.8–9: "We entred into the house of Philippe the Euangelist. . . . Nowe hee had foure daughters virgins, which did prophesie."

[1.3.8: John 18.22.]

1.3.39–40:   This be Damascus, be thou cursed Cain,
             To slay thy brother Abel, if thou wilt.

According to a medieval legend, Damascus was founded on the site where Cain slew Abel. The fictitious *Travels of Sir John Mandeville*, first printed by Pynson in 1496 and reprinted five times prior to the first performance of *1*

Henry VI (*STC* 17246–51), records that legend. See also Ranulf Higden's *Polychronicon* (*STC* 13438–40). The Bible's account of Cain slaying Abel occurs at Genesis 4.8.

1.3.55:   Thou wolf in sheep's array.

Matt. 7.15: "Beware of false Prophets, which come to you in sheepes clothing, but inwardely they are rauening wolues."

Closest parallel in Shakespeare's sources: During the siege of Orleans, Hall says that Talbot fought so fiercely that the Frenchmen fled "like shepe before the Wolffe" (3.58). See also Holinshed, who follows Hall's account word for word in this passage (3/601).

[1.3.56: Rev. 17.4.]

1.4.70–71:   *Sal.* O Lord, have mercy on us, wretched sinners!
                Gar. O Lord, have mercy on me, woeful man!

A common expression that occurs frequently not only in Scripture, but also in the Anglican liturgy.

Matt. 20.30: "Sonne of Dauid, haue mercie on vs."

Luke 17.13: "Iesus, Master, haue mercie on vs."

Luke 18.13: "O God, be mercifull to me a sinner."

Psalm 51, which David composed after his sin with Bathsheba, begins: "Haue mercie vpon mee (O God)."

The words, "Haue mercy vpon vs miserable sinners," occurs eight times in the opening petitions and responses of the Litany.

After each of the Ten Commandments was rehearsed in the Communion Service, the people responded: "Lord haue mercy vpon vs, and . . . ."

1.5.9:   Heavens, can you suffer hell so to prevail?

Compare Matt. 16.18, all versions but Geneva: "And the gates of hell shall not preuaile against it."

Geneva: "And the gates of hell shall not ouercome it."

If Shakespeare had Matthew 16.18 in mind, his reference could be to any Bible except the Geneva.

The Prayer Book Gospel reading for Saint Peter's day also has, "and the gates of hell shall not preuaile against it."

For the thought of why should evil triumph, compare Ps. 94.3: "Lord, how long shal the vngodly: how long shall the vngodly triumph?"

1.5.13:   Farewell, thy hour is not yet come.

John 7.30: "His houre was not yet come."
John 2.4: "Mine houre is not yet come."
Compare also John 13.1.

[1.5.34: Acts 8.1; 22.20.]

[1.5.39: Jer. 14.3; 2 Sam. 15.30; Esther 6.12.]

1.6.16:   When they shall hear how we have play'd the men.

Compare 1 Sam. 4.9: "Be strong and play the men."
All other versions except Coverdale (Matthew, Taverner, Great, Bishops')
have: "Be strong, and quite your selues like men," parallel to the Authorized
Version. Coverdale has: "Be stronge now an[d] manly." But the Geneva
reading, "play the men," was probably a common expression. Holinshed
uses it when recounting the battle of Verneuil. Holinshed says that when the
Duke of Alencon sought to encourage his soldiers, he "exhorted his people
to plaie the men" (3/588).

2.1.26–27: God is our fortress, in whose conquering name
            Let us resolve to scale their flinty bulwarks.

2 Sam. 22.2–3: "The Lord is my rocke and my fortresse, and he that
deliuereth me. God is my strength . . . my hie tower and my refuge."
If Shakespeare had 2 Samuel 22 in mind in this passage, then his reference
is to the Geneva Bible. All other versions have "castle" rather than "for-
tresse." The expression also occurs in the Psalms, but in both occurrences
Shakespeare is even closer to the Geneva Psalms than to the Psalter:
Ps. 31.3, Geneva: "For thou art my rocke and my fortresse."
Psalter (31.4): "For thou art my strong rocke, and my castell."
Ps. 18.2, Geneva: "The Lord is my rocke, and my fortresse."
Psalter (18.1): "The Lorde is my stonie rocke and my defence."
For "conquering name," compare Prov. 18.10: "The Name of the Lorde is
a strong tower."
For putting trust in God's name compare also:
Ps. 20.5: "We will . . . triumph in the name of the Lord our God."
Ps. 20.7: "Some put their trust in Charets, and some in Horses: but we
will remember the name of the Lord our God."

2.3.7–10:   Great is the rumor of this dreadful knight,
And his achievements of no less account;
Fain would mine eyes be witness with mine ears
To give their censure of these rare reports.

Shakespeare seems to have consciously patterned the words of the Countess on those of the Queen of Sheba at 2 Chron. 9.6: "Howbeit I beleeued not their report, vntil I came, and mine eyes had seene it."

Compare also 2.3.68, "I find thou art no less than fame hath bruited," with the latter part of 2 Chron. 9:6: "Thou exceedest the fame that I heard."

See also 1 Kings 10.7.

[2.4.88: Ps. 100.2 (100.3, Geneva); 119.73.]

2.5.8:   Like lamps whose wasting oil is spent.

Compare Matt. 25.8: "Giue vs of your oyle, for our lampes are out."

Perhaps an analogy rather than a reference, but compare *Antony and Cleopatra* 4.15.85: "Our lamp is spent, it's out."

2.5.8–9:   These eyes . . . / Wax dim.

For one's eyes to become dim was a common expression that occurs several times in Scripture, as at Gen. 27.1; 48.10; Deut. 34.7; 1 Sam. 4.15; Job 17.7; Lam. 5.17. The expression "wax dim" relative to eyesight occurs at 1 Sam. 3.2: "His eyes began to waxe dimme that he coulde not see."

At 1 Sam. 3.2–3 the Bishops' has: "And as at that time Eli lay in his place, his eyes began to waxe dimme, that he could not see. And yer [ere] the lampe of God went out, Samuel laide him downe to sleepe." The Coverdale, Matthew, Taverner, and Great Bibles likewise have "lampe," although the Geneva has "light."

If Shakespeare's lines, "These eyes, like lamps whose wasting oil is spent, / Wax dim," were inspired by this account in 1 Samuel, then he is least like the Geneva, and closer to the other versions of his day. The image of a lamp going out in 1 Samuel seems to have reminded Shakespeare of the parable of the foolish virgins whose lamps ran out of oil, and he apparently combined Matthew 25.8 with the account in 1 Samuel.

[2.5.11–12: John 15.5–6.]

2.5.14:   This lump of clay.

Compare Job 33.6: "I am also formed of the clay."
Compare Job 13.12: "Your memories may be compared vnto ashes, and your bodies to bodies of clay."
Compare Job 10.9: "Thou hast made me as the clay."
See also 2 Henry IV 1.2.7.
Although the notion that man is but clay became part of everyday speech, its origin was most likely Scripture.

2.5.21:   My soul shall then be satisfied.

Ps. 63.6 (63.5, Geneva): "My soule shall bee satisfied."
Jer. 50.19: "His soule shalbe satisfied."
Compare also Prov. 6:30; Isa. 53:11.

2.5.102–3:   Strong fixed is the house of Lancaster,
                   And like a mountain, not to be remov'd.

Compare Ps. 125.1: "Euen as the mount Sion: which may not bee re-moued, but standeth fast for euer."

[2.5.116, "pilgrimage": Gen. 47.9; Ps. 119.54. But the comparison of life to a pilgrimage had become proverbial. See Tilley L249.]

[3.1.4: Acts 7.60.]

3.1.25–26:   The King, thy sovereign, is not quite exempt
                    From envious malice of thy swelling heart.

Catechism: "To beare no malice not hatred in my heart."

3.1.68:   To join your hearts in love and amity.

Some have thought that "love and amity" is an echo of the Marriage Service: "That this woman may be louing and amiable to her husband." But Shakespeare borrowed the expression from Hall where it appears in the same context: that the Duke of Gloucester and Cardinal of Winchester should be reconciled to each other "in perfite love and amitie" (3.70).

The expression seems to have been fairly common. Holinshed records the efforts of Henry VI to bring "perpetuall loue and assured amitie" between the houses of York and Lancaster (3/647), and the word "amitie" occurs by itself several times in both Hall and Holinshed.

3.1.129–30:   Will you not maintain the thing you teach,
                But prove a chief offender in the same?

Compare Rom. 2.21: "Thou therefore which teachest another, teachest thou not thy selfe? thou that preachest, A man should not steale, doest thou steale?"

Perhaps an unconscious echo of a well-known Christian principle rather than a conscious reference to Romans chapter 2.

3.1.196:   Was in the mouth of every sucking babe.

Matt. 21.16: "By the mouth of babes and sucklings."
Ps. 8.2: "Out of the mouth of very babes and sucklings."
Ps. 8.2, Sternhold and Hopkins:

> Euen by the mouthes of sucking babes,
>   thou wilt confound thy foes:
> For in those babes thy might is seene,
>   thy graces they disclose.

3.2.106:   We are like to have the overthrow again.

Some think that this line may be an echo of the Geneva gloss on 2 Chron. 13.15: "Euen as the men of Iudah shouted, God smote Ieroboam." The gloss on "smote" is, "gaue him the ouerthrowe."

But the expression seems to have been common. George Cavendish used the expression in *The Life and Death of Cardinal Wolsey,* written ca. 1556–58, before the Geneva Bible appeared: "By that means we may other [either] escape or elles geve them an ouerthrowe" (EETS edition, 40).

Compare also *Julius Caesar* 5.2.5: "And sudden push gives them the overthrow."

3.2.110–11:   Now, quiet soul, depart when heaven please,
                For I have seen our enemies' overthrow.

Evening Prayer, *Nunc dimittis,* based on Luke 2.29–30: "Lord now lettest thou thy seruant depart in peace: according to thy word. For mine eyes haue seene: thy saluation."

3.2.112:   What is the trust or strength of foolish man?

Compare Jer. 17.5: "Cursed be the man that trusteth in man, and maketh flesh his arme."
Compare Ps. 146.2 (146.3, Geneva): "Put not your trust in princes, nor in any childe of man: for there is no helpe in them."
Compare also Ps. 118.8–9.

[3.2.122, "her old familiar": See 5.3.10–12, below.]

3.3.42:   Let thy humble handmaid speak to thee.

Compare 1 Sam. 25.24: "Let thine handmayde speake to thee."
If Shakespeare had 1 Samuel in mind in this passage, then his reference was to the Geneva Bible. All other versions have either "speake before thyne eares" (Coverdale), or "speake in thine audience" (Matthew, Taverner, Great, Bishops').

4.1.141–42:   Be provok'd
               To willful disobedience, and rebel!

Apparently a paraphrase of the title of the homily "Against Disobedience and Wilfull Rebellion."

4.1.191–92:   But that it doth presage some ill event.
               'Tis much, when sceptres are in children's hands.

Shakespeare's passage seems to be based on Hall's paraphrase of Isaiah 3.4: "Saiyng by hys prophet Esay: I shall geue you children to be your princes, and enfantes without wysedom, shall haue the gouernaunce of you" (sig. q6ᵛ; not in Bullough). Holinshed followed Hall's account word for word (Holinshed 3/656).
Isa. 3.4, Coverdale Bible, current when Hall published his chronicle in 1548: "And I shall geue you children to be youre princes / (sayeth the Lorde) and babes shall haue the rule of you."

The Matthew and Taverner Bibles are identical to the Coverdale Bible. The Great Bible has "them" and "their" rather than "you" and "youre": "I shal geue them children to be their princes, and babes shal haue the rule of you."

But Hall paraphrases Isaiah 3.4 in a completely different context. He makes it part of the Duke of York's oration to parliament claiming his right to the throne.

Compare also Eccles. 10.16: "Wo to thee, O lande, when thy King is a child." Shakespeare again follows his sources and makes a clear reference to Eccles. 10.16 in *Richard III* 2.3.11.

[4.2.26–27: Rev. 6.8.]

4.4.18:   Drops bloody sweat from his . . . limbs.

Compare the Litany, "By thine agonie and bloody Sweate," based on Luke 22.44: "But being in an agonie . . . his sweat was like droppes of bloud."

5.1.9:   To stop effusion of our Christian blood.

Compare the homily "Against Disobedience and Wilfull Rebellion," part 6: "Effusion of Christian blood, destruction of Christian men, decay and ruine of Christendome. . . ." The expressions "shedding of Christian bloud," "spent so much Christian blood," and "streams of Christian blood" also occur in part 6 of this homily.

But Shakespeare probably borrowed the expression from his sources rather than from the homily. The expression occurs twice in Hall (3.65, 71) and twice in Holinshed (3/651). Hall, in turn, seems to have borrowed the expression from earlier chronicles. The related expression "effusion of bloude" (rather than "effusion of Christen bloud") occurs in Fabyan's account (3.48, n. 2). Holinshed also has "the effusion of mans bloud" (3/605). The fact that all six occurrences appear in different contexts in the above three chronicles indicates that the expression was fairly common in the sixteenth century, and was not necessarily an echo of the homilies. "Effusion of our English bloud" occurs in part 1 of *The Troublesome Raigne of Iohn King of England* (Bullough 4.94, line 833).

Compare also *Henry V* 3.6.130, "th' effusion of our blood," and 5.4.52–53, below.

5.3.6:   Under the lordly Monarch of the North.

The devil was thought to inhabit the regions of the north. This was probably based on Isaiah 14.13 where Lucifer, understood to be Satan, boasts that he would exalt his throne "vpon the mount of the Congregation in the sides of the North." *Paradise Lost* portrays Satan as assembling his rebel angels in the "Quarters of the North" (5.689).

In Isaiah 14, the "mount of the Congregation" was Mount Moriah, the mount on which the temple was built, and where Israel assembled to worship. It was located north of Mount Zion, the original city of Jerusalem in Isaiah's time. Isaiah depicts Nebuchadnezzar (Lucifer) as boasting that he would conquer Jerusalem, and establish his throne on that northern mount where God's temple was located. But since Lucifer was often interpreted as symbolizing Satan, the devil was thought to live in northern regions.

Compare also Ps. 48.2: "The hill of Sion is a fayre place: . . . vpon the Northside lyeth the citie of the great king."

5.3.10–12:   Now, ye familiar spirits, that are cull'd
             Out of the powerful regions under earth,
             Help me this once.

The phrase "familiar spirits" seems to be borrowed from the account of Saul consulting the witch of Endor at 1 Samuel 28.8: "I pray thee, coniecture vnto me by the familiar spirite, and bring me him vp whome I shall name vnto thee." Like the witch of Endor, Joan of Arc is depicted as having a familiar spirit, a spirit link with the powers of hell.

"Regions" seems to be the correct reading in line 11. Marlowe has a similar line in *2 Tamburlaine* 4.3.32: "O thou that swaiest the region under earth." At 4.4.16 of *1 Henry VI*, the Folio's "Regions" was emended to "legions" by Rowe, and most editors have accepted Rowe's reading. Should "regions" be emended to "legions" in this passage, then the reference would be to Mark 5.9, "My name is Legion: for we are many." (See also Luke 8.30.) The context of 5.3.10–12 would allow for "legions": Joan of Arc invoking legions of evil spirits to aid her. But "regions" is probably what Shakespeare wrote.

[5.3.31, "unchain": 2 Peter 2.4; Jude 6.]

5.4.44:   Stain'd with the guiltless blood of innocents.

Compare Jer. 2.34: "In thy wings is founde the bloud of the soules of the poore innocents."

Compare also Deut. 21.9: "The crie of innocent blood."

5.4.47–48:   You judge it straight a thing impossible
                 To compass wonders but by help of devils.

Compare Matt. 9.33–34 and parallel Scriptures: "The multitude mar-
ueiled, saying, The like was neuer seene in Israel. But the Pharises said, He
casteth out deuils, through the prince of deuils."
Perhaps an unconscious echo rather than a reference.

5.4.52–53:   Whose maiden blood, thus rigorously effus'd,
                 Will cry for vengeance at the gates of heaven.

Compare Gen. 4.10: "The voyce of thy brothers blood cryeth vnto me
from the earth."
Compare Deut. 21.9: "So thou shalt take away the crie of innocent
blood."
See 5.1.9, above.

5.4.63:   The fruit within my womb.

Gen. 30.2: "Am I in Gods steade, which hath withholden from thee the
fruite of the wombe?"
Luke 1.42: "Blessed art thou among women, because the fruite of the
wombe is blessed."
Ps. 127.4 (127.3, Geneva): "The fruite of the wombe."
See also Isa. 13.18.

5.4.89:   The gloomy shade of death.

The related expression, "shadow of death," occurs frequently in Scripture
especially in the book of Job, which Shakespeare knew well. Shakespeare
may have changed "shadow of death" to "shade of death" in order to achieve
the required meter. See Job 3.5; 10.21–22; 12.22; 16.16; 24.17; 28.3; 34.22;
38.17.
Compare also Ps. 23.4: "The valley of the shadowe of death," Matt. 4.16,
Luke 1.79, and other Scriptures.

5.5.21:   To love and honor Henry as her lord.

With echoes of the Marriage Service: "Wilt thou obey him, and serue him,
loue, honour, and keepe him?"

5.5.91: King Henry's faithful and anointed queen.

Derived ultimately from Scripture. In Israel, the king was called "the Lords anointed." See *1 Henry IV* 4.3.40, and the comments thereon. The expression was common in Shakespeare's time and occurs in both Hall and Holinshed.

5.5.92–93: For your expenses and sufficient charge,
             Among the people gather up a tenth.

The idea of gathering a tithe or tenth has its roots primarily in Scripture. The tithe is first mentioned in Genesis. After Abraham returned from warfare with much booty and was blessed by Melchizedek, Abraham "gaue him tythe of all" (Gen. 14.17–20). The Pentateuch sets forth an elaborate code for tithing, and this became the standard in Christianity.

Lev. 27.30–32: "Also all the tithe of the land . . . is the Lords: it is holy to the Lorde." By Shakespeare's time, however, the idea of giving a tenth was so common that it may have lost much of its biblical significance.

2 Henry VI

In 1594 and 1595 two anonymous plays were published that have since elicited much controversy. In 1594, *The First Part of the Contention betwixt the Two Famous Houses of York and Lancaster, with the Death of the Good Duke Humphrey* appeared in quarto, and the following year *The True Tragedy of Richard Duke of York, and the Death of Good King Henry the Sixt* was printed. Both plays were again published in quarto in 1600. A third edition appeared in 1619, but this time the two plays were published together under the title *The Whole Contention between the Two Famous Houses, Lancaster and York.*

For a long time it was thought that these plays had been written by such men as Greene, Peele, Nashe, and Marlowe, and that Shakespeare had revised them into *2* and *3 Henry VI*. Thus it was said that when in his 1592 pamphlet, *Groats-worth of Wit*, Greene attacked Shakespeare as "an vpstart Crow, beautified with our feathers," and at the same time parodied a line from *3 Henry VI*, he was attacking Shakespeare for wholesale plagiarism of plays written by himself and others.

Today, however, most scholars agree that the 1594 and 1595 quartos are not sources, but pirated editions of Shakespeare's *2 and 3 Henry VI*, pieced together from memory and from the parts of one or more actors in the plays. But the problem does not end there. Since the 1594 quarto was called the *first* part of the contention, and since internal evidence in the play suggests it, some think that Shakespeare wrote *2* and *3 Henry VI* first, and only when these plays proved successful did he preface them with *1 Henry VI* to exploit the success of the earlier plays.

It may well be that *1 Henry VI* was written after its sister plays. If so, that would make *2 Henry VI* one of Shakespeare's earliest plays, and his earliest history play. But although we cannot be sure of the order in which the three plays were written, it appears safe to conclude that *2 Henry VI* was written entirely by Shakespeare, without collaboration with others.

Shakespeare's main source for the play was Edward Hall's *Union of the Two Noble and Illustre Families of Lancaster and York* (1548). Secondary sources include chronicles by Holinished, Grafton, Fabyan, and Hardyng. Shakespeare also used Foxe's *Acts and Monuments*, principally for the exposure of the false miracle. Some favor Grafton as Shakespeare's primary source, mainly because the false Simpcox miracle is not in Hall but appears in Grafton. While Shakespeare may have gotten the Simpcox miracle from Grafton, it is more likely that he got it from the very popular *Acts and Monuments* of Foxe. In other respects, Grafton's account is much like Hall's, whom Grafton follows closely.

Shakespeare found few biblical references in these works. There are very few biblical references in those portions of Hall's chronicle that deal with the events covered in *2 Henry VI,* and the same applies to Shakespeare's secondary sources. The many biblical references that occur throughout the play are Shakespeare's own. Shakespeare's use of Scripture in the play can be seen in the way he drew the character of the king. Hall depicts Henry as "a man of a meke spirite, and of a simple witte, preferrying peace before warre, reste before businesse, honestie before profite, and quietnesse before laboure. . . . There could be none, more chaste, more meke, more holy, nor a better creature. . . . He gaped not for honor, nor thirsted for riches, but studied onely for the health of his soule: the savyng wherof, he estemed to bee the greatest wisedome" (3.105). But Hall makes no biblical references when depicting Henry as a meek, pious ruler, void of ambition. Shakespeare, however, gives the entire play a religious cast, and puts many biblical references and religious expressions in the mouths of his characters.

Some of these religious utterances strongly suggest Scripture, but do not seem to be biblical references. When Henry is introduced to his queen, he says,

> O Lord, that lends me life,
> Lend me a heart replete with thankfulness!
>
> (1.1.19–20)

Are these words parallel to the many expressions of thankfulness and of dependence on God recorded in Scripture, especially in the Psalms? Thinking that a miracle has been performed, the king tells Simpcox:

> God's goodness hath been great to thee.
> Let never day nor night unhallowed pass,
> But still remember what the Lord hath done.
>
> (2.1.82–84)

Here, again, each line contains strong overtones of Scripture, but no actual references seem to be involved. The play contains many similar passages that are difficult to deal with, passages that are best classified as religious expressions rather than actual biblical references. Other passages that appear to be closer to Scripture than the above examples, but that still may not be conscious references (as at 1.3.157, 2.1.151, and 3.2.136), are included below, but they have been placed within brackets to indicate their doubtful nature.

In the list that follows, page numbers preceded by the number 3, as (3.111), refer to volume 3 of Bullough. References to passages from Holinshed's *Chronicles* that are not included in Bullough, are to the second edition of 1587, volume 3 (*STC* 13569, variant 2). These are also indicated by the number 3, but are followed by a slash, as (3/595), to distinguish them from references to volume 3 of Bullough.

1.1.113:   By the death of Him that died for all.

A religious oath used for emphasis. The expression "died for all," however, is probably based on 2 Cor. 5.14–15: "If one be deade for all, . . . he died for al."

1.2.72:   But, by the grace of God. . . .

A common religious expression that derives from Scripture.
1 Cor. 15.10: "But by the grace of God, I am that I am."
See also Luke 2.40; Acts 11.23; 13.43; 14.26; 15.40; 1 Cor. 1.4; 3.10; etc.

1.2.72–73:   By the grace of God . . .
            Your Grace's title shall be multiplied.

Perhaps a play on 1 Peter 1.2: "Grace and peace be multiplied vnto you."

[1.3.37–38: Matt. 23.37; Luke 13.34; Ps. 36.7; 57.1; 61.4; 91.4.]

1.3.57:   His champions are the prophets and apostles.

For the probable origin of this expression, compare Eph. 2.20: "Built vpon the foundation of the Apostles and Prophets."
Compare 1 Cor. 12.28: "First, Apostles, secondly Prophets."

[1.3.58: Eph. 6.17.]

1.3.141–42:   Could I come near your beauty with my nails,
             I could set my ten commandements in your face.

The ten fingers are compared to the Ten Commandments since the Decalogue was "written with the finger of God." Ex. 31.18; Deut. 9.10. The comparison was not uncommon. In the play *Locrine*, first published in 1595 and attributed to Shakespeare (it was also included in the Third and Fourth Folios, 1664 and 1685), Strumbo says of his wife: "Althogh I trembled, fearing she would set her ten commandements in my face . . ." (4.2.43–44; *The Shakespeare Apocrypha*, ed. C.F. Tucker Brooke).

[1.3.157: Ps. 119.124; Jer. 21.2.]

1.3.188:   God is my witness.

Compare Rom. 1.9: "God is my witnes."
Compare also Gen. 31.50; 1 Sam. 12.5.
Used for emphasis, the expression "God is my witness" had become embedded in everyday speech in Shakespeare's day, although its origin was probably Scriptural. The expression also occurs in Holinshed's account of Henry VI, although in a completely different context, the reconciliation of Gloucester and Winchester: "I take first God to my witnes, and after all the world, that . . ." (3/595).

[1.3.214: Jer. 1.19; 15.20; 2 Chron. 14.11; Ps. 13.4.]

1.3.215:   O Lord, have mercy upon me!

A common religious expression. Compare Ps. 6.2: "Haue mercy vpon me, O Lorde."
Ps. 9.13: "Haue mercy vpon me, O Lord."
Ps. 51.1: "Haue mercie vpon mee (O God)."
Compare also *1 Henry VI* 1.4.70–71, and the comments thereon.

1.4.25–26:   By the eternal God, whose name and power
             Thou tremblest at.

The above words are spoken to the conjured spirit. Compare Jas. 2.19: "Thou beleeuest that there is one God: thou doest wel: the deuils also beleeue it, and tremble."
Homily "Of the True, Liuely, and Christian Faith," part 1: "This faith, by the holy Apostle Saint Iames, is compared to the fayth of Diuels, which beleeue GOD to bee true and iust, and tremble for feare."

1.4.39:   Descend to darkness and the burning lake!

Rev. 19.20: "Were aliue cast into a lake of fire, burning with brimstone."
References to the "burning lake" are often to classical sources, as at *Titus Andronicus* 4.3.44–45: "I'll dive into the burning lake below, / And pull her out of Acheron by the heels." See also Sackville's "Induction" in *The Mirror for Magistrates:* "Rude Acheron, a lothsome lake to tell / That boyles and bubs vp swelth as blacke as hell" (480–81), as well as Kyd's *Spanish Tragedy* 3.12.8–11.

In this passage, however, Shakespeare is probably referring to Scripture since he employs none of the usual terms associated with the classical lake of fire, and then makes a clear biblical reference to the devil in the next line. Revelation 20.10 associates the devil with the lake of fire: "And the deuill that deceyued them, was cast into a lake of fire."

1.4.40:   False fiend, avoid!

Matt. 4.10: "Auoide Satan."
Prayer Book, Gospel reading, first Sunday in Lent: "Then saith Iesus vnto him, Auoyd Satan."
Matt. 4.10, Bishops': "Get thee hence behind me, Satan."
Only the Bishops' Bible, from 1572 and on (when the Bishops' New Testament was revised by Giles Lawrence, professor of Greek at Oxford), has, "Get thee hence behind me, Satan," at Matt. 4.10. All other versions have, "Auoide Satan," as did the Bishop's Bible prior to 1572. Thus Shakespeare's "False fiend, avoid!" could reflect any Bible except the Bishops'.

2.1.7:   To see how God in all his creatures works!

Compare 1 Cor. 12.6: "God is the same, which worketh all in all."
Compare Eph. 1.11: "According to the purpose of him, which worketh al things after the counsell of his owne will."
Compare Phil. 2.13: "It is God which worketh in you."
Compare Heb. 13.21: "Working in you that which is pleasant in his sight."

2.1.17–18:   Were it not good your Grace could fly to heaven?
              King. The treasury of everlasting joy.

Matt. 6.20: "Laye vp treasures for your selues in heauen."
Luke 12.33: "A treasure that can neuer faile in heauen."

See also Matt. 19.21.

Communion Service, second offertory sentence: "Lay vp for your selues treasures in heauen."

Compare Spenser's pastoral elegy *Astrophel*, where Spenser uses the expression "treasury of joy" without biblical overtones:

> And her faire brest the threasury of ioy,
> She spoyld thereof, and filled with annoy.
>
> (161–62)

Shakespeare may be combining the expression "treasury of joy" with Scripture.

2.1.20:   The treasure of thy heart.

Matt. 6.21; Luke 12.34: "For where your treasure is, there wil your heart be also."

2.1.34:   Blessed are the peacemakers on earth.

Matt. 5.9: "Blessed are the peacemakers."

2.1.35–36:   Let me be blessed for the peace I make
                Against this proud Protector with my sword!

Compare Matt. 10.34: "I came not to send peace, but the sword."
Seeking to make peace between Gloucester and the cardinal, the king quotes Matthew 5.9. But if Shakespeare intended the cardinal's answer to be a pun on "piece," the resemblance to Matthew 10.34 was probably unintentional.

2.1.51–52:   *Medice, teipsum–*
                Protector, see to't well, protect yourself.

Luke 4.23, Vulgate: "Medice cura teipsum."
Geneva: "Ye will surely say vnto me this prouerb, Physicion, heale thy selfe."
"Physician, heal thyself" was a well-known proverb in Shakespeare's day (see Tilley P267), even as it was in Jesus' day. Shakespeare's omission of "cura," however, is strange.

2.1.64–65:   Now God be prais'd, that to believing souls
                   Gives light in darkness, comfort in despair!

Morning Prayer, *Benedictus:* "To giue light to them that sit in darkenesse."
Evening Prayer, third collect: "Lighten our darknes we beseech thee, O Lord."
Luke 1.79: "To giue light to them that sit in darkenes."
2 Sam. 22.29: "Thou art my light, O Lorde: and the Lord will lighten my darkenes."
Ps. 18.28: "Thou also shalt light my candle: the Lord my God shall make my darknesse to be light."
Compare Micah 7.8: "When I shall sit in darkenes, the Lord shalbe a light vnto me."
Compare also Isa. 42.16; Ps. 112.4
Morning and Evening Prayer, recited daily, would be Shakespeare's primary source for this reference.

2.1.68:   Great is his comfort in this earthly vale.

Compare the homily "Against Idlenesse": "Cast him out of Paradise into this wofull vale of miserie."
Compare the homily "Against Disobedience and Wilfull Rebellion," part 1: "Banishment out of Paradise . . . into this wretched earth and vale of misery."
Compare Ps. 84.6: "The vale of miserie." ("Vale of Baca," Geneva.)

2.1.69:   Although by his sight his sin be multiplied.

Compare John 9.41: "If ye were blinde, ye should not haue sinne: but now ye say, We see: therefore your sinne remaineth."

2.1.72–73:   Good fellow, tell us here the circumstance,
                   That we for thee may glorify the Lord.

This account is clearly patterned after the healing of the blind man in John 9. Compare the following texts:
9.10: "How were thine eyes opened?"
9.15: "Againe the Pharises also asked him, howe he had receiued sight."
9.26: "Then said they to him againe, What did he to thee? how opened he thine eyes?"

For line 73, "That we for thee may glorify the Lord," compare John 9.24: "Giue glory vnto God." (Bishops': "Giue God the praise.")

See also Matt. 5.16: "And glorifie your Father which is in heauen," which is the first sentence in the Communion offertory.

2.1.74–79:   What, hast thou been long blind and now restor'd?
             Simp. Born blind, and't please your Grace.
             Wife. Ay indeed was he.
             Suf. What woman is this?
             Wife. His wife, and't like your worship.
             Glou. Hadst thou been his mother, thou couldst have better
             told.

2.1.95–96:   How long hast thou been blind?
             Simp. O, born so, master.

Again, parallel to the account in John 9, where the Pharisees seek to verify the blind man's receiving sight.

9.18–20: "Then the Iewes did not beleue him (that he had bene blinde, and receyued his sight) vntill they had called the parentes of him that had receiued sight. And they asked them, saying, Is this your sonne, whom ye say was borne blind? How doeth he now see then? His parents answered them, and sayde, We knowe that this is our sonne, and that he was borne blinde."

[2.1.151: Ps. 94.3–4.]

2.1.158:   Made the lame to leap.

Isa. 35.6: "Then shall the lame man leape."

2.1.179:   Sorrow and grief have vanquish'd all my powers.

Compare Ecclus. 38.18: "The heauines of the heart breaketh the strength."

Perhaps an analogy rather than a reference. See *Antony and Cleopatra* 4.15.33 where the reference to Ecclus. 38.18 is more obvious.

2.1.182–83:   O God, what mischiefs work the wicked ones,
              Heaping confusion on their own heads thereby!

Ps. 7.15–17: "Beholde, he trauaileth with mischiefe: he hath conceiued sorow. . . . For his trauel shal come vpon his own head: and his wickednes shal fall on his own pate."

Geneva (7.14–16): "Behold, he shall trauaile with wickednes: for he hath conceiued mischiefe. . . . His mischiefe shall returne vpon his owne head, and his crueltie shal fall vpon his owne pate."

Ps. 14.8: "They are all such workers of mischiefe." Geneva (14.4): "Workers of iniquitie."

Ps. 140.9: "Let the mischiefe of their owne lippes fall vpon the head of them." Geneva: "Let the mischiefe of their owne lippes come vpon them."

2.1.191–92:   Convers'd with such
             As, like to pitch, defile nobility.

Ecclus. 13.1: "He that toucheth pitche, shalbe defiled with it."

2.1.200–201:   Poise the cause in justice' equal scales,
             . . . whose rightful cause prevails.

Compare Job 31.6: "Let God weigh me in the iust balance, and he shall know mine vprightnes."

Compare Virgil's account of the battle between Aeneas and Turnus:

Jupiter holds the scales in his own hand: empty, they balance:
And then he puts in the scales the different fates of the two men,
To see which weight sinks down, meaning defeat and death.
                                 (*Aeneid* 12.725–27)

2.2.73–74:   Till they have snar'd the shepherd of the flock,
             That virtuous prince.

Matt. 26.31: "I will smite the shepheard, and the sheepe of the flocke shalbe scattered."

Zech. 13.7: "Smite the shephearde, and the sheepe shall be scattered."

2.3.2–7:   In sight of God and us, your guilt is great;
           Receive the sentence of the law for sins
           Such as by God's book are adjudg'd to death.

    · · · · · · · · · · · · · ·

           The witch in Smithfield shall be burnt to ashes.

Ex. 22.18: "Thou shalt not suffer a witch to liue."

Deut. 18.10–12: "Let none be founde among you that . . . vseth witch-craft, or a regarder of times, or a marker of the flying of soules, or a sorcerer, or a charmer, or that counselleth with spirites, or a soothsayer, or that asketh counsel at the dead. For all that do such thinges are abomination vnto the Lord."

See also Lev. 20.6

2.3.18–19:   Ah, Humphrey, this dishonor in thine age
               Will bring thy head with sorrow to the ground!

Gen. 42.38: "Ye shall bring my gray head with sorow vnto the graue."
See *3 Henry VI* 2.5.40.

2.3.24–25:   God shall be my hope,
               My stay, my guide, and lanthorn to my feet.

For God shall be "my hope," compare Ps. 39.8 (39.7, Geneva): "And now Lord, what is my hope: truely my hope is euen in thee."

Ps. 71.4 (71.5, Geneva): "For thou, O Lord God, . . . art my hope, euen from my youth."

See also Jer. 17.7, 17; Ps. 146.4 (146.5, Geneva).

For the thought that God is "my stay," compare Ps. 18.18, Geneva: "The Lord was my stay." (Psalter: "The Lord was my vpholder.") Psalm 18 also appears at 2 Sam. 22. Thus, 2 Sam. 22.19 and Ps. 18.18 have identical readings in the Geneva.

Ps. 71.6, Geneva: "Vpon thee haue I bene stayed from the wombe." (Psalter, 71.5: "Through thee haue I bene holden vp euer since I was borne.")

Isa. 50.10: "Let him trust in the Name of the Lord, and stay vpon his God." (Bishops': "holde him by his God.")

Isa. 48.2: "For they . . . staye themselues vpon the God of Israel, whose Name is the Lord of hostes." (Bishops': "For they . . . are grounded vpon.")

See also Isa. 10.20, Geneva.

That God is one's stay is a reading that is more characteristic of the Geneva Bible in the above texts, although the Bishops' has "the Lord stayed me vp" at 2 Sam. 22.19.

For God being "my guide," compare Ps. 48.13 (48.14, Geneva): "For this God is our God for euer and euer: he shalbe our guide vnto death."

Ps. 31.4 (31.3, Geneva): "Be thou also my guide."

Ps. 73.23 (73.24, Geneva): "Thou shalt guide me with thy counsell."

Compare Ps. 42.9, Sternhold and Hopkins, which has both "guide" and "stay": "O Lord thou art my guide and stay, / my rock and my defence." The Psalter simply has "the God of my strength" at the corresponding text (42.11 in the Psalter).

See also Isa. 58.11; Jer. 3.4.

God as a "lanthorn to my feet" is a reference to Ps. 119.105: "Thy worde is a lanterne vnto my feete: and a light vnto my paths."

Compare also Prov. 6.23: "For the commandement is a lanterne, and instruction a light."

3.1.69–71:   Our kinsman Gloucester is as innocent

. . . .

As is the sucking lamb or harmless dove.

The expression "sucking lamb" occurs at 1 Sam. 7.9: "Samuel tooke a sucking lambe, and offred it."

For "harmless dove" compare Matt. 10.16, Bishops': "Be ye therefore wise as the serpents, and harmelesse as the Doues." (Geneva: "Innocent as doues.")

On the innocence of lambs, compare Luke 10.3: "I sende you forth as lambes among wolues."

Compare Isa. 11.6: "The wolfe also shall dwell with the lambe, and the leopard shal lye with the kid."

Compare 1 Peter 1.19: "As of a Lambe vndefiled, and without spot."

See also John 1.29.

3.1.77–78:   Is he a lamb? his skin is surely lent him,
             For he's inclin'd as is the ravenous wolves.

Matt. 7.15: "Beware of false Prophets, which come to you in sheepes clothing, but inwardely they are rauening wolues."

[3.1.79: 2 Cor. 11.14.]

3.1.86:   God's will be done!

Derived ultimately from the Lord's Prayer. Compare Matt. 6.10: "Thy wil be done."
See also Luke 11.2.

3.1.191–92:   Thus is the shepherd beaten from thy side,
               And wolves are gnarling who shall gnaw thee first.

The images of shepherd, sheep and wolves are overwhelmingly derived from Scripture.
Compare John 10.1–16, especially verses 11–13: "I am the good shepheard: the good shepheard giueth his life for his sheepe. But an hierling, and he which is not the shepheard, neither the sheep are his own, seeth the wolfe comming, and he leaueth the sheepe, and fleeth, and the wolfe catcheth them, and scattereth the sheepe. So the hierling fleeth, because he is an hierling, and careth not for the sheepe."
Compare also Matt. 26.31: "I will smite the shepheard, and the sheepe of the flocke shalbe scattered."
See 2.2.73–74, above.

[3.2.57–58: Matt. 5.44.]

3.2.76–77:   What? art thou like the adder waxen deaf?
              Be poisonous too.

Ps. 58.4–5: "As the poyson of a Serpent: euen like the deafe Adder that stoppeth her eares. Which refuseth to heare the voyce of the charmer."

[3.2.136: Gen. 18.25; Ps. 9.8; 94.2; Rev. 20.12.]

3.2.140:   For judgment only doth belong to thee.

Compare these parallel statements that were probably Shakespeare's model:
Ps. 3.8: "Saluation belongeth vnto the Lorde."
Ps. 62.11: "Power belongeth vnto God."
Ps. 94.1: "O Lord God to whom vengeance belongeth: thou God to whom vengeance belongeth, shew thy selfe."
Dan. 9.7: "O Lord, righteousnes belongeth vnto thee."
Heb. 10.30: "Vengeance belongeth vnto me."

3.2.154:   That dread King that took our state upon him.

Compare Prayer Book, collect for Christmas Day: ". . . thy onely begotten Sonne, to take our nature vpon him."
Collect, Sunday next before Easter: ". . . our Sauiour Iesus Christ to take vpon him our flesh."
Compare also Phil. 2.7; John 1.14.

3.2.155:   To free us from his Father's wrathful curse.

Based on the doctrine of man's fall and ransom. The language is borrowed from Scripture.
Gal. 3.13:   "Christ hath redeemed vs from the curse of the Law, when he was made a curse for vs."
See also Gen. 3.17–19 relative to God's curse on man after the fall.

3.2.232–33:   What stronger breastplate than a heart untainted!
               Thrice is he arm'd that hath his quarrel just.

Compare Wisdom 5.18–20: "He shall put on righteousnes for a brestplate, and take true iudgement in steade of an helmet. . . . He will sharpen his fierce wrath for a sword."
Compare Eph. 6.14: "Hauing on the brestplate of righteousnes."
Perhaps an analogy rather than a reference. Compare Tilley I81: "Innocence bears its defense with it."

3.2.285–86:   And therefore by His majesty I swear,
               Whose far-unworthy deputy I am.

That kings and secular rulers were God's duly-appointed deputies was a theme stressed by Elizabeth's government. Romans 13 was cited to support that claim and was frequently quoted in the homilies.
Rom. 13.1–4: "Let euery soule be subiect vnto the higher powers: for there is no power but of God: and the powers that be, are ordeined of God. . . . For Princes are not to be feared for good workes, but for euil. . . . For he is the minister of God to take vengeance on him that doth euil."
Homily "Concerning Good Order, and Obedience to Rulers and Magistrates," part 1: Rulers are "set in authority by GOD, for as much as they bee GODS Lieutenants, GODS Presidentes, GODS Officers, GODS Commissioners, GODS Iudges, ordained by GOD himselfe, of whom onely they haue all their power, and all their authority."

See also all six parts of the homily "Against Disobedience and Wilfull Rebellion."

Compare the references at *Richard III* 5.3.108, 113 and *King John* 2.1.87.

[3.2.395: Gen. 46.4.]

3.3.24: See how the pangs of death do make him grin!

2 Sam. 22.5: "The pangs of death haue compassed me."
The Bishops' version of the Psalms also has "panges of death" at Ps. 18.3 (18.4, Geneva), where the Psalter has "sorowes of death." But it is unlikely that Shakespeare had the Bishops' Psalms in mind, since that version of the Psalms was published only four times, in the editions of 1568, 1569, 1572 (where it appeared side by side in parallel columns with the Psalter), and 1585. In all other editions of the Bishops' Bible the Anglican Psalter, the version of the Psalms used in the services of the Anglican Church, was published. Thus, Shakespeare's reference is most likely to 2 Sam. 22.5. Not recorded in Tilley or Dent.

3.3.31: Forbear to judge, for we are sinners all.

Compare Matt. 7.1: "Ivdge not, that ye be not iudged." (See also Luke 6.37.)
Compare Rom. 3.23: "For all haue sinned."

[3.3.32: See above at 3.2.395.]

4.1.71–72: Ay, kennel, puddle, sink, whose filth and dirt
            Troubles the silver spring where England drinks.

Variations on the expression "puddle and sink" also occur in the homilies, but these were probably common expressions used by both Shakespeare and the homilies, rather than a reference to the homilies on the part of Shakespeare.
Compare the homily "Against Disobedience and Wilfull Rebellion," part 3: "He that nameth rebellion . . . nameth the whole puddle and sinke of all sinnes against GOD."
Compare also the homily "Against Adultery," part 2: "Wee should finde the sinne of whoredome, to be that most filthy lake, foule puddle, and stinking sinke, whereunto all kindes of sinnes and euils flow."
But compare *Troilus and Cressida* 5.1.76 where Thersites sarcastically says: "Sweet draught! . . . Sweet sink, sweet sewer." At *Antony and*

Cleopatra 1.4.61–62 we have, "Thou didst drink / The stale of horses and the gilded puddle." These comparisons to filthy sewers, puddles, and sinks were probably common expressions used to emphasize something's depravity.

4.1.74:   For swallowing the treasure of the realm.

The expression "treasure of the realm" also occurs in part 3 of the homily "Against Disobedience and Wilfull Rebellion": "By the spending and wasting of monie and treasure of the Prince and Realme." But as in the previous passage (4.1.71–72), nothing more than a common expression is probably involved, and Shakespeare's immediate source was Hall who calls Suffolk, "the moste swallower up and consumer of the kynges treasure" (3.111).

4.2.16:   Yet it is said, labor in thy vocation.

Compare 1 Cor. 7.20: "Let euery man abide in the same vocation wherein he was called."
That every man should labor in his vocation or calling was a well-known proverb in Shakespeare's day. See Tilley C23, C480, M104. The homily "Against Idlenesse" stressed that theme: "Euery one ought, in his lawfull vocation and calling, to giue himself to labour." Also, "Earnestly apply your selues, euery man in his vocation, to honest labour." "Euery one . . . ought . . . in some kind of labour to exercise himselfe, according as the vocation whereunto GOD hath called him shall require." The words "labour" and "vocation" are used in combination with each other several more times throughout the homily.
Homily "Concerning Good Order, and Obedience to Rulers and Magistrates": "Euery degree of people in their vocation, calling and office, hath appointed to them their duty and order."
Compare the Catechism: "To learne and labour truely to get mine owne liuing."
Compare the Commination Service: "Seeking alwayes his glory, and seruing him duely in our vocation."
Compare the Geneva (not the Tomson) note on 2 Thess. 3.10: "None ought to liue idely, but ought to giue himselfe to some vocation, to get his liuing by." See also Eph. 4.1.

4.2.35:   For our enemies shall fall before us.

Cade may be borrowing Scriptural language to give color to his rebellion. Compare Lev. 26.8: "Your enemies shall fall before you." But this may also be a pun on his name: Latin *cado*, I fall.

[4.2.99: Derived ultimately from Isa. 7.14.]

4.2.134: Adam was a gardener.

Gen. 2.15: "The Lord God tooke the man, and put him into the garden of Eden, that he might dresse it and keepe it."

[4.4.11: Matt. 26.52.]

4.4.38: They know not what they do.

Compare Luke 23.34: "They know not what they doe."
The Geneva was the first version to use "know," followed by the Rheims New Testament. All other versions have "wote not what they do." Although Shakespeare may have been using a common expression, he was probably aware that the king's words echoed Scripture.
See the comment on *Romeo and Juliet* 1.1.65 in the volume *Biblical References in Shakespeare's Tragedies*.

4.4.55: God, our hope, will succor us.

Compare Ps. 71.4 (71.5, Geneva): "For thou, O Lord God, art the thing that I long for: thou art my hope, euen from my youth."
Compare Ps. 39.8 (39.7, Geneva): "And now Lord, what is my hope: truely my hope is euen in thee."
Compare Jer. 17.13: "O Lord, the hope of Israel."
See also Jer. 14.8; 17.17; Joel 3.16.
See 2.3.24–25, above.

4.7.107–8: He has a familiar under his tongue.

Compare 1 Sam. 28.7: "Seeke me a woman that hath a familiar spirit."
Compare the reference at *1 Henry VI* 5.3.10–12 and the comments thereon.

4.8.28–31: Let them . . . ravish your wives and daughters before your faces.

Compare the homily "Against Disobedience and Wilfull Rebellion," part 3: "What are the forceable oppressions of matrons and mens wiues, and the violating and deflowring of virgins and maides, which are most rife with rebels?" Also, rebels "abuse by force other mens wiues, and daughters, and rauish virgins and maydens, most shamefully, abominably, and damnably."

Though himself a rebel, Cade tells his followers that they can expect treatment such as that described in the homily against rebellion if they lay down their arms. But Cade's words are most likely an analogy rather than a reference to the homily, since women were frequently ravished in warfare. The same thought occurs in *Gorbuduc*: "The wives shall suffer rape, the maids deflowered" (5.2.209). *Gorbuduc* was first performed in 1562; the homily "Against Disobedience and Wilfull Rebellion" was written after the Northern Rebellion of 1569.

Moreover, Cade's words in this passage should not be confused with what he says at 4.7.121–23: "There shall not a maid be married, but she shall pay to me her maidenhead ere they have it." These words seem to refer to the feudal custom whereby the lord of the manor had the right to spend the first night with the bride of any of his vassals. The theme of the entire passage is of the tribute he will receive and the rights he will enjoy when he rules England. The passage at 4.8.28–31, on the other hand, is parallel in meaning to that in *Gorbuduc*: their wives and daughters would be ravished by the victors. Neither passage seems to be based on the homily, but on what was commonly understood to be the aftermath of defeat in warfare.

4.9.13:   Then, heaven, set ope thy everlasting gates.

Ps. 24.7, 9: "Lift vp your heads, O ye gates, and be ye lift vp ye euerlasting doores."

Sternhold and Hopkins: "Ye Princes open your gates, stand open, / the euerlasting gate."

[4.10.18–19: 1 Tim. 6.6.]

4.10.22–23:   Sufficeth that I have maintains my state
             And sends the poor well pleased from my gate.

Perhaps inspired by Job 31.19–21: "If I haue seene any . . . poore without couering . . . when I sawe that I might helpe him in the gate. . . ."

5.1.159–60:   Nay, we shall heat you thoroughly anon.
             Clif. Take heed, lest by your heat you burn yourselves.

Perhaps based on the account of the fiery furnace in Daniel, whose excessive heat slew those that heated it.

Dan. 3.22: "Because the Kings commandement was strait, that the fornace shoulde bee exceeding hote, the flame of the fire slewe those men that brought forth Shadrach, Meshach and Abednego."

5.1.182–83:   It is great sin to swear unto a sin,
              But greater sin to keep a sinful oath.

This point is made clear in the homily "Against Swearing and Periury," part 2: "But if a man at any time shall, either of ignorance or of malice, promise and sweare to doe any thing which is either against the law of Almighty GOD, or not in his power to performe: let him take it for an vnlawfull and vngodly oath."

Again: "Yee haue heard how damnable a thing it is, either to forsweare ourselues, or to keepe an vnlawfull, and an vnaduised oath."

5.1.187–88:   To reave the orphan of his patrimony,
              To wring the widow from her custom'd right.

With strong overtones of the rights of the "fatherlesse and widow," frequently mentioned in Scripture.

Compare Deut. 10.18: "Who doth right vnto the fatherlesse and widow."

Compare Deut. 27.19: "Cursed be he that hindreth the right of the stranger, the fatherles, and the widowe."

See also Deut. 14.29; 16.11; 24.19–21; 26.12–13; Ps. 146.9; Isa. 1.17; Jer. 7.6; 22.3; etc.

Compare the tragedy of Eleanor, Duchess of Gloucester, added to the 1578 edition of *The Mirror for Magistrates* (STC 1252.5): "By the same acte, from me did then withdraw. / Such right of dower, as widowes haue by law" (153–54).

5.1.214:   For you shall sup with Jesu Christ to-night.

Evidently a combination of Rev. 19.9 and 3.20.

Rev. 19.9: "Blessed are they which are called vnto the Lambes supper."

Rev. 3.20: "I wil come in vnto him, and wil sup with him, and he with me."

See also Luke 23.43.

Compare *Hamlet* 4.3.16–18, 33.

[5.2.33–34: Ezek. 14.21; 5.12–13; Isa. 66.16.]

5.2.36:   Hot coals of vengeance!

Compare Ps. 140.10: "Let hot burning coales fall vpon them."
Compare Jude 7: "As Sodom and Gomorrhe . . . suffer the vengeance of eternall fire."
See the reference at *Richard II* 1.2.8 and the comments thereon.

5.2.40–42:   O, let the vile world end,
             And the premised flames of the last day
             Knit earth and heaven together!

A general reference to the Bible's descriptions of the end of the world.
Compare 2 Peter 3.10: "But the day of the Lord will come as a thief in the night, in the which the heauens shal passe away with a noyse, and the elements shall melte with heate, and the earth with the workes, that are therein, shalbe burnt vp."
Compare 2 Peter 3.12: "The day of God, by the which the heauens being on fire, shalbe dissolued, and the elements shall melt with heat."
A similar passage occurs in Ovid's *Metamorphoses*. Jove was determined to destroy the world with his thunderbolts, but "he stayed his hand in fear lest perchance the sacred heavens should take fire from so huge a conflagration, and burn from pole to pole. He remembered also that 'twas in the fates that a time would come when sea and land, the unkindled palace of the sky and the beleaguered structure of the universe should be destroyed by fire." (1.254–58, Loeb ed.)
Arthur Golding's translation of the same passage:

And now his lightning had he thought on all the earth to throw:
But that he feared least the flames perhaps so hie should grow
As for to set the heauen a fire, and burne vp all the skie.
He did remember furthermore how that by destenie,
A certaine time should one day come, wherein both Sea and Lond
And Heauen it selfe should feele the force of Vulcans scorching brond.

Shakespeare knew Ovid well, both in the original Latin and in Golding's translation. But it is probable that "flames of the last day" is a reference to Scripture, and that the majority of his audience would have been reminded of the Bible's description of the fiery end of the world. In the following line (5.2.43), Shakespeare refers to another well-known text in Scripture about the end of the world:

5.2.43:   Now let the general trumpet blow his blast.

1 Cor. 15.52: "At the last trumpet: for the trumpet shall blowe."

5.2.50–51:   My heart is turn'd to stone; and while 'tis mine,
                    It shall be stony.

Compare 1 Sam. 25.37: "His heart died within him, and he was like a
stone."
Compare Ezek. 11.19: "I will take the stonie heart out of their bodies."
See 2 Henry IV 4.5.107, and the comments thereon.

5.2.71:   Priests pray for enemies.

Matt. 5.44: "Loue your enemies: blesse them that cursse you: . . . and
pray for them which hurt you, and persecute you."
See also Luke 6.27–28.

5.2.73:   Can we outrun the heavens?

Compare Ps. 139.6–7 (139.7–8, Geneva): "Whither shall I go then from
thy spirite: or whither shall I goe then from thy presence? If I clime vp into
heauen, thou art there: if I go downe to hell, thou art there also."
Compare also Amos 9.1–3: "He that fleeth of them, shall not flee away:
and he that escapeth of them, shal not be deliuered. Though they digge into
the hell, thence shall mine hande take them: though they clime vp to heauen,
thence will I bring them downe. And though they hyde them selues in the
toppe of Carmel, I will search and take them out thence: and though they
bee hid from my sight in the bottome of the sea, thence will I command the
serpent, and hee shall byte them."
Compare also Jer. 23.24.
At best analogies rather than references. Shakespeare is most likely expressing a common religious idea rather than making a conscious reference
to Scripture.

3 Henry VI

The Third Part of King Henry VI first appeared in print in 1595 under the title *The True Tragedy of Richard Duke of York, and the Death of Good King Henry the Sixt*. It was republished in 1600 and 1619 before finally appearing in an authorized edition in the First Folio. There is general agreement among scholars today that the 1595 octavo (rather than "quarto") was not the source of Shakespeare's play, as had been once thought, but a pirated version of the play. Although the title page of the 1619 quarto (the first edition of the play to bear Shakespeare's name) claimed that the play had been "newly corrected and enlarged," the play was not printed from an authorized text until it appeared in the Folio. The text of the three pirated editions is two-thirds as long as that of the Folio.

The play must have been written by 1592, for in that year Robert Greene attacked Shakespeare as an "vpstart Crow, beautified with our feathers, that with his *Tygers hart wrapt in a Players hyde*, supposes he is as well able to bombast out a blanke verse as the best of you: and beeing an absolute *Iohannes fac totum*, is in his owne conceit the onely Shake-scene in a countrey." The attack appeared in Greene's death-bed treatise, *Groats-worth of Wit*, and was a clear parody of York's words to Queen Margaret, "O tiger's heart wrapp'd in a woman's hide" (1.4.137). Greene's anger was directed at the fact that an actor, who would normally be unable to earn a living without Greene and his fellow playwrights, was himself writing plays, so that the playwrights were in danger of being displaced by the "vpstart Crow" who was both actor and dramatist. Thus by 1592 Shakespeare had become sufficiently known as both an actor and playwright (a *Iohannes fac totum*) to elicit the wrath of professional playwrights upon whom the actors would be much less dependent in the future.

Shakespeare's principal source for the play was Edward Hall's *Union of the Two Noble and Illustre Families of Lancaster and York* (1548). But Shakespeare also read the second edition of Holinshed's *Chronicles* (1587), borrowing from it whatever seemed suitable. The biblical reference at 1.4.90–95 in which Queen Margaret mocks York "as the Jewes did unto Christ" (3.210), is an outstanding example. The other sources that are listed for part 2 of the play must also have been in Shakespeare's mind when he wrote part 3, but there are no certain traces of them in part 3. His three main sources were the chronicles of Hall, Holinshed, and Grafton, but the latter two are so similar to Hall, whom they followed closely, that most of the time it is impossible to distinguish which chronicle is being used.

Shakespeare found relatively few biblical references in his chronicle sources. Hall's theme was moral. He sought to demonstrate God's providence toward England and repeatedly points out that those who commit evil will sooner or later be punished. Yet his account contains very few biblical references. Inspired by Hall's theme of divine retribution, Shakespeare adds biblical references that reflect that theme (1.4.168; 2.2.129; 2.6.55). The chronicles by Holinshed and Grafton likewise have very few biblical references. Holinshed's complete life of Henry VI, which covers the material in all three parts of the play, contains some fourteen references. As already noted, Shakespeare borrowed only one of them, the mocking of Christ prior to his crucifixion, at 1.4.90–95.

An example of how Shakespeare added biblical references to what he found in his sources can be seen in the passage in Hall relating the death of Warwick's brother. Hall simply says: "He [Lord Fitzwater] was slayne, and with hym the Bastard of Salisbury, brother to the erle of Warwycke, a valeaunt yong gentelman" (3.181). At 2.3.14–23 Shakespeare expands that statement into a passage that contains at least three biblical references.

There may be influences from *The Mirror for Magistrates*, *The Faerie Queene*, and other works in the play, but these were influences, not sources. The passage at 2.1.21–24, which is so similar to Psalm 19, may have been inspired by Shakespeare's reading of *The Faerie Queene*. But there are some 350 other biblical references in the first three books of Spenser's poem (published in 1590) that Shakespeare did not borrow, and Shakespeare's resemblance to *The Faerie Queene* may be accidental.

In the list that follows, page numbers preceded by the number 3, as (3.210), refer to volume 3 of Bullough.

1.1.24:   I vow by heaven these eyes shall never close.

Compare Ps. 132.4: "I will not suffer mine eyes to sleepe, nor mine eye lids to slumber."

The spirit of both passages is much the same. Warwick swears that he will not close his eyes till he sees York on England's throne, while the Psalmist records David's resolve that he will never rest till he builds a temple for God.

1.1.42:   Hath made us by-words to our enemies.

Compare Ps. 44.15 (44.14, Geneva): "Thou makest vs to be a byworde among the Heathen."

The Geneva has "a prouerbe" rather than "a byworde" at Psalm 44.

Job 17.6: "Hee hath also made mee a byworde of the people."

"Byword" occurs six times in the Authorized King James Bible, but it does not occur in the Bishops' Bible in any of those texts, including the Bishops' version of Psalm 44. In the corresponding six texts, it only occurs at Job 17.6 in the Geneva. Not in Tilley or Dent. Shakespeare was no doubt using a common expression, but one that he heard most often in church when Psalm 44 was read.

1.1.161:   May that ground gape, and swallow me alive.

Num. 16.32–33: "The earth opened her mouth, and swallowed them vp. . . . So they . . . went downe aliue into the pit."

The same event is related at Deut. 11.6 and Ps. 106.17, as well as in the homily "Concerning Good Order, and Obedience to Rulers and Magistrates," part 2: "And therefore the earth opened and swallowed them vp aliue." See also *Richard III* 1.2.65.

1.1.242:   The trembling lamb environed with wolves.

With strong overtones of the frequent biblical illustrations involving sheep and wolves. See *2 Henry VI* 3.1.191–92 and the comments thereon.

[1.4.37: Ps. 123.1–2.]

1.4.56:   When a cur doth grin.

Compare Ps. 59.6, 14: "They grinne like a dogge."

1.4.90–95:   And I, to make thee mad, do mock thee thus.

            . . . .
            York cannot speak unless he wear a crown.
            A crown for York! and, lords, bow low to him;
            Hold you his hands whilest I do set it on.

Matt. 27.29: "And platted a crowne of thornes, and put it vpon his head, . . . and bowed their knees before him, and mocked him, saying, God saue thee King of the Iewes."

Shakespeare borrowed this reference from Holinshed: "Some write that the duke was taken alive, and in derision caused to stand upon a molehill, on whose head they put a garland in steed of a crowne, . . . and having so crowned him with that garland, they kneeled downe afore him (as the Jewes did unto Christ) in scorne, saieng to him; Haile king without rule, haile king without heritage, haile duke and prince without people or possessions. And at length having thus scorned him with these and diverse other the like despitefull words, they stroke off his head" (3.210). This passage does not occur in Hall.

1.4.112:   Whose tongue more poisons than the adder's tooth!

Ps. 140.3: "They haue sharpened their tongues like a serpent: Adders poyson is vnder their lippes."

1.4.168:   My blood upon your heads!

2 Sam. 1.16: "Thy blood be vpon thine owne head."
2 Sam. 3.29: "Let the blood fall on the head of Ioab."
A common biblical expression. See also Josh. 2.19; 1 Kings 2.32; Matt. 27.25; Acts 5.28.

1.4.177:   Open thy gate of mercy, gracious God!

Compare the song "The Lamentation of a Sinner":

O Lord turne not away thy face, from him that lieth prostrate:
Lamenting sore his sinfull life, before thy mercy gate.
Which gate thou openest wide to those, that do lament their sinne:
Shut not that gate against me Lord, but let me enter in.

"The Lamentation of a Sinner" was one of a group of miscellaneous prayers, songs, creeds, and passages of Scripture that were put into meter and set to music, and either prefixed or appended to various editions of Sternhold and Hopkins' metrical Psalms. Not all editions contained the same selection of songs and prayers, but "The Lamentation of a Sinner" was a well-known religious song in Shakespeare's day.
Compare also the expression "the gates of righteousnesse" at Ps. 118.19: "Open me the gates of righteousnesse: that I may go into them."
Compare *Henry V* 3.3.10, and the comments thereon.

2.1.21–24: See how the morning opes her golden gates,
            And takes her farewell of the glorious sun!
            How well resembles it the prime of youth,
            Trimm'd like a younker prancing to his love!

With clear overtones of Ps. 19.5 (19.4–5, Geneva): "In them hath he set a tabernacle for the sunne: which commeth forth as a bridegrome out of his chamber, and reioyceth as a Gyant to runne his course."

Compare Ps. 19.4, Sternhold and Hopkins: "In them the Lord made for the Sun, a place of great renowne: / Who like a bridegrome ready trimd, doth from his chamber come."

Compare *The Faerie Queene* 1.5.2.(1–4):

> At last the golden Orientall gate
> Of greatest heauen gan to open faire,
> And *Phoebus* fresh, as bridegrome to his mate,
> Came dauncing forth, shaking his deawie haire.

[2.2.7: Rom. 12.19.]

[2.2.127–28: Acts 23.12, 21.]

2.2.129: Their blood upon thy head.

See above at 1.4.168.

2.2.163–65: But when we saw our sunshine made thy spring,
             And that thy summer bred us no increase,
             We set the axe to thy usurping root.

Luke 3.9: "Now also is the axe laid vnto the roote of the trees: therefore euery tree which bringeth not forth good fruite, shalbe hewen downe."

Shakespeare's reference seems to be primarily to Luke 3.9. But compare also Luke 13.6–7: "He came and sought fruit thereon, and found none. Then said he . . . cut it downe: why keepeth it also the ground baren?"

2.3.15: Thy brother's blood the thirsty earth hath drunk.

Gen. 4.10–11: "The voyce of thy brothers blood cryeth vnto me from the earth . . . which hath opened her mouth to receiue thy brothers blood."

2.3.17:   And in the very pangs of death he cried.

Compare 2 Sam. 22.5: "The pangs of death haue compassed me."
The Bishops' version of the Psalms also has "panges of death" at Ps. 18.3
(18.4, Geneva) where the Psalter has "the sorowes of death." But it is
unlikely that Shakespeare had the Bishops' Psalms in mind, since that
version of the Psalms was seldom published. See *2 Henry VI* 3.3.24 and the
comments thereon. Thus, if Shakespeare had Scripture in mind in this
passage, his reference was most likely to 2 Sam. 22.5.

[2.3.22: Gen. 49.33. Compare also Gen. 35.18; Matt. 27.50; Acts 5.10.]

2.3.23:   Then let the earth be drunken with our blood!

A common biblical expression. Compare Judith 6.4: "Their mountaines
shall be drunken with their bloud."
Compare Isa. 49.26: "They shalbe drunken with their owne bloode."
Compare Rev. 17.6: "I sawe the woman drunken with the bloud of
Saintes."
Compare also Deut. 32.42; Jer. 46.10; Ezek. 39.19.

2.3.37:   Thou setter-up and plucker-down of kings.

Dan. 2.21: "He taketh away kings: he setteth vp kings."
Compare also Ps. 75.8 (75.7, Geneva): "God is the iudge: hee putteth
downe one, and setteth vp another."
Sternhold and Hopkins (75.6): "The Lord our God he is, the righteous
iudge alone: / He putteth downe the one and sets, another in the throne."

2.5.40:   Would bring white hairs unto a quiet grave.

Compare Gen. 42.38: "Ye shall bring my gray head with sorow vnto the
graue."
See *2 Henry VI* 2.3.18–19.

[2.5.69: Luke 23.34.]

2.6.1:   Here burns my candle out; ay, here it dies.

Compare Job 18.6: "His candle shalbe put out with him."
Compare Job 21.17: "How oft shall the candle of the wicked bee put out?"
Compare also Ps. 18.28.

2.6.55:   Measure for measure must be answered.

Compare Mark 4.24: "With what measure ye mete, it shall be measured
vnto you."
Compare also Matt. 7.2; Luke 6.38.

[2.6.68: Job 19.1 (19.2. AV).]

3.1.17:   Thy balm wash'd off wherewith thou wast anointed.

In ancient Israel, the king was called "the Lords anointed," since oil was
poured over his head at his installation.
   1 Sam. 10.1: "Then Samuel tooke a viole of oyle and powred it vpon his
head, and kissed him, and sayde, Hath not the Lorde anoynted thee to bee
gouernour ouer his inheritance?"
   See also 1 Sam. 16.13; 1 Kings 1.33–39.
   Compare *1 Henry IV* 4.3.40 and the comments thereon, and *Richard II*
3.2.54–55.

3.1.24–25:   Let me embrace thee, sour adversities,
             For wise men say it is the wisest course.

Compare Ecclus. 2.4–5: "Whatsoeuer commeth vnto thee, receiue it
patiently, and be patient in the change of thine affliction. For . . . euen so are
men acceptable in the fornace of aduersitie."
   Shakespeare may have had a proverb in mind. Compare Tilley A42:
"Adversity makes men wise." But the earliest occurrence of this proverb that
Tilley lists is this passage from Shakespeare at 3.1.24–25. Dent, however,
lists an earlier occurrence.
   Closest parallel in Hall is Hall's statement that King Henry never sought
vengeance on those who injured him, but always "rendered to almightie
God, his creator, hartie thankes, thinking that by this trouble, and adver-
sitie, his synnes were to him forgotten and forgeven" (3.207).

[3.1.64: 1 Tim. 6.6–8. But compare Tilley C623, the proverb Shakespeare probably had in
   mind.]

3.1.76: I was anointed king.

See above at 3.1.17.

[3.2.126: Isa. 11.1, Bishops'.]

3.3.29: Of England's true-anointed lawful king.

See above at 3.1.17.

3.3.51: I come, in kindness and unfeigned love.

2 Cor. 6.6: "By kindnes, by the holy Ghost, by loue vnfained."
Prayer Book, Epistle, first Sunday in Lent: "In kindnesse, in the holy Ghost, in loue vnfained."
Shakespeare's primary source for this reference is most likely the Prayer Book, although most English Bibles (Tyndale, Coverdale, Matthew, Taverner, Great, and the pre-1572 editions of the Bishops') also had "in" rather than "by" at 2 Cor. 6.6. Moreover, the sense of Warwick's words lends itself to "in kindness" rather than "by kindness."

3.3.157: Proud setter-up and puller-down of kings!

See 2.3.37, above.

4.1.21–23: God forbid that I should wish them sever'd
Whom God hath join'd together; ay, and 'twere pity
To sunder them that yoke so well together.

Matt. 19.6: "Let not man therefore put asunder that, which God hath coupled together."
Marriage Service: "We are gathered together heere in the sight of God . . . to ioyne together this man and this woman in holy Matrimonie." "Any impediment why yee may not bee lawfully ioyned together in Matrimonie."
Shakespeare's reference is primarily to the Prayer Book. All Protestant Tudor Bibles have "coupled together" (or "coupled") rather than "ioyned together" at Matt. 19.6 and Mark 10.9.

4.4.20:   And bear with mildness my misfortune's cross.

Luke 14.27: "Whosoeuer beareth not his crosse . . . can not be my disciple."
See also Matt. 10.38; 16.24; Mark 8.34; 10.21; Luke 9.23.
Shakespeare's passage is closest to Luke 14.27. The other texts have either "taketh" or "take vp" one's cross, rather than "bear" one's cross, although the meaning of all the texts is the same: the need to endure hardship.
Compare also *Richard III* 3.1.4–5; 3.1.126–27.

[4.8.48: John 1.16. Compare *Romeo and Juliet* 2.3.86.]

[4.8.49: Isa. 11.6.]

5.1.26:   Confess who set thee up and pluck'd thee down.

See 2.3.37 and 3.3.157 above.

5.1.90–91:   To keep that oath were more impiety
              Than Jephthah when he sacrific'd his daughter.

A reference to Jephthah who made a vow to God that if God gave him victory over the Ammonites, he would sacrifice "for a burnt offring" whatever came first out of his house to greet him. His only daughter was first to greet him, and he "did with her according to his vowe." Judges 11.30–39.
This incident is mentioned in the homily "Against Swearing and Periury," part 2: "And Iephtah when God had giuen to him victorie of the children of Ammon, promised (of a foolish deuotion) vnto God, to offer for a sacrifice vnto him that person which of his owne house should first meete with him after his returne home. By force of which fonde and vnaduised oath, hee did slay his owne and onely daughter. . . . Thus the promise which hee made (most foolishly) to God . . . most cruelly hee performed."

5.2.11–15:   Thus yields the cedar to the axe's edge,
              Whose arms gave shelter to the princely eagle,
              Under whose shade the ramping lion slept,
              Whose top-branch overpeer'd Jove's spreading tree,
              And kept low shrubs from winter's pow'rful wind.

Compare Ezek. 31.3–8: "Beholde, Asshur was like a cedar in Lebanon with faire branches, and with thicke shadowing boughes, and shot vp very hye, and his toppe was among the thicke boughes. . . . Therefore his height was exalted aboue all the trees of the fielde. . . . All the foules of the heauen made their nestes in his boughes, and vnder his branches did all the beastes of the fielde bring foorth their yong. . . . The cedars in the garden of God could not hide him."

Some have considered Shakespeare's mention of "Jove's spreading tree" a reference to Virgil's *Georgics:*

> But in the midday heat let them seek out a shady dell, where haply Jove's mighty oak with its ancient trunk stretches out giant branches, or where the grove, black with many holms, lies brooding with hallowed shade.
>
> (3.331–34)

While Shakespeare's passage combines details from many sources, he seems closest to Scripture. Tilley lists many similar proverbs at S941 ("Many strokes fell great oaks"), but the trees felled in these proverbs are oaks rather than cedars. Shakespeare probably had those proverbs in mind at 2.1.54–55. But the cedar in this passage seems to be based on Scripture. Compare also the reference to a cedar at *Richard III* 1.3.263.

5.4.44–49:   For did I but suspect a fearful man,
                  He should have leave to go away betimes,
                  Lest in our need he might infect another,
                  And make him of like spirit to himself.
                  If any such be here—as God forbid!—
                  Let him depart before we need his help.

Deut. 20.8: "Let the officers speake further vnto the people, and say, Whosoeuer is afraide and faint hearted, let him goe and returne vnto his house, least his brethrens heart faint like his heart."

Compare Hall: "The lusty kyng Edward . . . made proclamacion that all men, whiche were afrayde to fighte, shoulde incontinent departe, and to all men that tarried the battell, he promised great rewardes" (3.181).

While Shakespeare's lines are primarily based on Hall, Shakespeare added details from Scripture to what he found in Hall. Hall's account says nothing about fearful soldiers departing lest they infect other soldiers with fear. That idea seems to be based on Deuteronomy 20.

5.4.74–75:   My tears gainsay; for every word I speak,
                  Ye see I drink the water of my eye.

Compare Ps. 80.5: "Thou feedest them with the bread of teares: and giuest them plenteousnesse of teares to drinke."

5.5.7–8:   So part we sadly in this troublous world,
           To meet with joy in sweet Jerusalem.

Compare Rev. 21, where "the holie citie newe Ierusalem" is used as a symbol of heavenly joy: "And I Iohn saw the holie citie newe Ierusalem come downe from God out of heauen, prepared as a Bride trimmed for her husbande. . . . And he caried me away in the spirite to a greate and an hie mountain, and he shewed me the great citie, holy Ierusalem, descending out of heauen from God" (Rev. 21.2, 10).

[5.5.75–76: Matt. 5.33.]

5.6.7:   So flies the reakless shepherd from the wolf.

Compare John 10.12–13: "But an hierling, and he which is not the shepheard, . . . seeth the wolfe comming, and he leaueth the sheepe, and fleeth, and the wolfe catcheth them, and scattereth the sheepe. So the hierling fleeth."
See also *2 Henry VI* 3.1.191–92, and the comments thereon.
The closest parallel in Shakespeare's sources comes from Hall's chronicle: King Edward sought "to circumvent or trappe the erle of Warwycke, knowing perfitly that if he had once mastred the chief belwether, the flocke wolde sone be dispercled" (3.192). Shakespeare is considerably closer to Scripture.

[5.6.11: Prov. 28.1. But more likely a proverb. See Tilley F117.]

5.6.52:   Not like the fruit of such a goodly tree.

Matt. 7.17–18: "So euery good tree bringeth forth good fruite. . . . A good tree can not bring forth euill fruite."

[5.6.60: Luke 23.34.]

[5.7.13–14: Ps. 110.1; Matt. 22.44.]

5.7.33–34:   So Judas kiss'd his master,
             And cried "All hail!" when as he meant all harm.

Matt. 26.49, all versions except Geneva: "When he came to Iesus, he said, Haile master: and kissed him."

Geneva: "Hee came to Iesus, and sayde, God saue thee, Master, and kissed him."

Prayer Book, Gospel reading, Sunday before Easter: "And foorthwith hee came to Iesus, and said, Haile, Master, and kissed him."

Both in this passage and at *Richard II* 4.1.169–70 Shakespeare has Judas greeting Jesus with the words "All hail!" when he betrayed him. But no English Bible has "All hail!" Except for the Geneva, all Protestant English Bibles of the day, as well as the Prayer Book, have "Haile master." The Rheims New Testament has "Haile Rabbi." Shakespeare's "All hail!" seems to be borrowed from the medieval play, *The Agony and the Betrayal,* a York mystery play. In that play Judas greets Jesus with the words, "All hayll, maistir" (243).

At Matt. 28.9, the resurrected Jesus greets his disciples with the words "All hail," according to all versions of Shakespeare's day except Tyndale (1526), Coverdale, and the Geneva. Tyndale's first edition of the New Testament as well as the Coverdale Bible have, "God spede you." The Geneva has, "God saue you." All other versions, including Tyndale's 1535 New Testament, have "All haile."

But it is unlikely that Matt. 28.9 influenced this passage in *3 Henry VI* or the related passage in *Richard II.* There is no mention of Judas or of the betrayal in Matthew 28. Rather, Shakespeare's "All hail!" seems to be based on the York mystery play about the betrayal. Shakespeare evidently had seen more than one cycle of mystery plays during his childhood. See the reference on *Hamlet* 3.2.13–14 in the volume *Biblical References in Shakespeare's Tragedies* where the influence of the Coventry cycle is evident.

Richard III

Shakespeare's *Richard III* was an immensely popular play. Written about 1592, it first appeared in print in 1597 and was reprinted five more times in quarto before appearing in the First Folio of 1623. It is Shakespeare's longest history play, and longer than any other Shakespeare play except *Hamlet*. *Richard III* is the tragedy of a ruthless Machiavel who would not hesitate to destroy anyone in his way, and whose crimes against others cry out for divine retribution.

Shakespeare's sources for the play are many and complex. The single most important source for all succeeding narratives about the life of Richard was Sir Thomas More's *The History of King Richard the Third*, written about 1513; the first authoritative English edition of More's text was printed in 1557. But it is unlikely that Shakespeare read More's account. Shakespeare's primary sources were the second edition of Holinshed's *Chronicles* (1587), which reprinted most of More's *History,* and Edward Hall's chronicle, *The Union of the Two Noble and Illustre Families of Lancaster and York,* first published in 1548. It is difficult to determine which of these two chronicles was Shakespeare's main source, since Holinshed borrowed heavily from Hall, but it is clear from various details in the play that he used both of them.

Any consideration of Shakespeare's sources must also include the anonymous play *The True Tragedy of Richard the Third,* printed defectively in 1594 (most likely a pirated text), and based on an earlier play that may have influenced Shakespeare. But the extent, if any, to which Shakespeare borrowed from that earlier play is uncertain. Parts of the 1594 *True Tragedy* are so similar to *Richard III* that it is clear that one of these two plays borrowed extensively from the other. If the original play, of which the 1594 text is a garbled version, preceded Shakespeare's play, then it could have been an important source for Shakespeare. But if the original *True Tragedy* followed *Richard III*, then it was inspired by Shakespeare's play. Another explanation for the similarities between *Richard III* and *The True Tragedy* might be that those responsible for publishing *The True Tragedy* in 1594 had recollected lines from Shakespeare's play, added them to their text, and published it to capitalize on the success of Shakespeare's play. Whatever the correct explanation, the biblical references in *Richard III* that have parallels in *The True Tragedy* are noted in the following list.

Other histories and chronicles available to Shakespeare include those by

Polydore Vergil, Hardyng, Grafton, Fabyan, and Stow. But these works are so similar to each other (since they all borrowed freely from each other, often word for word), and they are so like Holinshed and Hall, Shakespeare's main sources, that if Shakespeare consulted them, it is hardly possible to identify which one he used. Moreover, Holinshed drew upon most of these earlier accounts.

Lesser sources include *The Mirror for Magistrates*, primarily for the Clarence scenes. Shakespeare was also influenced by several of Seneca's tragedies; *Richard III* is the most Senecan of Shakespeare's plays. There are also echoes of Marlowe, Kyd, *The Troublesome Raigne of Iohn King of England*, and other works, but none of these seem to have influenced Shakespeare's biblical references.

Shakespeare found a number of biblical references in Holinshed and Hall. Holinshed's account contains some seventeen references (to King David, to Lucifer, Israel's captivity in Egypt, Matt. 19.26, etc.), including several Latin paraphrases of Scripture, but Shakespeare borrowed very few of these. The overwhelming majority of biblical references in Shakespeare's play are his own. The outstanding biblical reference in the play is probably the reference to Ecclesiastes 10.16 at 2.3.11: "Woe to that land that's govern'd by a child," which derives from More's *History* and occurs in subsequent accounts, including Holinshed and Hall, although not in *The True Tragedy*.

Half of the biblical references in the play occur in act 1, and it is in act 1 that Shakespeare invents more freely than in the rest of the play. The remaining references are divided up almost equally between the other four acts. Many of the items in the following list may be analogies rather than conscious references to Scripture, but they seem to be sufficiently close to Scripture either verbally or in context to justify including them for the reader's consideration. On the other hand, comparisons such as, "The killing of the Princes is a massacre of the innocents, and their mother is like Rachel weeping for her children," are not included, these comparisons being too farfetched and general to be considered valid references.

In the list that follows, page numbers preceded by the number 3, as in (3.258), refer to volume 3 of Bullough. Bullough omits reproducing Holinshed's account of Richard in his study of Shakespeare's sources for the play, since Holinshed's account is so much like Hall's, which Bullough chose to include. Thus, references to Holinshed are to the second edition of 1587, volume 3 (*STC* 13569, variant 2), and are also indicated by the number 3, but are followed by a slash, as (3/735), to distinguish them from references to volume 3 of Bullough. References to More's history of Richard are to the Yale edition of *The Complete Works of St. Thomas More*, volume 2 (1963), edited by Richard Sylvester. *The True Tragedy* is represented by the 1929 Malone Society reprint, since the text that appears in Bullough is not complete.

[1.1.138: The Apostle John's name used as an oath. Folio reading; all six quartos have "by Saint Paul," rather than "by Saint John," Saint Paul being Richard's usual oath in the rest of the play, as at 1.2.36, 41; 1.3.45; 3.4.76; 5.3.216. Shakespeare borrowed this oath from his sources. See 3.4.76–77, below.]

1.2.47–48: Thou hadst but power over his mortal body,
            His soul thou canst not have.

Compare Matt. 10.28: "Feare ye not them which kill the bodie, but are not able to kill the soule."

But compare Holinshed (3/735) relative to the murder of the two princes: "They gaue vp to God their innocent soules into the ioies of heauen, leauing to the tormentors their bodies dead in the bed." Hall's account of the princes's murder is identical (3.279), as is More's (85).

Compare also King Edward's words on his deathbed in the anonymous play, *The True Tragedy of Richard the Third:* "I commit my soule to almighty God, . . . my bodie to the earth" (186–87).

At best an anology rather than a reference. The body/soul concept of man is a common one, and the parallel passages in Shakespeare's sources are not spoken about Henry VI, as in Shakespeare's play.

1.2.63: O earth! which this blood drink'st, revenge his death!

Gen. 4.11: "Thou art cursed from the earth, which hath opened her mouth to receiue thy brothers blood."

Compare Richard's words in *The True Tragedy:* "My Nephues bloods, Reuenge, reuenge, doth crie" (1883).

[1.2.64: Luke 9.54.]

1.2.65: Or earth gape open wide and eat him quick.

Num. 16.30, 32: "The earth open her mouth, and swallowe them vp. . . . The earth opened her mouth, and swallowed them vp."

See also Ps. 106.17; Deut. 11.6.

Compare also "earth gapes" at 4.4.75, and *Hamlet* 1.2.244.

1.2.69: Which renders good for bad, blessings for curses.

Matt. 5.44: "Blesse them that cursse you: doe good to them that hate you, and pray for them which hurt you."

Rom. 12.14: "Blesse them which persecute you: blesse, . . . and curse not."

1 Peter 3.9: "Not rendring euill for euill, . . . but contrariwise blesse." See also 1 Thess. 5.15.

[1.2.73: John 8.44.]

[1.2.108: Luke 9.62, AV only but no Tudor version.]

1.3.174:   When thou didst crown his warlike brows with paper.

Gloucester refers to the time when Queen Margaret mocked his father's claim to the throne with a paper crown prior to killing him, in the same manner that Christ was mocked prior to his crucifixion. Matthew 27.29. See the reference at *3 Henry VI* 1.4.90–95, and the comments thereon.

1.3.178:   His curses then, from bitterness of soul.

The expression "bitterness of soul" occurs several times in Scripture.
Compare Job 10.1: "Will speake in the bitternes of my soule."
Compare Job 21.25: "Another dyeth in the bitternes of his soule."
Compare also Prov. 14.10; Isa. 38.15. Not recorded in Tilley or Dent.

[1.3.220: 1 Kings 18.17–18; 1 Chron. 2.7.]

1.3.221:   The worm of conscience still begnaw thy soul!

Compare Geneva gloss "l" on Isa. 66.24: "Meaning, a continuall torment of conscience, which shall euer gnawe them and neuer suffer them to be at rest."

There are several references to troubled consciences in Shakespeare's sources (Holinshed 3/755, 756, 757; Hall 3.273, 291, 293; *The True Tragedy* 1405, 1878), but none of them employ the words "gnaw" or "begnaw" along with "conscience" as does the Geneva note at Isa. 66.24. However, although neither Tilley nor Dent record a similar proverb, both Shakespeare and the translators of the Geneva Bible were probably employing a common expression, rather than Shakespeare making a reference to this note in the Geneva Bible.

Closest verbal parallel in Shakespeare's sources; "The wild worme of vengeance wauering in his head" (Holinshed 3/746).

[1.3.229: Matt. 23.15.]

1.3.263:   Our aery buildeth in the cedar's top.

Compare Ezek. 17.3: "The great egle with great wings . . . tooke the hiest branch of the cedar."
Compare Ezek. 17.22: "I will also take off the toppe of this hie cedar."
The closest parallel in Shakespeare's sources appears in a completely different context. In the anonymous ballad, *The Rose of England,* the part that the Stanleys played in helping Richmond to the throne is referred to under the guise of an eagle (3.346–49). But there is no reference to a cedar. Shakespeare is considerably closer to Scripture.

1.3.286–87:   I will not think but they ascend the sky,
                       And there awake God's gentle-sleeping peace.

Compare Ps. 44.23: "Up Lord, why sleepest thou: awake and be not absent from vs for euer."
Compare Ps. 78.66 (78.65, Geneva): "So the Lorde awaked as one out of sleepe."
Compare also 4.4.24: "When didst thou sleep when such a deed was done?"
Closest verbal parallel in Shakespeare's sources, said of Richard in a completely different context: "He needed now no more . . . either to wake, or to breake his golden sleepe" (Holinshed 3/752).

1.3.315–16:   A virtuous and a Christian-like conclusion—
                       To pray for them that have done scathe to us.

Matt. 5.44: "Pray for them which hurt you, and persecute you."
Luke 6.28: "Pray for them which hurt you."
See above at 1.2.69.

1.3.326:   Clarence, who I indeed have cast in darkness.

Matt. 8.12: "The children of the kingdome shalbe cast out into vtter darkenes."

Matt. 22.13: "Cast him into vtter darkenes."
The expression also occurs at Matt. 25.30.

1.3.334:   Tell them that God bids us do good for evil.

Matt. 5.44: "Doe good to them that hate you, and pray for them which hurt you."
1 Thess. 5.15: "See that none recompence euill for euil vnto any man: but euer follow that which is good."
Rom. 12.21: "Be not ouercome of euil, but ouercome euil with goodnes."
See also Luke 6.27.
This biblical reference, as well as those at 1.2.69 and 1.3.315–16, which exhort men to render good for evil, were added by Shakespeare. There are no corresponding passages in his sources.

1.3.337:   And seem a saint, when most I play the devil.

Compare 2 Cor. 11.13–14: "Such false Apostles are deceitfull workers, and transforme them selues into the Apostles of Christ. And no marueile: for Satan him selfe is transformed into an Angel of light."
Like Satan who tempted Christ with Scripture (Matt. 4.1–11; Luke 4.1–13), so also Richard disguises his villainy "with a piece of scripture," and with texts "stol'n forth of holy writ" (1.3.333, 336).

[1.4.37: Gen. 35.18; Matt. 27.50; Acts 5.10.]

1.4.58:   A legion of foul fiends.

Mark 5.9: "My name is Legion: for we are many."

1.4.74:   My soul is heavy, and I fain would sleep.

Matt. 26.38, Tyndale, Coverdale, Matthew, Taverner, Great: "My soule is heauy."
Geneva: "My soule is very heauie."
Bishops': "My soule is exceeding heauy."
Rheims: "My soul is sorowful."
Compare also Matt. 26.43: "He came, and founde them a sleepe againe: for their eyes were heauie."

1.4.76–77:   Sorrow breaks seasons and reposing hours,
                     Makes the night morning and the noontide night.

Compare Job 17.11–12: "The thoughts of mine heart haue changed the nyght for the daye, and the lyght that approched, for darkenesse."

1.4.136–37:   A man cannot lie with his neighbor's wife.

Commination Service: "Cursed is he that lieth with his neighbors wife."
Deut. 27.20: "Cursed bee he that lieth with his fathers wife."

1.4.189–90:   I charge you, as you hope to have redemption
                     By Christ's dear blood shed for our grievous sins.

A general reference to Christian doctrine rather than to a specific text. The closest parallels in Scripture are:
Matt. 26.28: "This is my bloud . . . that is shed for many, for the remission of sinnes."
Rev. 5.9: "Thou was killed, and hast redeemed vs . . . by thy blood."
1 Peter 1.18–19: "Yee were not redeemed with corruptible things, . . . but with the precious blood of Christ."
Compare also the Litany: "Thy people whom thou hast redeemed with thy most precious blood."

1.4.195:   The great King of kings.

Rev. 19.16: "THE KING OF KINGS, AND LORDE OF LORDES."
Rev. 17.14: "He is Lord of Lordes, and King of Kings."
1 Tim. 6.15: "The King of Kings, and Lord of Lords."

1.4.196:   Hath in the table of his law commanded.

A general reference to the Ten Commandments in Exodus 20.
Ex. 32.15–16: "The two Tables of the Testimonie."
Ex. 34.28: "Hee wrote in the Tables the words of the couenant, euen the ten commandements."

1.4.197:   That thou shalt do no murther.

A reference to the sixth commandment as it appears in the Prayer Book in both the Catechism and the Communion Service: "Thou shalt doe no murther." All Protestant Tudor Bibles have "Thou shalt not kill" at Exodus 20, where the Ten Commandments first appear. The Douay Old Testament has "Thou shalt not murder," but the Douay was not published until 1609–10, long after *Richard III* appeared.

At Matthew 19.18, the Bishops' also has "Thou shalt doe no murder," and the Rheims New Testament has "Thou shalt not murder." But it is probably safe to infer that Shakespeare primarily echoes the Catechism in this passage, since he had been drilled in the Catechism as a child.

The Ten Commandments also appear in Deuteronomy 5, but only the Douay Old Testament, unavailable to Shakespeare, has "murder": "Thou shalt not murder" (5.17). All other English Bibles have either "Thou shalt not kill" or "Thou shalt not slay" at Deut. 5.17.

1.4.199–200:   Take heed; for he holds vengeance in his hand,
               To hurl upon their heads that break his law.

   Rom. 12.19: "Vengeance is mine."
   Rom. 13.4: "He is the minister of God to take vengeance on him that doth euil."
   See also Deut. 32.35: "Vengeance and recompence are mine."

1.4.201–206:   And that same vengeance doth he hurl on thee
               For false forswearing and for murther too.
               Thou didst receive the sacrament . . .

               .   .   .   .
               And like a traitor to the name of God
               Didst break that vow.

   Compare Matt. 5.33: "Thou shalt not forsweare thy selfe, but shalt performe thine othes to the Lord."
   Compare Eccles. 5.3–4 (5.4–5, AV): "When thou hast vowed a vowe to God, deferre not to pay it. . . . It is better that thou shouldest not vow, then that thou shouldest vow and not pay it."
   Compare also Deut. 23.21.

1.4.209–10:   How canst thou urge God's dreadful law to us,
              When thou hast broke it in such dear degree?

Compare Rom. 2.21–23: "Thou therefore which teachest another, teachest thou not thy selfe? . . . Thou that gloriest in the Lawe, through breaking the Law dishonourest thou God?"

Compare also Jas. 2.11.

Most likely an analogy rather than a reference.

1.4.215–19:   If God will be avenged for the deed,
              O, know you yet he doth it publicly.
              Take not the quarrel from his pow'rful arm;
              He needs no indirect or lawless course
              To cut off those that have offended him.

A well-known theme in Elizabethan England. Compare part 1 of the homily "Concerning Good Order, and Obedience to Rulers and Magistrates": "Wee reade in the booke of Deuteronomie, that all punishment pertaineth to GOD, by this sentence, Vengeance is mine, and I will reward. . . . No man (of his owne priuate authority) may bee iudge ouer other, may punish, or may kill. But we must referre all iudgement to GOD, to Kings, and Rulers, Iudges vnder them, which be GODS officers to execute iustice, and by plaine wordes of Scripture, haue their authoritie and vse of the sword graunted from GOD."

Compare Rom. 12.19: "Auenge not your selues, but giue place vnto wrath: for it is written, Vengeance is mine: I wil repay, saith the Lord."

Deut. 32.35, 43: "Vengeance and recompence are mine: . . . he wil auenge the blood of his seruants, and will execute vengeance vpon his aduersaries."

Compare also Luke 18.7–8.

1.4.217:   His pow'rful arm.

Compare Ex. 15.16: "Because of the greatnes of thine arme."

Compare Job 40.4 (40.9, AV): "Hast thou an arme like God?"

Compare Ps. 89.14 (89.13, Geneva): "Thou hast a mightie arme: strong is thy hand, and high is thy right hand."

See also Ps. 44.3–4 (44.3, Geneva); 89.22 (89.21, Geneva); Isa. 40.10; 51.9; 62.8; etc.

1.4.220:   Who made thee then a bloody minister?

Rom. 13.4, 6: "For he is the minister of God to take vengeance on him that doth euill. . . . For they are Gods ministers."

The self-appointed executioner who took the law into his own hands was "a bloody minister," in contrast to God's duly-appointed minister.

1.4.241–42:   *Clar.* O, do not slander him, for he is kind.
              1 Mur. Right, as snow in harvest.

Prov. 25.13: "As the cold of the snow in the time of haruest."
Compare also Prov. 26.1: "As the Snow in the sommer, and as the raine in the haruest are not meete. . . ."

[1.4.248: Heb. 12.2.]

1.4.249:   Make peace with God.

Compare Rom. 5.1, Tyndale, Matthew, Taverner, Great, Bishops': "We are at peace with God."
Coverdale: "We haue peace with God."
Geneva: "Wee haue peace towarde GOD."
Rheims: "Let vs haue peace toward God."
Compare also Isa. 27.5: "That he may make peace with me."
But the expression was probably common and may not be a conscious reference to any one Scripture.

1.4.272–73:   How fain, like Pilate, would I wash my hands
              Of this most grievous murther!

Matt. 27.24: "Pilate . . . tooke water and washed his hands before the multitude, saying, I am innocent of the bloud of this iust man."

2.1.13:   The supreme King of kings.

See above at 1.4.195.

2.1.50–53:   We have done deeds of charity,
             Made peace of enmity, . . .

             .   .   .   .
             A blessed labor.

Compare Matt. 5.9: "Blessed are the peacemakers."

[2.1.83: Ps. 33.13 (33.13–14, Geneva.)]

[2.1.124: Gen. 1.26; 9.6; Rom. 8.29.]

2.2.41–42:   Why grow the branches when the root is gone?
                 Why wither not the leaves that want their sap?

Compare John 15.4–6: "The branch cannot beare fruite of it selfe, except it abide in the vine. . . . He is cast forth as a branche, and withereth."
Perhaps an analogy rather than a reference. In *The True Tragedy*, Shore's wife makes a similar statement when she hears of King Edward's death: "For when the tree decaies / Whose fruitfull branch haue flourished many a yeare. . . ." (262–63).

2.2.107–108:   God bless thee, and put meekness in thy breast,
                  Love, charity, obedience, and true duty!

Compare 1 Tim. 6.11: "Followe after righteousnes, godlines, faith, loue, patience, and meekenes."
Probably an analogy based on Christian principles rather than a conscious reference to the text in Timothy.

[2.2.109: Gen. 25.8; 35.29.]

2.2.151–52:   My other self, my counsel's consistory,
                  My oracle, my prophet.

Compare 2 Sam. 16.23: "And the counsell of Ahithophel which hee counseled in those dayes, was like as one had asked counsell at the oracle of God: so was all the counsell of Ahithophel."
Perhaps an analogy rather than a reference.

2.3.11:   Woe to that land that's govern'd by a child!

Eccles. 10.16: "Wo to thee, O lande, when thy King is a child."
Homily "Against Disobedience and Wilfull Rebellion," part 1: "Againe the

Scriptures, of vndiscreet and euill Princes, speake thus, Woe be to thee (O thou land) whose King is but a child."

Shakespeare borrowed this reference from his sources. It appears in Hall ("Woe to that realm whose King is a child," 3.274), as well as in Holinshed, who cites it in both Latin and English: "*Vae regno cuius rex puer est:* Wo is that realme that hath a child to their king" (3/730). Both Hall and Holinshed no doubt borrowed the reference from More's *History of King Richard the Third*; More likewise has Buckingham quoting the text in both Latin and English: "*Veh regno cuius rex puer est.* Woe is that Realme, that hathe a chylde to theyre Kynge" (74).

In the Vulgate, Ecclesiastes 10.16 reads, "Vae tibi terra, cuius rex puer est."

Compare the reference at *1 Henry VI* 4.1.191–92.

2.3.38–44: Truly, the hearts of men are full of fear.

.   .   .   .

. . . as by proof we see
The water swell before a boist'rous storm.

Compare Luke 21.25–26: "The sea and the waters shal roare. And mens hearts shall fayle them for feare."

Shakespeare's primary source, however, was probably Holinshed rather than Scripture. Holinshed has, "They neither wist what they feared: . . . men's hearts . . . misgiue them; as the sea without wind swelleth . . . before a tempest" (3/721). But in Holinshed's narrative these words appear simply as a simile, with no hint that Scripture is being echoed. The same is true of More's account, Holinshed's ultimate source: "Mens hartes of a secret in-stinct of nature misgiueth them. As the sea without wind swelleth of himself somtime before a tempest" (44). Hall's account is somewhat different. Shakespeare is closer to Holinshed and More.

[2.4.62–63: Mark 13.12; Matt. 10.21.]

3.1.4–5: Our crosses on the way
Have made it tedious.

Derived ultimately from Jesus' words about bearing one's cross.
Matt. 16.24: "Let him forsake him selfe, and take vp his crosse."
See also Matt. 10.38; Mark 8.34; 10.21; Luke 9.23; 14.27.
Compare *3 Henry VI* 4.4.20.

3.1.9–11:   Nor more can you distinguish of a man
            Than of his outward show, which, God he knows,
            Seldom or never jumpeth with the heart.

Compare 1 Sam. 16.7: "Man looketh on the outwarde appearance, but the Lorde beholdeth the heart."

Perhaps an analogy rather than a reference. The closest parallel in Shakespeare's sources are Hall's comments about the slain Richard III: "God whiche knewe his interior cogitacions at the hower of his deathe" (3.300).

   [3.1.14: Ps. 140.3; Rom. 3.13.]

3.1.126–27:   My Lord of York will still be cross in talk.
              Uncle, your Grace knows how to bear with him.

Some have suggested that Shakespeare is here playing on the words "cross" and "bear" in Luke 14.27, Bishops': "Whosoeuer doeth not beare his crosse." The Tyndale, Matthew, Taverner, and Great Bibles are parallel to the Bishops'.

Geneva, Coverdale: "Whosoeuer beareth not his crosse."

But the context of Shakespeare's lines is considerably different from Jesus' words in Luke 14.27. See 3.1.4–5, above, where Shakespeare's context is parallel to Scripture.

3.2.111:   Come the next Sabbath.

The first two quartos have "sabaoth."

Q3–Q6, as well as the Folio, have "Sabboth."

Q8 (1634) has "Sabbath."

In Hebrew, the word "sabaoth" means "hosts," as in the expression, "the Lord of hosts" *(ts^{e}vaoth)*. But it is clear that those responsible for the first two quartos thought "sabaoth" was equivalent to "sabbath." See *The Merchant of Venice* 4.1.36, and the note thereon in *The Riverside Shakespeare*. See also the reference at *1 Henry VI* 1.1.31, and the comments thereon.

   [3.4.10–11: 1 Sam. 16.7.]

3.4.76–77:   Off with his head! Now by Saint Paul I swear
             I will not dine until I see the same.

Some authorities feel that Richard's oath not to dine until Hastings's head was cut off is an allusion to Acts 23.12: "Certaine of the Iewes . . . bound them selues with an oth, saying, that they would neither eate nor drinke, till they had killed Paul." The fact that Richard swears by Saint Paul supposedly strengthens this conclusion.

However, Shakespeare borrowed Richard's oath from his sources. In Hall's account, Richard not only swears "by sainct Poule . . . I wyll not dyne tyll I se thy head off" when he arrests Hastings (3.265), but also threatens Lord Stanley at the Battle of Bosworth that if Stanley refused to fight on his side, "he sware by Christes passion that he woulde stryke of his sonnes hedde before he dined" (3.299). Both of these oaths also appear in Holinshed (3/723, 760). Richard's oath relative to Hastings also occurs in the anonymous play, *The True Tragedy of Richard the Third:* "By the blessed Saint *Paule* I sweare, I will not dine till I see the traitors head" (951–53), as well as in More's account (49).

Shakespeare may have been aware of the similarity between his sources and the account in Acts, but it is probably safer to conclude that he was not making a conscious biblical reference in this passage.

3.4.92–93:   Now thy heavy curse
               Is lighted on poor Hastings' wretched head!

A common expression that probably had its origin in Scripture, and by Shakespeare's time had become proverbial.

Compare Tilley C924: "Curses return upon the heads of those that curse."

Compare Josh. 2.19: "His blood shall be vpon his head."

Compare 1 Sam. 25.39: "The Lord hath recompensed the wickednesse of Nabal vpon his owne head."

See *Henry VIII* 2.1.137–39 for additional biblical parallels.

[3.4.96–97: Jer. 17.5; Ps. 146.2 (146.3, Geneva); Commination Service. But Shakespeare's immediate source was probably Holinshed (3/723) rather than Scripture or the Prayer Book.]

3.4.99–101:   Like a drunken sailor on a mast,
                Ready with every nod to tumble down
                Into the fatal bowels of the deep.

Prov. 23.34, of a drunk person: "Thou shalt be as one that sleepeth in the middes of the sea, and as he that sleepeth in the toppe of the mast."

Homily "Against Gluttony and Drunkennesse": "Solomon, who . . .
forbiddeth the very sight of wine [sayeth] . . . thou shalt bee as one that
sleepeth in the middes of the sea, and as he that sleepeth on the toppe of the
maste."

[3.5.27–28: Rev. 20.12.]

3.5.41:   Think you we are Turks or infidels?

Compare the Prayer Book, third collect for Good Friday: "Haue mercie
vpon all Jewes, Turkes, Infidels, and Heretikes."

3.7.73–77:   But on his knees at meditation;

   . . . .

Not sleeping, to engross his idle body,
But praying, to enrich his watchful soul.

Compare the words "sleeping," "praying," and "watchful" with Matt.
26.40–41: "He came vnto the disciples, and founde them a sleepe, and saide
to Peter, What? coulde ye not watch with me one houre? Watch, and pray."

[3.7.146–47: Matt. 11.29–30.]

[3.7.167: Matt. 12.33.]

4.3.38:   The sons of Edward sleep in Abraham's bosom.

Luke 16.22: "The begger dyed, and was caryed by the Angels into
Abrahams bosome."

4.4.22–23:   Wilt thou, O God, fly from such gentle lambs,
           And throw them in the entrails of the wolf?

Compare John 10.12: "An hierling . . . seeth the wolfe comming, and he
leaueth the sheepe, and fleeth."
If Shakespeare is making a conscious reference to Scripture in this passage,
then the reference was probably suggested to him by his sources, where the
wolf-lamb image occurs several times. See 3.258, 287, 293 in Hall, and
3/716, 750, 756 in Holinshed, where Holinshed borrows the same three

passages from Hall. The passages at 3.258 in Hall and 3/716 in Holinshed are drawn, ultimately, from More, who writes that when the Duke of Gloucester was made the king's protector, "the lamb was betaken to the wolfe to kepe" (24–25).

In *The True Tragedy*, the comparison occurs in a different context. When Lord Stanley is reunited with his son George, who had been taken hostage by Richard III, George compares his experience to "a lambe kept by a greedie Woolfe" (2140–41).

[4.4.24: Ps. 44.23; 78.66 (78.65, Geneva). See 1.3.286–87, above.]

[4.4.30: Rev. 17.6.]

4.4.51:   That foul defacer of God's handiwork.

Compare Isa. 64.8: "We are all the worke of thine hands."
Compare Job 34.19: "They be all the worke of his hands."
Compare also Job 14.15; Isa. 45.11; Ps. 119.73; 100.2 (100.3, Geneva); etc.

[4.4.60: Rom. 1.9; Gen. 31.50; 1 Sam. 12.5.]

[4.4.111: Jer. 27.8, 11, 12.]

4.4.140–42:   That forehead . . .
              Where should be branded . . .
              The slaughter of the prince.

Most likely a reference to Cain, who was branded with a mark for killing his brother. Gen. 4.15: "The Lord set a marke vpon Kain."

Closest parallel in Shakespeare's sources: "If thy faults were so written in thy forehead as mine is, it would be as wrong with thee" (*The True Tragedy* 1175–76). But the context is considerably different, these words being spoken by Shore's wife.

4.4.151:   Rail on the Lord's anointed.

2 Sam. 19.21: "Shal not Shimei die for this, because he cursed the Lords anoynted?"

In ancient Israel, the king was called "the Lords anointed." See 1 Sam. 16.6; 24.7, 11 (24.6, 10, AV); 26.9, 16; 2 Sam. 1.14; Lam. 4.20; Ps. 2.2.

The expression occurs several times in Shakespeare's sources.

Compare the references at *1 Henry IV* 4.3.40 and *King John* 3.1.136 and the comments thereon.

4.4.184:   Either thou wilt die by God's just ordinance.

An indirect reference to the biblical death penalty for murder.

Compare Gen. 9.6: "Who so sheadeth mans blood, by man shal his blood be shed."

Compare Ex. 21.23: "But if death folowe, then thou shalt pay life for life."

Compare Lev. 24.17: "He also that killeth any man, he shall be put to death."

See also Deut. 19.21.

[4.4.318–19: Job 42.10.]

4.4.345–46:   *K. Rich.* Tell her the King, that may command, entreats.
              Q. Eliz. That at her hands which the King's King forbids.

A reference to the biblical injunctions against incest, summarized in the Anglican Church's Table of Kindred and Affinity drawn up by Archbishop Parker in 1563, and given full status of law by Canon 99 in 1604.

Richard sought to marry his niece to strengthen his claim to the throne. The Table of Kindred and Affinity stipulated that 'a man may not marry his brother's daughter', based on Lev. 18.16–17: "Thou shalt not discouer the shame of thy brothers wife: for it is thy brothers shame. Thou shalt not discouer the shame of the wife and of her daughter, neither shalt thou take her sonnes daughter, nor her daughters daughter, to vncouer her shame: for they are thy kinsfolks, and it were wickednes."

Richard reigned from 1483–85, prior to Archbishop Parker's time, but the religious prohibitions against incest were known before the break with Rome. Hall has: "All men, and the mayden her selfe moost of all, detested and abhorred this unlawfull and in maner unnaturall copulacion" (3.288). Hall's *Chronicle* first appeared in 1548, after the separation from Rome, but long before the Table of Kindred and Affinity was drawn up.

4.4.385–86:   Two tender bedfellows for dust,
              Thy broken faith hath made the prey for worms.

Probably an echo of Job 21.26: "They shall sleepe both in the dust, and the wormes shall couer them."

See also Job 17.14.

4.4.418: Shall I be tempted of the devil thus?

With clear overtones of the Devil's temptation of Jesus.
Matt. 4.1: "Then was Iesus led . . . to be tempted of the deuill."
Luke 4.2: "Fourtie dayes tempted of the deuil."

5.1.23–24: Thus doth he force the swords of wicked men
To turn their own points in their masters' bosoms.

Compare Ps. 37.15: "Their sworde shall goe through their owne heart."
Compare Ps. 7.17 (7.16, Geneva): "His trauel shal come vpon his own head: and his wickednes shal fall on his own pate."
Compare also Ps. 9.15–16; 1 Kings 2.32–33.
Perhaps an analogy rather than a reference, as the thought is common.

5.3.12: The King's name is a tower of strength.

Prov. 18.10: "The Name of the Lorde is a strong tower."
Shakespeare probably had Prov. 18.10 in mind in this passage. If so, then his reference is to the Geneva Bible. All other versions have: "The name of the Lord is a strong castle."
But compare Ps. 61.3: "For thou hast bene my hope, and a strong towre for me against the enemie."

[5.3.19–21: Matt. 16.2.]

5.3.108, 113: O Thou whose captain I account myself,

. . . .

Make us thy ministers of chastisement.

Compare Rom. 13.4: "For hee is the minister of God: . . . for he is the minister of God to take vengeance on him that doth euil."
A well-known Tudor doctrine that was often rehearsed in the homilies. See part 1 of the homily "Concerning Good Order, and Obedience to Rulers

and Magistrates," as well as all six parts of the homily "Against Disobedience and Wilfull Rebellion."

Richmond proclaims himself to be God's duly-appointed minister of chastisement, and not a rebel as defined in the homilies. In his oration to his soldiers prior to the Battle of Bosworth, he refers to his forces as, "The scourges of God against tyrants" (Holinshed 3/758; see also Hall 3.296).

Compare also the references at *2 Henry VI* 3.2.285–86 and *King John* 2.1.87.

See 1.4.220, above.

5.3.110:   Put in their hands thy bruising irons of wrath.

Ps. 2.9 (of King David, the Lord's anointed): "Thou shalt bruise them with a rod of iron."

Shakespeare appears to have had the Psalter in mind in this passage. The Geneva has, "Thou shalt krush them with a scepter of yron."

Shakespeare's choice of the word "wrath" may have been influenced by verse 5 of this Psalm: "Then shall he speake vnto them in his wrath."

See also Rev. 2.27.

5.3.124:   My anointed body.

See above at 4.4.151.

[5.3.138, 151: Ps. 91.11; Matt. 4.6; Luke 4.10.]

[5.3.150: Ps. 4.8, Geneva: "sleepe in peace." The Psalter (4.9) has: "lay me downe in peace, and take my rest."]

5.3.241–42:   The prayers of holy saints and wronged souls,
**   . . . stand before our faces.**

Compare Rev. 6.9–10: "I saw . . . the soules of them, that were killed for the worde of God. . . . And they cryed with a loude voyce, saying, How long, Lord, . . . doest not thou iudge and auenge our blood?"

Compare Rev. 5.8: "The prayers of the Saints."

Closest parallel in Shakespeare's sources: "Whose guiltlesse blood craues daily at Gods hands, / Reuenge for outrage done to their harmelesse liues"

(*The True Tragedy* 1648–49). Richmond is the speaker in both plays.
See also *The True Tragedy* 1783–84.

[5.3.258: Gen. 45.18.]

[5.5.24–26: Matt. 10.21; Micah 7.6. See the reference at *Richard II* 4.1.136–41 and the comments thereon. See also the stage directions at *3 Henry VI* 2.5.54 and at 2.5.78.]

Richard II

Richard II is a play about a successful rebellion in which the rightful king is deposed by a relative who had no legal claim to the throne. But to Elizabethans, a rebellion against the duly-constituted monarch was a heinous sin comparable to the rebellion of Satan against God. It mattered not that the deposed king was hated by his subjects and was unfit to rule, and that his successor was not only fit, but had been terribly wronged by his evil predecessor. The king was God's anointed against whom no one could rightly rebel.

The play was very popular. Five quarto editions were published before the First Folio appeared in 1623 (1597, two in 1598, 1608, and 1615). But the famous deposition scene (4.1.154–318), enough to make any monarch uneasy, was not published until Q4, in 1608. Even Q4–5 (1608, 1615) present an inferior, probably reported, text of the deposition. That scene was no doubt performed on the stage, but was not allowed to be published during Elizabeth's reign. On 7 February 1601, the day before the Earl of Essex attempted to overthrow the queen, his followers persuaded Shakespeare's company to perform the play at the Globe and paid them an honorarium of forty shillings for doing so. If the rebels thought that the play would encourage Londoners to support their rebellion, they were mistaken. Although Shakespeare's company was exonerated of any complicity, a few months later Queen Elizabeth said: "I am Richard II. know ye not that? . . . This tragedy was played 40^tie times in open streets and houses."

Shakespeare's sources for *Richard II* are a matter of dispute. While most authorities agree that his main source was Holinshed, the agreement stops there. Shakespeare may have consulted more than a dozen works, including two French manuscripts. But so eminent an authority as John Dover Wilson discounted that many sources. In the introduction to his edition of the play, he postulated a lost play as Shakespeare's main source, and said that that lost play along with Daniel's *Civil Wars* and the anonymous play *Thomas of Woodstock* "are together sufficient to account for all the facts."

Dover Wilson's arguments for a lost play as Shakespeare's main source have not been generally accepted, and it appears likely that Shakespeare did consult a large number of sources when writing the play. His main sources were the second edition of Holinshed's *Chronicles* (1587), Daniel's epic poem *The Civil Wars between the Two Houses of Lancaster and York* (1595), the anonymous play *Thomas of Woodstock* (written ca. 1591–95; first printed in 1870), and Lord Berners's translation of *The Chronicle of Sir John Froissart* (1523–63; STC 11396–97). Secondary sources include two French manuscripts: the *Chronicque de la Traïson et Mort de Richart Deux Roy Dengleterre*, evidently written by a member of Queen Isabella's entourage, and the *Histoire du Roy d'Angleterre Richard*, written by Jean Créton, who accompanied King Richard on his expedition to Ireland in 1399. Holinshed, Hall, and Daniel all used the *Traïson;* Holinshed refers four times to the *Traïson* and three times to Créton as sources. From these two sources Shakespeare probably borrowed the comparison of Richard's betrayal to Christ's. Holinshed refers to the archbishop as a Pilate (see 4.1.239–42, below), and at 4.1.169–70 Shakespeare borrows the wording of a medieval mystery play when he refers to Judas. But the emphasis on Richard's betrayal as being parallel to Christ's occurs only in the *Traïson*, in Créton, and in Shakespeare, and Shakespeare's inspiration for that parallel evidently came from them.

Other secondary sources probably include Hall's chronicle (1548), since Shakespeare begins his play precisely where Hall begins his chronicle: the quarrel between Mowbray and Bolingbroke. Hall's huge chronicle begins with the life of Henry IV, and Hall begins that narrative by introducing Bolingbroke, the future Henry IV, as Mowbray accuses him before Richard II. There may also be an echo of Hall at 3.4.84–86, but Holinshed borrowed so much from Hall that it is difficult to find solid evidence that Shakespeare used Hall.

Shakespeare certainly knew *The Mirror for Magistrates*, which from the first edition (1559) contained the tragedies not only of Richard, but also of Gloucester, Mowbray, Norfolk, and Northumberland. Yet Shakespeare does not seem to have used it. There may also be a few faint echoes of Lyly's *Euphues*. There are firmer echoes of Cicero's *Tusculan Disputations*, either in Latin or in Dolman's translation (STC 5317); John Eliot's translation of lines from Du Bartas (1593; STC 7574); and Thomas Lodge's poem "Truth's Complaint over England" (1584; in STC 16653).

There are relatively few biblical references in most of these sources. There are no more than six references in those portions of Holinshed's *Chronicles* that cover the same events as Shakespeare's play. One of these references is to Pilate, but as we have seen, that reference occurs in a completely different context and does not seem to have been Shakespeare's principal inspiration for the references to Pilate in *Richard II*. The three other primary sources likewise contain few references. There are no biblical references at all in those chapters of Froissart's long chronicle that deal with the closing years of Richard's life that are covered in Shakespeare's play. Daniel's poem is almost completely devoid of biblical references. As pointed out at 3.3.88, 4.1.136–41, and 4.1.322–23 in the list of references, Daniel has expressions and ideas that find parallels in the homilies, but almost no clear references. Two possible biblical references in Daniel are indicated at 5.1.69 and 5.6.43. The situation with *Woodstock* is somewhat different. Shakespeare borrowed more biblical references from it than from any of his other sources. The play does not have many references; the text that we have has just under three thousand lines and contains at most some fourteen references. Two of the clearest occur at 2134 ("So many wyld boores rootes & spoyles our lands"; a reference to Ps. 80.13: "The wilde Bore of the wood doeth roote it vp"), and at 2026–28 (with its images of "Rauening wooInes," "Silly sheepe," and "sloothfull Shephard," most likely based on John 10), but Shakespeare used neither of them. The references that he did use are indicated in the text below, although some of these may be striking parallels to Scripture rather than conscious biblical references.

As for Shakespeare's secondary sources, the most significant biblical borrowing is the betrayal of Christ theme taken from Créton and the *Traïson*. But these works contain very few additional references to Scripture, none of which Shakespeare used, and the same is true of the other sources, or those portions of them that he seems to have consulted. As was Shakespeare's usual practice, the many biblical references in the play are largely his own.

In the list that follows, page numbers preceded by the number 3, as in (3.386), refer to volume 3 of Bullough. Passages from the *Traïson*, from Créton, from Hall, Daniel, and Froissart that are not included in Bullough are from the editions of those works listed in the bibliography. References to *Thomas of Woodstock* are to the Malone Society edition of 1929, since the text in Bullough is not complete.

1.1.104–106:   Which blood, like sacrificing Abel's, cries,
                  Even from the tongueless caverns of the earth,
                  To me for justice.

Gen. 4.10: "What hast thou done? the voyce of thy brothers blood cryeth vnto me from the earth."

The account of Cain and Abel is recorded at Genesis 4.1–17. "Sacrificing Abel's" probably refers to the offering Abel made to God, "the first fruites of his sheepe, and of the fatte of them" (Gen. 4.4). Cain's offering consisted "of the fruite of the ground."

[1.1.114: Prov. 6.16–17.]

[1.1.160: Matt. 5.9.]

1.1.174–75: Lions make leopards tame.
          Mow. Yea, but not change his spots.

Jer. 13.23: "Can the blacke More change his skin? or the leopard his spottes?"
   A clear reference to the Geneva Bible. All other versions have "catte of the mountaine" instead of "leopard."

1.2.8: Will rain hot vengeance on offenders' heads.

   Compare Gen. 19.24: "Then the Lorde rained vpon Sodom and vpon Gomorah brimstone, and fire."
   Compare Luke 17.29: "It rained fire and brimstone from heauen, and destroyed them all."
   Compare Jude 7, Tyndale, Coverdale, Matthew, Geneva: "As Sodom and Gomorrhe . . . suffer the vengeance of eternall fire." (Taverner: "the vengeaunce of euerlasting fyre.")
   The Great, Bishops', and Rheims lack "vengeance" at Jude 7. These versions have, "The paine of eternal fire."
   Compare Ps. 11.7 (11.6, Geneva): "Upon the vngodly he shal raine snares, fire, and brimstone."
   Compare Ps. 140.10: "Let hot burning coales fall vpon them."
   Compare Ezek. 38.22: "I will cause to raine vpon him . . . fire, and brimstone."
   Compare the reference at *2 Henry VI* 5.2.36.

1.2.20: His summer leaves all faded.

   Compare Ps. 1.3, Geneva: "Whose leafe shall not fade."
   Psalter (1.4): "His leafe also shall not wither."
   Compare Isa. 1.30: "For ye shalbe as an oke, whose leafe fadeth."
   All other versions (Coverdale, Matthew, Taverner, Great, Bishops'): "Whose leaues are fallen awaye."
   If Shakespeare had Scripture in mind in this passage, then he is closer to the Geneva Bible than to the Psalter in the first Psalm, and closer to the Geneva Bible than to any other Bible at Isa. 1.30. But Shakespeare's line may be an analogy rather than a reference to Scripture.

1.2.22–24: That womb,
          . . . that self mould, that fashioned thee
          Made him a man.

Compare Job 31.15: "He that hath made me in the wombe, hath he not made him? hath not he alone facioned vs in the wombe?"

Compare Job 33.6, all versions except Geneva: "Before God, I am euen as thou: for I am fashioned and made euen of the same moulde."

Geneva: "I am according to thy wish in Gods stead: I am also formed of the clay."

Shakespeare is least like the Geneva Bible at Job 33.6 and closer to all the other versions of the day. But all translations have "womb," "made," and "fashioned," at Job 31.15, although with varying word order.

1.2.38–41ᵃ: His deputy anointed in His sight,

. . . .

. . . for I may never lift
An angry arm against His minister.

In ancient Israel, the king was called "the Lords anointed," since oil was poured over his head at his installation. See 1 Samuel 10.1. David several times said that he could not raise his hand against "the Lords anointed."

1 Sam. 26.9, 11: "Dauid saide . . . who can lay his hand on the Lords anointed, and be giltlesse? . . . The Lord keepe me from laying mine hand vpon the Lordes anointed." See also 1 Sam. 24.7, 11 (24.6, 10, AV).

The phrase is used frequently in the homilies. See *1 Henry IV* 4.3.40 and *3 Henry VI* 3.1.17 and the comments thereon.

Shakespeare's immediate source for 1.2.38, however, may have been the anonymous play, *Thomas of Woodstock*. Prior to the battle between the king's forces and those of his uncles, Lancaster (Gaunt) and York, Richard tells his foes that they drew their swords against "the hyest gods Anoynted Deputye / Breakeing your holly oathes to heauen & vs" (2778–79).

The idea that the king was God's anointed was so common in Shakespeare's day, that in a play about a rebellion against the king, Shakespeare probably would have referred to Richard as God's anointed even if there had been no parallel line in *Thomas of Woodstock*. In Shakespeare's play, John of Gaunt speaks these words, while in the anonymous play the speaker is Richard. But since Shakespeare borrowed the following line (2779) from the anonymous play at 4.1.234–35, listed below, *Woodstock* could also have been his inspiration for the reference to the king as God's anointed at 1.2.38.

1.2.38–41ᵇ: His deputy . . .
Hath caus'd his death, the which if wrongfully,
Let heaven revenge, for I may never lift
An angry arm against His minister.

The Tudors stressed the theme that secular rulers were God's duly-appointed deputies or ministers. Romans 13 was frequently quoted in the homilies to support that claim.

Rom. 13.4: "For hee is the minister of God: . . . for he beareth not the sword for nought: for he is the minister of God to take vengeance on him that doth euil."

Gaunt says that even if Richard has wrongfully caused the death of Gloucester, they must patiently wait on heaven for vengeance, and not rebel against the king. Compare part 2 of the homily "Concerning Good Order, and Obedience to Rulers and Magistrates": "Whereby Christ taught vs plainely, that euen the wicked rulers haue their power and authoritie from GOD, and therefore it is not lawfull for their Subiects to withstand them, although they abuse their power: . . . to perswade obedience to gouernours, yea, although they bee wicked and wrong doers." The same part of the homily later says: "Wee must in such case patiently suffer all wrongs, and iniuries, referring the iudgement of our cause onely to GOD."

See *2 Henry VI* 3.2.285–86 and *King John* 2.1.87 and the comments thereon for additional passages from the homilies. See also the reference at *Richard III* 5.3.108, 113 where Richmond claims to be God's minister of chastisement.

Compare the prayer for the Queen in the Communion Service: "So rule the hart of thy chosen seruaunt Elizabeth, our Queene, and gouernour, that she (knowyng whose Minister she is). . . ."

For the words, "Let heaven revenge," compare Rom. 12.19: "Auenge not your selues . . . for it is written, Vengeance is mine: I wil repay, saith the Lord." See also the reference at *Richard III* 1.4.215–19 and the comments thereon.

The closest parallel in Shakespeare's sources to Gaunt's "Let heaven revenge" are the words of Woodstock's (the Duke of Gloucester's) murderer just before the murder. Lapoole says that his conscience bids him refrain from murder, "& tells me that his Innocent blood thus spilt / Heauen will reuenge" (2422–23).

1.2.43:   To God, the widow's champion and defense.

Ps. 68.5: "He is a father of the fatherlesse, and defendeth the cause of the widowes."

Ps. 146.9: "The Lord . . . defendeth the fatherlesse and widow."

Shakespeare is closer to the Psalter in both texts. Instead of "defendeth," the Geneva has "a Iudge of the widowes" in the former text, and "relieueth the fatherles and widowe" at Ps. 146.9.

See the parallel passages at *King John* 3.1.108 and *2 Henry VI* 5.1.187–88 and the comments thereon.

1.3.101–102:   God defend the right!
            Bull. Strong as a tower in hope, I cry amen.

Compare Ps. 61.3: "For thou hast bene my hope, and a strong towre for me against the enemie."

Compare Prov. 18.10: "The Name of the Lorde is a strong tower."

Both Hall and Holinshed have "God aid him that hath the right" (3.386, 393), parallel to 1.3.101, this being the usual formula uttered before the combat. The *Traïson* has, "Dieux aide au droit" (20). To this Shakespeare adds the biblical reference in line 102, a passage that appears in none of his sources.

If Shakespeare's reference in this passage is to Prov. 18.10, then he had the Geneva Bible in mind. Only the Geneva has "strong tower." All other versions have, "The name of the Lord is a strong castle." But his reference may have been primarily to Ps. 61.3.

1.3.202:   My name be blotted from the book of life.

Rev. 3.5, Bishops': "I will not blot out his name out of the booke of life."

The Bishops' is the only Bible of Shakespeare's day that has "blot out" at Rev. 3.5. All the other versions, including the Rheims New Testament, have "put out." Shakespeare's line seems to reflect the Bishops' Bible in this passage.

No version, not even the Bishops', has "blot out" at the parallel passage in Ex. 32.32–33: "If thou wilt not, wipe me, I pray thee, out of thy booke which thou hast written. And the Lorde sayde vnto Moses, I will put him out of my booke that hath sinned agaynst me" (Bishops'). At Ps. 69.29 (69.28, Geneva) the Psalter has, "Let them bee wiped out of the booke of the liuing."

The expression "book of life" also occurs in Rev. 17.8; 20.12, 15; 21.27; Phil. 4.3. See 4.1.236, below.

[1.3.236: Rev. 10.10. But see Tilley M1265.]

1.3.304:   I'll bring thee on thy way.

Compare Gen. 18.16: "Abraham went with them to bring them on the way."

Compare 1 Cor. 16.6: "That ye may bring mee on my way."

See the parallel expression at *Othello* 3.4.197. But Shakespeare was probably using a common expression rather than making a conscious reference to Scripture.

1.4.23–28: Ourself and Bushy . . .
> Observ'd his courtship to the common people,
> How he did seem to dive into their hearts
> With humble and familiar courtesy,
> What reverence he did throw away on slaves,
> Wooing poor craftsmen with the craft of smiles.

Compare 2 Sam. 15.5–6 concerning Absalom: "And when any man came neere to him, and did him obeisance, hee put forth his hande, and tooke him, and kissed him. And on this maner did Absalom to all Israel, that came to the King for iudgement: so Absalom stale the heartes of the men of Israel."

Holinshed does not say that Bolingbroke courted the favor of the masses as he left England, but that the people ran after him: "So he tooke his jornie over into Calis, and from thence went into France, where he remained. A woonder it was to see what number of people ran after him in everie towne and street where he came, before he tooke the sea, lamenting and bewailing his departure, as who would saie, that when he departed the onelie shield, defense, and comfort of the commonwealth was vaded and gone" (3.394).

Daniel likewise expresses the dismay and anger of the populace at Bolingbroke's banishment, and how the "open multitude" ran after him at his departure:

> At whose departure hence out of the land,
> O how the open multitude reueale
> The wondrous loue they bare him vnderhand,
> . . . .
> Vnto the shore with teares, with sighes, with mone
> They him conduct. . . .
>
> (1.67–68)

A few stanzas later, Daniel briefly explains the reason for their anger. He says that in the past,

> For this good Duke had wonne them in this sort
> By suckring them and pittying of their ill.
>
> (1.71)

While this brief passage in Daniel (1.71) could have been Shakespeare's inspiration for 1.4.23–28, it is more likely that he patterned his lines on the well-known account in 2 Samuel. Notice the word "hearts" in both Shakespeare and Scripture. Daniel's account that Bolingbroke had "wonne them . . . / By suckring them and pittying of their ill" may have reminded Shakespeare of the biblical account about Absalom, so that he changed his main source, Holinshed, and made Bolingbroke woo the populace rather than have them run after him to lament his banishment.

Froissart likewise has no hint that Bolingbroke courted the favor of the people when banished. Like Holinshed, he says that the citizens of London came out in force to weep at his departure: "There were in the stretes mo thanne fourtie thousande men, wepyng and cryeng after hym, that it was pytie to here" (Books 3 and 4, cap. 226).

It is likely, therefore, that Shakespeare patterned Bolingbroke's conduct towards the people on the account about Absalom in 2 Samuel 15. Compare the references at *1 Henry IV* 3.2 50–54 and 4.3.82–84.

2.1.42:   This other Eden, demi-paradise.

Gen. 2.8: "The Lord God planted a garden Eastward in Eden, and there he put the man whom he had made."

In Genesis 13.10, Eden is referred to as "the garden of the Lord." At Ezekiel 28.13, the king of Tyre is said to be "in Eden the garden of God" on account of his wealth and the beauty of his city. John of Gaunt compares England to Eden's beauty.

The closest parallel in Shakespeare's sources is Thomas Lodge's poem "Truth's Complaint over England," published in 1584. In praising England's enviable situation as a blessed island, he says that it "should seeme the seate [to] bee, / Of Paradise, if it from sinne were free." (In the volume *An Alarum Against Vsurers,* STC 16653, p. 37ᵛ.) Lodge's poem seems to have been Shakespeare's source of inspiration not only for this line of Gaunt's deathbed speech, but for several other lines as well.

2.1.55–56:   As is the sepulchre in stubborn Jewry
             Of the world's ransom, blessed Mary's Son.

These terms originate with Scripture. "Sepulchre" is the standard word for Christ's grave in the Gospels, as at Matt. 27.60–66; 28.1–8. Thus we have the "Church of the Holy Sepulchre" in Jerusalem.

For Christ as a ransom, see Matt. 20.28: "To giue his life for the ransome of many."

Bishops': "To giue his life a ransome for many."

See also 1 Tim. 2.6: "Who gaue him selfe a raunsome for all men."

While some versions (Tyndale, Coverdale, Matthew, Taverner, Great, Rheims) have "redemption" at Matt. 20.28, all except the Rheims New Testament have "ransom" at 1 Tim. 2.6. The Rheims has "a redemption for al" at that text.

2.1.98: Thy anointed body.

See 1.2.38–41ª, above.

2.2.3–4: Lay aside life-harming heaviness
          And entertain a cheerful disposition.

Compare Ecclus. 30.23, Bishops': "As for sorowe and heauinesse, driue it farre from thee: for heauinesse hath slayne many a man."

The Geneva has "sorowe" rather than "heauinesse" in the above text. But compare Ecclus. 30.21, 22, 24 in the Geneva: "Giue not ouer thy minde to heauines, and vexe not thy selfe in thine owne counsell. The ioye of the heart is the life of man, and a mans gladnes is the prolonging of his dayes. . . . Enuie and wrath shorten the life, and carefulness bringeth age before the time."

Compare also Ecclus. 38.18, 20: "For of heauines commeth death, and the heauines of the heart breaketh the strength. . . . Take no heauines to heart."

2.2.76: For God's sake speak comfortable words.

Compare the Communion Service: "Heare what comfortable wordes our Sauiour Christ saith vnto all that truely turne to him."

Compare 2 Sam. 14.17: "The word of my lorde the King shall nowe bee comfortable."

Compare Zech. 1.13: "And the Lorde answered the Angel that talked with me, with good wordes and comfortable wordes."

Compare Ecclus. 18.14: "My sonne, . . . vse no discomfortable wordes."

Noble thinks that Shakespeare's reference is primarily to Ecclus. 18.14 in this passage, more so than to the Communion Service or any of the other texts, since at 3.2.36 Richard says, "Discomfortable cousin." The expression "comfortable words," however, seems to have been a common one in Shakespeare's day. In his *Life and Death of Cardinal Wolsey*, written ca. 1556–58, Cavendish used that expression at least seven times (102, 121 [twice], 132 [twice], 161, 173). It appears in Hall's account of Richard III (3.294) as Richmond encourages his troops at the Battle of Bosworth. It also occurs in *Lancelot of the Laik*, the Scottish paraphrase and adaptation of the Lancelot story, written ca. 1485–1500: "And confortable wordis to them schew" (2654). Even Chaucer has "And with wordes to comforte" in *The House of Fame* (572).

It would appear, therefore, that Shakespeare was using a common expression, but one that he also repeatedly heard in the Communion Service.

2.2.79.   Where nothing lives but crosses, cares, and grief.

"Crosses" in the sense of distress or suffering derives ultimately from Scripture.

Compare Matt. 16.24: "If any man wil followe me, let him . . . take vp his crosse, and followe me."

See also Matt. 10.38; Mark 8.34; 10.21; Luke 9.23; 14.27.

2.3.96:   The anointed King.

See 1.2.38–41ᵃ, above.

2.3.104–105:   Chastise thee,
                And minister correction to thy fault!

In Richard's absence, York was the appointed "lord governor of England" (2.1.220). As such, he was God's minister of chastisement against evildoers as described at Rom. 13.4: "For hee is the minister of God: . . . for he beareth not the sword for nought: for he is the minister of God to take vengeance on him that doth euil."

See 1.2.38–41ᵇ above, and the comments thereon.

[2.3.120: Gen. 4.12. See 5.6.43, below.]

[2.4.19–20: Rev. 9.1; 8.10; Luke 10.18.]

3.1.5–6:   Yet, to wash your blood
          From off my hands, here in the view of men.

Matt. 27.24: "When Pilate sawe that hee auailed nothing, . . . he tooke water and washed his hands before the multitude, saying, I am innocent of the bloud of this iust man."

See 4.1.239–42, below.

3.1.21:   Eating the bitter bread of banishment.

Compare 1 Kings 22.27: "Feed him with bread of affliction, and with water of affliction."

Compare Isa. 30.20: "The Lorde hath giuen you the bread of aduersitie, and the water of affliction."

See also Deut. 16.3; 2 Chron. 18.26.

3.1.34:   The pains of hell.

Compare Ps. 18.4 (18.5, Geneva): "The paines of hell came about me."

Compare Ps. 116.3: "The paynes of hell gat holde vpon me."

A reference to the Psalter. The Geneva has "sorowes of the graue" in the former passage, and "griefes of the graue" at Ps. 116.3.

   [3.2.24–26: Luke 19.40.]

3.2.36–46:   Know'st thou not
             That when the searching eye of heaven is hid
             Behind the globe, that lights the lower world,
             Then thieves and robbers range abroad unseen
             In murthers and in outrage boldly here,
             But when from under this terrestrial ball
             He fires the proud tops of the eastern pines
             And darts his light through every guilty hole,
             Then murthers, treasons, and detested sins,
             The cloak of night being pluck'd from off their backs,
             Stand bare and naked, trembling at themselves?

Compare Job 24.13–17: "These are they, that abhorre the light: they knowe not the wayes thereof, nor continue in the paths thereof. The murtherer riseth early and killeth the poore and the needie: and in the night he is as a thiefe. The eye also of the adulterer waiteth for the twylight, and sayeth, None eye shall see me, and disguiseth his face. They digge through houses in the darke, which they marked for them selues in the daye: they knowe not the light. But the morning is euen to them as the shadowe of death."

Closest parallel in Shakespeare's sources:

> Alacktheday, the night is made a vayle
> To shaddowe mischeife.
>
> (*Woodstock* 128–29)

Shakespeare is closer to Scripture. Woodstock's (Gloucester's) context in the above passage is that although they have failed to poison us tonight, our enemies may try a "Second strattagem" to destroy us under cover of night (126).

3.2.54–55: Not all the water in the rough rude sea
            Can wash the balm off from an anointed king.

See 1.2.38–41[a], above for "anointed king." Compare also the passage at *3 Henry VI* 3.1.17, and the comments thereon.

3.2.56–57: Men cannot depose
            The deputy elected by the Lord.

See 1.2.38–41[b], above.

3.2.60–62: God for his Richard hath in heavenly pay
            A glorious angel; then if angels fight,
            Weak men must fall, for heaven still guards the right.

Compare Ps. 34.7: "The angell of the Lorde taryeth rounde about them that feare him: and deliuereth them."

Compare Ps. 91.11: "For he shall giue his angels charge ouer thee: to keepe thee in all thy wayes."

Compare Matt. 26.53: "Thinkest thou, that I can not nowe pray to my Father, and he wil giue me mo then twelue legions of Angels?"

Compare also Matt. 18.10.

Closest parallel in Shakespeare's sources are Woodstock's (the Duke of Gloucester's) words to his murderer:

> Thou canst not kill me villayne
> Gods holly angle guards a Iust mans life

And with his radiant beames as bright as fire
Will guard & keepe his righteous Innocence.

(2516–19)

3.2.129:   O villains, vipers, damn'd without redemption!

Compare Matt. 23.33: "O serpentes, the generation of vipers, howe should yee escape the damnation of hell?"

Compare also the expression "generations of vipers" at Matt. 3.7; 12.34; Luke 3.7.

The Bishops' Bible has, "But shalt destroye them without redemption" at Deut. 20.17. The Geneva has, "But shalt vtterly destroy them."

A proverb may also be involved. Tilley has: "There is no redemption from hell" (R60).

3.2.132:   Three Judases, each one thrice worse than Judas!

A reference to Judas, the apostle who betrayed Christ. See Matt. 26.14–16, 21–25.

The *Traïson's* reference to Judas is applied to the aged Earl of Northumberland whom Henry had sent as a messenger to Richard. Northumberland assured Richard that the only thing Henry desired of the king was peace, and that his lands and titles be restored, although Northumberland had actually prepared an ambush to capture Richard. After a mass had been chanted, Northumberland "placed his hand upon the body of our Lord which was upon the altar, in the presence of the King and of the lords, and swore that all that he had said to the King from Henry of Lancaster was true; in which he perjured himself wickedly and falsely" (199; Benjamin Williams' English translation). For so doing, the author of the *Traïson* says that he "can only be likened to Judas or to Guenelon" (198–99). French original: "Lequel peut bien estre compare a Judas ou a Guenelon" (49). Guenelon was a notorious traitor during the time of Charlemagne.

See 4.1.169–70, below, where Richard specifically compares his betrayal to Christ's. These references to Judas and to Christ's betrayal in the *Traïson*, as well as the reference to Pilate in Créton, seem to have inspired the idea in Shakespeare's play that Richard's betrayal by his followers was parallel to Christ's.

[3.2.134, "their spotted souls": Heb. 9.14; 1 Peter 1.19; 2 Peter 3.14; Eph. 5.27; James 1.27.]

3.2.167–68:   As if this flesh which walls about our life
              Were brass impregnable.

Compare Job 6.12: "Is my strength the strength of stones? or is my flesh of brasse?"

Some have suggested the influence of Marlowe in this passage, since in *Doctor Faustus* Faustus boasts, "I'le have them wall all *Germany* with Brasse (115). While the image of being "walled" with brass could have been inspired by Marlowe, Shakespeare probably had Job in mind when he compared man's flesh with brass.

See 4.1.283–84, below, for another possible borrowing from *Doctor Faustus*.

3.2.194–95:   Men judge by the complexion of the sky
              The state and inclination of the day.

Compare Matt. 16.2–3: "When it is euening, ye say, Faire wether: for the skye is red. And in the morning ye say, To day shalbe a tempest: for the skie is red and lowring."

3.3.77–78:   Show us the hand of God
              That hath dismiss'd us from our stewardship.

Another reference to the well-known Tudor doctrine, repeatedly stressed in the homilies, that civil rulers are appointed by God, and that only He has the power to remove them. See 3.2.56–57 and 1.2.38–41[b], above.

Compare the following excerpts from the homily "Concerning Good Order, and Obedience to Rulers and Magistrates":

Part 1: "Let vs consider the Scriptures of the holy Ghost, which perswade and command vs all obediently to bee subiect, first and chiefely to the Kings Maiestie, supreme gouernour ouer all, and the next to his honourable counsell, and to all other noble men, Magistrates, and officers, which by GODS goodnesse, be placed and ordered. For Almighty GOD is the onely authour and prouider for this forenamed state and order, as it is written of GOD, in the booke of the Prouerbs: Thorow mee kings doe raigne, thorow mee counsellers make iust lawes, thorow mee doe princes beare rule, and all iudges of the earth execute iudgement."

Part 1: "Obedience, submission, and subiection to the high powers, which bee set in authority by GOD, for as much as they bee GODS Lieuetenants, GODS Presidentes, GODS Officers, GODS Commissioners, GODS Iudges, ordained of GOD himselfe, of whom onely they haue all their power, and all their authority."

Part 2, quoting 1 Samuel, where David says of King Saul: "As sure as the Lord liueth, the Lord shall smite him, or his day shall come to die, or he shall descend or goe downe into battaile, and there perish, the Lord keepe me from laying my handes vpon the Lords anoynted. . . . Here is euidently prooued that we may not withstand, nor in any wise hurt an anointed King, which is GODS lieftenant, vice-gerent, and highest minister in that countrey where he is King."

Part 3: "The violence and iniury that is committed against authoritie, is committed against GOD, the common weale, and the whole Realme, which GOD will haue knowen, and condignly or worthily punished one way or other."

The word "stewardship," however, may be an echo of the parable of the Unjust Steward: "Then the steward said within him selfe, What shal I do: for my master wil take away from mee the stewardship?" (Luke 16.3) The only other occurrence of the word in Shakespeare is at 2.2.59.

3.3.82–83:   And though you think that all, . . .
             Have torn their souls.

Compare the parallel expression at Job 18.4: "Thou art as one that teareth his soule in his anger." But the similarity may be accidental.

[3.3.85–87: 2 Kings 6.17; 19.35.]

3.3.88:   Your children yet unborn and unbegot.

Evidently an echo of the homily "Against Disobedience and Wilfull Rebellion." See 4.1.322–23, below, and the comments thereon.

3.3.101:   The King of heaven.

The expression "King of heauen" occurs at Dan. 4.34 (4.37, AV), but the expression was probably common in Shakespeare's day.

3.4.73:   Thou old Adam's likeness, set to dress this garden.

Gen. 2.15: "The Lord God tooke the man, and put him into the garden of Eden, that he might dresse it."

3.4.75–76: What Eve, what serpent, hath suggested thee
　　　　　　　To make a second fall of cursed man?

Gen. 3.13: "God saide vnto the woman, Why hast thou done this? And the woman said, the serpent beguiled me."

Gen. 3.17: "To Adam he saide, Because thou hast obeyed the voyce of thy wife, . . . cursed is the earth for thy sake."

[3.4.78: 1 Cor. 15.47; Gen. 3.19.]

3.4.84–86: Their fortunes both are weigh'd.
　　　　　　　In your lord's scale is nothing but himself,
　　　　　　　And some few vanities that make him light.

Compare Dan. 5.27: "Thou art wayed in the balance, and art found to [too] light."

Compare Ps. 62.9, Geneva: "The children of men are vanitie: . . . vpon a balance they are altogether lighter then vanitie."

Psalter: "The children of men, they are but vaine: . . . vpon the weights, they are altogether lighter then vanitie."

Perhaps analogies rather than references, although the verbal similarities are striking. The closest parallel in Shakespeare's sources is Hall's account of Richard's death in his life of Henry IV. Hall says that Richard was slain by those "whom he had brought vp and norished: so that all menne maye perceyue and see, that fortune wayeth princes and pore men all in one balance" (fol. xv; sig. c.i.ʳ).

4.1.99–100: And his pure soul unto his captain Christ,
　　　　　　　 Under whose colors he had fought so long.

Compare the Baptism Service: "Manfully to fight vnder his banner, . . . and to continue Christs faithfull souldier and seruant vnto his liues end."

Compare also 2 Tim. 2.3–4: "Suffer affliction as a good souldiour of Iesus Christ. . . . because he would please him that hath chosen him to be a souldier."

The Bishops' Bible has the word "captaine" at Heb. 2.10 ("the captaine of their saluation") and at Matt. 2.6 ("a captaine, that shall gouerne my people Israel"). The Geneva has "Prince" and "gouernour" at these texts. But Shakespeare is closest to the Baptism Service.

4.1.103–4:   Sweet peace conduct his sweet soul to the bosom
             Of good old Abraham!

Luke 16.22: "Was caryed by the Angels into Abrahams bosome."
Homily "Against the Feare of Death," part 1: "Death, which sent *Lazarus*
the poore miserable man by Angels anon vnto Abrahams bosome, a place of
rest, pleasure, and consolation."

4.1.125–26:   Shall the figure of God's majesty,
              His captain, steward, deputy, elect. . . .

See the reference at 1.2.38–41^b, above. See also 3.2.56–57 and 3.3.77–78,
above.

4.1.127:   Anointed, crowned, . . .

See 1.2.38–41^a, above. Shakespeare's immediate source was Holinshed. In
Holinshed, Bishop Carlisle likewise tells the nobles that they had no right to
"proceed to the judgement of an anointed king" (3.411). But whether in
Holinshed or Shakespeare, the term "anointed" when applied to kings
derives from Scripture.

4.1.136–41:   And if you crown him, let me prophesy,
              The blood of English shall manure the ground,
              And future ages groan for this foul act.
              Peace shall go sleep with Turks and infidels,
              And in this seat of peace tumultuous wars
              Shall kin with kin and kind with kind confound.

Standard Tudor doctrine. These lines recapitulate the evils of rebellion as
set forth in the homilies. Carlisle says that as a result of Bolingbroke's
rebellion against Richard, all sorts of evils and civil wars will result. Compare the following excerpts from the homily "Against Disobedience and
Wilfull Rebellion":
Part 1: Rebels "assemble companies and bands of rebels, to breake the
publique peace so long continued, . . . and being Englishmen, to robbe,
spoyle, destroy and burne in England Englishmen, to kill and murther their
owne neighbours and kinsefolke, their owne countreymen."
Part 3: "So is it yet more euident that all the calamities, miseries, and
mischiefes of warre, be more grieuous and doe more follow rebellion, then

any other warre, . . . Houses, Villages, Townes, Cities, to be taken, sacked, burned, and destroyed. . . . These mischiefes are wrought in rebellion by them that should be friends, by countreymen, by kinsemen, . . . the brother to seeke, and often to worke the death of his brother, the sonne of the father, the father to seeke or procure the death of his sons, . . . to disinherite their innocent children and kinsemen."

Part 6: "Streames of Christian blood, shed by the rebellions of ignorant subiects against their naturall Lords and Emperours, whom they haue stirred thereunto by such false pretences."

Compare the opening stanza of Daniel's *Civil Wars:*

> I sing the civill warrs, tumultuous broyles,
>
> Whilst Kin their Kin, brother the brother foyles.
>
> (3.434–35)

Compare also the Bishop of Carlisle's words at 4.1.322–23, below.

4.1.143–44:   This land be call'd
              The field of Golgotha and dead men's skulls.

Matt. 27.33: "They came vnto the place called Golgotha, (that is to say, the place of dead mens skulles)."

See also Mark 15.22; John 19.17; Prayer Book, Gospel reading for Good Friday.

4.1.145–46:   O, if you raise this house against this house,
              It will the woefullest division prove.

Mark 3.25: "If a house be deuided against it selfe, that house cannot continue."

See also Matt. 12.25; Luke 11.17.

[4.1.147: Gen. 3.17, Geneva.]

4.1.169–70:   Did they not sometimes cry "All hail!" to me?
              So Judas did to Christ.

No English Bible has "All hail!" when Judas greets Jesus. All Protestant English versions except the Geneva have "Haile master" at Matt. 26.49. The Geneva, possibly to avoid the word "Haile" with its Catholic connotations, has, "God saue thee, Master." The Rheims New Testament has "Haile Rabbi."

Shakespeare's "All hail!" seems to be borrowed from the medieval play *The Agony and the Betrayal,* a York mystery play. In that play Judas greets Jesus with the words, "All hayll, maistir" (243).

See *3 Henry VI* 5.7.33–34 for another example in which Shakespeare probably echoes the same mystery play.

Although the expression "All hail!" comes from a mystery play, Shakespeare's inspiration for comparing Richard's betrayal to Christ's seems to have come from the *Traïson* and from Créton. In the *Traïson,* when Richard saw that he had been betrayed by Northumberland, he said to his companions: "Ah! my good and faithful friends, we are all betrayed, and given without cause into the hands of our enemies; for God's sake have patience, and call to mind our Saviour, who was undeservedly sold and given into the hands of his enemies" (201). The original French text, which Shakespeare seems to have read, has: "Ha mes bons loyaulx amis nous sommes tous trahiz et mis entre les mains de nos ennemis sanz cause pour Dieu auez pascience et vous souuiengne de nostre Saulueur qui fu vendu et mis entre la main de ses ennemis sanz ce quil leust deseruy" (52).

When captured by Henry and imprisoned in Flint castle, Richard and his companions expressed such anguish that the Bishop of Carlisle attempted to comfort them with the words: "If we must die, let us accept death willingly, and call to mind the passion of our Saviour and of the holy martyrs in Paradise" (206). French original: "Et se a mourir fault prenons la mort en gre et ayons memoire de la passion de notre Saulueur et des sains martirs qui sont en Paradiz" (56).

See 3.2.132, above.

4.1.170–71:   He, in twelve,
             Found truth in all but one; I, in twelve thousand, none.

Compare John 13.10–11: "Ye are cleane, but not all. For he knewe who should betraye him: therefore said he, Ye are not all cleane."

Compare John 13.18: "I speake not of you all."

Compare Eccl. 7.30 (7.28, AV): I haue found one man of a thousande: but a woman among them all haue I not founde."

4.1.234–35:   The deposing of a king,
             And cracking the strong warrant of an oath.

Compare the homily "Against Disobedience and Wilfull Rebellion," part 3: "And besides the dishonour done by rebels . . . by their breaking of their oath made to their Prince. . . ."

Again, part 3: "Rebels by breach of their faith giuen, and the oath made to their Prince, bee guiltie of most damnable periurie."

Shakespeare's primary source for this passage, however, was probably the anonymous play, *Thomas of Woodstock*. Just prior to the battle between Richard's forces and those of his uncles, Richard tells his foes that they are drawing their swords against God's anointed, and thus "breakeing your holly oathes to heauen & vs" (2779). See the reference at 1.2.38–41ª, above.

4.1.236:   Mark'd with a blot, damn'd in the book of heaven.

Rev. 3.5, Bishops': "I will not blot out his name out of the booke of life." See 1.3.202, above, and 4.1.274–75, below.

4.1.239–42:   Though some of you, with Pilate, wash your hands,
                 Showing an outward pity, yet you Pilates
                 Have here deliver'd me to my sour cross,
                 And water cannot wash away your sin.

Matt. 27.24: "When Pilate sawe that hee auailed nothing, . . . he tooke water and washed his hands before the multitude, saying, I am innocent of the bloud of this iust man."

Matt. 27.26: "Deliuered him to be crucified." (Also John 19.16.)

See also 3.1.5–6, above.

For "wash away your sin," compare Acts 22.16: "Be baptized, and washe awaye thy sinnes."

Shakespeare's reference to Pilate is evidently based on Créton's *Histoire du Roy d'Angleterre Richard:*

Lors dist le duc henry moult hault aux communes de ladicte ville; Beaux seigneurs, vecy votre roy; regardez que vous en volez faire. Et ilz respondirent a haute voix, nous voulons quil soit mene a wemonstre: Et ainsi il leur delivra. A celle heure il me souvint il de pilate, le quel fist batre notre seigneur ihesu crist a lestache, et apres le fist mener devant le turbe des Juifs disant, beaux seigneurs, vecy votre roy; lesquelz respondirent, nous voulons quil soit crucifie. Alors pilate en lava ses mains disant, Je sui innocent du sanc iuste. Et ainsi leur delivera notre seigneur. Assez sembablement fist le duc henry quant son droit seigneur livra au turbe de londres: afin telle que silz le faisoient mourir quil peust dire, ie sui innocent de ce fait icy (377–78).

English translation of John Webb (1824):

> Then spake Duke Henry quite aloud to the commons of the said city,
> "Fair Sirs, behold your king! consider what you will do with him!" And
> they made answer with a loud voice, "We will have him taken to West-
> minster." And so he delivered him unto them. At this hour did he
> remind me of Pilate, who caused our Lord Jesus Christ to be scourged at
> the stake, and afterwards had him brought before the multitude of the
> Jews, saying, "Fair Sirs, behold your king!" who replied, "let him be
> crucified!" Then Pilate washed his hands of it, saying, "I am innocent of
> the just blood." And so he delivered our Lord unto them. Much in the
> like manner did Duke Henry, when he gave up his rightful lord to the
> rabble of London, in order that, if they should put him to death, he
> might say, "I am innocent of this deed" (179).

The reference to Pilate in Holinshed occurs in a completely different
context. Holinshed mentions Pilate at the time that Richard confronted
Bolingbroke's army at Flint Castle. When Richard descended from the castle
walls to speak to Bolingbroke (3.3.186–209 in the play), the Archbishop of
Canterbury urged the king "to be of good comfort, for he should be assured,
not to have anie hurt, as touching his person." Holinshed adds the comment
that the archbishop "prophesied not as a prelat, but as a Pilat" (3.403).

4.1.270:   Fiend, thou torments me ere I come to hell!

Compare Matt. 8.29: "Art thou come hither to torment vs before the
time?"
If this passage in Shakespeare, spoken by Richard, is a conscious echo of
Matthew 8.29, then it presents an interesting contrast to the references in the
play wherein Richard compares himself to Christ betrayed by Judas. Matthew 8.29 is spoken by the devils that Jesus was about to cast out of the two
possessed men.

4.1.274–75:   The very book indeed
              Where all my sins are writ.

Compare Rev. 20.12: "The bookes were opened, . . . and the dead were
iudged of those things, which were written in the bookes, according to their
workes."
The thought behind Richard's words is drawn from Scripture, although no
one text exactly corresponds with his words. Compare 4.1.236, above.

4.1.283–84:   Was this the face
              That like the sun, did make beholders wink?

There are several biblical parallels, but they may be analogies rather than references.

Compare Rev. 1.16: "And his face shone as the sonne."

Compare the account of the transfiguration at Matt. 17.2: "And his face did shine as the Sunne."

Compare Ex. 34.35: "The children of Israel saw the face of Moses, howe the skin of Moses face shone bright: therefore Moses put the couering vpon his face."

But see the parallel sun image at 3.2.50, where no biblical reference is involved: "Shall see us rising in our throne, the east." Moreover, line 283 may have been inspired by Marlowe's *Doctor Faustus*: "Was this the face that Launcht a thousand ships?" (1768). Shakespeare may have combined a line borrowed from Marlowe with a sun image based on Scripture, although the similarity to Scripture in line 284 could also have been unintentional.

See 3.2.167–68, above, for another possible borrowing from Marlowe's *Doctor Faustus*.

4.1.322–23:   The woe's to come; the children yet unborn
              Shall feel this day as sharp to them as thorn.

The Bishop of Carlisle's words again reflect the homily "Against Disobedience and Wilfull Rebellion." Part 4 of that homily says: Rebels "vndoe all men where they come, that the childe yet vnborne may rue it, and shall many yeeres hereafter curse them."

See 3.3.88, above, and *Henry V* 1.2.287–88 where the same passage in the homily is referred to.

In book 1 of *The Civil Wars* Daniel has: "The babes unborne, shall o be borne to bleed / In this thy quarrell if thou doe proceede" (3.439) These words are spoken to Bolingbroke by the Genius of England in a vision that he sees on the first night of his return from banishment.

Compare also Ex. 20.5.

5.1.24:   Our holy lives must win a new world's crown.

A reference to the "crowne of life" held out as a reward for Christians.

James 1.12: "He shal receiue the crowne of life, which the Lorde hath promised to them that loue him."

2 Tim. 4.8: "Henceforth is layde vp for mee the crowne of righteousnes, which the Lorde the righteous iudge shall giue me at that day."

1 Peter 5.4: "Ye shall receiue an incorruptible crowne of glorie."

See also 1 Cor. 9.25; Rev. 2.10.

The closest parallel in Shakespeare's sources are Lancaster's (John of Gaunt's) words about Edward, the Black Prince, father of Richard II:

> But heauen fore stauld his diademe on earth
> To place hime with a royall Crowne in heauen.
>
> (*Woodstock* 43–44)

5.1.31–32:   Wilt thou, . . .
             Take the correction, mildly kiss the rod . . .?

While "kiss the rod" was proverbial from at least the time of Tyndale, and is recorded in both Tilley and Dent (R156), the expression "rod of correction" and variations of it are probably based on Scripture.

Compare Prov. 22.15: "The rodde of correction shall driue it away from him."

Compare Prov. 23.13: "Withhold not correction from the child: if thou smite him with the rodde, he shall not dye."

5.1.49:   And some will mourn in ashes.

Mourning in ashes, particularly in sackcloth and ashes, is biblical.

Compare Luke 10.13: "They had a great while agone repented, sitting in sackecloth and ashes."

Compare also Dan. 9.3, Jonah 3.6, Esther 4.3, and the reference at *King John* 4.1.110.

[5.1.58–59: James 1.15. See also *2 Henry IV* 3.1.76–77 where Shakespeare uses the same expression.]

5.1.69:   My guilt be on my head.

An expression that finds many parallels in Scripture. See the reference at *Henry VIII* 2.1.137–39 and the comments thereon. The origin of all of these related expressions was probably Scripture. See also 2 Sam. 1.16; 3.28–29; 1 Kings 2.37.

Daniel has: "The sinne be on their head that this haue wrought (3.440, stanza 91).

5.2.6:   Threw dust and rubbish on King Richard's head.

5.2.30:   But dust was thrown upon his sacred head.

Compare 2 Sam. 16.13: "As Dauid and his men went by the way, Shimei
. . . threw stones against him, and cast dust."
The contexts are similar. In each case a king is being unseated: Richard by
Bolingbroke, and King David by his son Absalom.

5.3.31:   My tongue cleave to my roof within my mouth.

Ps. 137.6: "Let my tongue cleaue to the roofe of my mouth."
Job 29.10: "Their tongue cleaued to the roofe of their mouth."
Ezek. 3.26: "I will make thy tongue cleaue to the roofe of thy mouth."

[5.3.85: Matt. 18.8; 5.30.]

[5.3.102: Matt. 15.8.]

5.3.103:   He prays but faintly.

Compare Ecclus. 7.10: "Be not faint hearted, when thou makest thy
prayer."

5.3.104:   We pray with heart and soul, and all beside.

Matt. 22.37: "With all thine heart, with al thy soule, and with all thy
minde."
See also Deut. 4.29; 6.5; 10.12; 30.6; Mark 12.30; Luke 10.27 for other
occurrences of the expression "with all thine heart, and with all thy soule,"
which originates with Scripture.

5.3.107–10:   His prayers are full of false hypocrisy,
                 Ours of true zeal and deep integrity;
                 Our prayers do outpray his, then let them have
                 That mercy which true prayer ought to have.

This passage seems to echo the parable of the Pharisee and the Publican
who went to the temple to pray, as recorded at Luke 18.10–14. Especially

the request to let our prayers have "that mercy which true prayer ought to have," seems to echo Luke 18.13: "O God, be mercifull to me a sinner." The prayer of the pharisee, "O God, I thanke thee that I am not as other men," was "full of false hypocrisy." Jesus said that the publican's prayer was accepted rather than the pharisee's, and the Duchess says, "Our prayers do outpray his."

But the context of Jesus' parable differs considerably from Shakespeare's. The point of the parable is humility versus haughtiness, a spirit of contrition rather than self-righteousness.

5.3.131:   I pardon him as God shall pardon me.

Matt. 6.14–15: "For if ye do forgiue men their trespaces, your heauenly Father wil also forgiue you. But if ye do not forgiue men their trespaces, no more will your Father forgiue you your trespaces."

Eph. 4.32. "Forgiuing one another, euen as God for Christs sake forgaue you."

See also Matt. 18.35; Mark 11.25.

5.3.146:   Come, my old son, I pray God make thee new.

Baptism Service: "O mercifull God, grant that the old Adam in these children may be so buried, that the new man may be raised vp in them."

Eph. 4.22–24: "Cast off . . . the olde man, . . . and put on the newe man, which after God is created in righteousnes."

See also 2 Cor. 5.17, Col. 3.9–10, and Tilley M170.

5.5.15–17:   "Come, little ones," and then again,
              "It is as hard to come as for a camel
              To thread the postern of a small needle's eye."

Mark 10.14: "Suffer the litle children to come vnto mee."

Mark 10.24–25: "Howe hard is it. . . . It is easier for a camel to go through the eye of a needle."

See also Matt. 19.14, 24; Luke 18.16, 25.

Baptism Service: "Suffer little children to come vnto me."

[5.5.61–62: 1 Sam. 16.14–23. But this was a commonly accepted notion in Shakespeare's day. Compare *The Merchant of Venice* 5.1.82–88.]

5.5.88:   Since pride must have a fall.

Prov. 16.18: "Pride goeth before destruction, and an hygh minde before
the fall."
See also Prov. 29.23.

[5.5.91: Gen. 9.2.]

5.5.108:   That hand shall burn in never-quenching fire.

An indirect reference to biblical descriptions of hell.
Mark 9.43: "Then hauing two handes, to go into hell, into the fire that
neuer shalbe quenched."
See also Matt. 18.8; Rev. 21.8.

5.6.43:   With Cain go wander.

Gen. 4.12–14: "A vagabond and a runnagate shalt thou be in the earth.
Then Kain said to the Lorde, . . . Behold, thou cast me out this day from
the earth, . . . and shalbe a vagabond, and a runnagate in the earth."
Compare also Bolingbroke's words at 2.3.120, above.
The closest parallel in Shakespeare's sources occurs in Daniel's poem:
"The out-cast of the world" (3.459, stanza 81). Daniel's context is identical
with Shakespeare's. Both statements are said of Exton, Richard's murderer.
Shakespeare seems to have transformed that line in Daniel into an explicit
biblical reference.

King John

King John appeared in print for the first time in 1623 when it was published in the First Folio. It does not seem to have been an outstanding play in Shakespeare's day, and it seldom appears on the modern stage. In his *Palladis Tamia*, Francis Meres lists it as one of Shakespeare's better plays. But Meres wrote in 1598, before Shakespeare's greatest works were written. The date of composition is a problem, but 1594–96 is probably the safest guess.

Shakespeare's main source for the play was *The Troublesome Raigne of Iohn King of England*, published anonymously in two parts in 1591. Shakespeare seldom followed his sources as closely as he followed *The Troublesome Raigne*, scene by scene and episode by episode, but he changed the emphasis of the play and greatly reduced its anti-papal bias. Most of all, Shakespeare's style is vastly superior to the uninspired lines of *The Troublesome Raigne*.

The Troublesome Raigne was reprinted in quarto in 1611 with the words "Written by W. Sh." on its title page. A third quarto appeared in 1622 that expanded "W. Sh." to "W. Shakespeare." There are those who believe that *The Troublesome Raigne* was not Shakespeare's source, but that Shakespeare's play preceded it, and that *The Troublesome Raigne* was a pirated text derived from Shakespeare's play. In that case, *King John* would be one of Shakespeare's earliest plays, written about 1590, while *The Troublesome Raigne* came out the following year, closely imitating Shakespeare's play in an effort to cash in on whatever success it may have had and on the reputation of its author.

After having considered the evidence carefully, I am convinced that the arguments put forward in favor of this theory have little merit. *The Troublesome Raigne* has few of the characteristics of a pirated or imitated text. Most of all, the complete absence of any trace of Shakespeare's vastly superior language and imagery strongly argues that *The Troublesome Raigne* did not copy Shakespeare's play. The evidence heavily favors the conclusion that Shakespeare worked from *The Troublesome Raigne*, most likely keeping a copy of the play in front of him, and greatly improving it as he went along.

Although *The Troublesome Raigne* conveys a strong religious message, depicting King John as a Protestant martyr who courageously attempted to resist the evils of Rome, it contains very few biblical references. The only reasonably clear reference in the entire first part of the play is the expression "receive a Prophets rewarde" (lines 1312–13), most likely based on Matthew 10.41. Two other possible references occur in lines 994–95 and 1711–12. Part 2 of the play, although shorter, contains some twelve biblical references, but Shakespeare borrowed none of them. As was his usual practice, the many biblical references in the play are almost entirely his own.

Shakespeare's secondary sources include Holinshed and Foxe; he may also have borrowed a few ideas from several other very minor sources. The portions of Holinshed's life of King John that correspond to Shakespeare's play contain at most some eight biblical references, but Shakespeare borrowed none of them. The passage at 5.6.29–30 in the list of references contains the only biblical reference that Shakespeare seems to have borrowed from his sources, it being from Foxe's *Book of Martyrs (Acts and Monuments)* either directly or indirectly through Grafton's *Chronicle*, which incorporated most of Foxe's account.

Medieval chroniclers had depicted King John as a reprobate for defying the Pope and imposing heavy exactions on the monasteries. This view of John began to change when John Bale wrote his violently anti-Catholic play, *King Johan*, ca. 1538, after he had been converted to Protestantism. This play, a transition between the old morality and the later history plays, started the dramatic tradition to which *King John* belongs. *The Troublesome Raigne* continued that tradition, but when Shakespeare reworked *The Troublesome Raigne*, he turned away from religious propaganda that characterized both drama and Foxe's prose account. Shakespeare could hardly have known Bale's work, which was not published until 1838. But it was one of the earliest works, if not the earliest, to apply the term "Usurped Power" to the Pope, as pointed out at 3.1.153–60, below.

In the list that follows, page numbers preceded by the number 4, as in (4.53), refer to volume 4 of Bullough. Line numbers for *The Troublesome Raigne* are for the text that appears in Bullough, pages 72–151 of volume 4. A reference such as (1.48) means part 1 of the play, line 48; (2.1092) refers to line 1092 of part 2.

[1.1.19: Ex. 21.24; Deut. 19.21; Matt. 5.38; Gen. 9.6. But see Tilley B458. *The Troublesome Raigne* has "prepare for bloodie warres" (1.48). Shakespeare's passage is closer to Scripture, though not a clear biblical reference.]

1.1.23: And so depart in peace.

Compare the Prayer Book, Evening Prayer, *Nunc dimittis:* "Lord now lettest thou thy seruant depart in peace," based on Luke 2.29: "Lord, now lettest thou thy seruant depart in peace."

The Troublesome Raigne has "convay him safely to the sea" (1.61). Shakespeare seems to have transformed that line into a recognizable reference to the Prayer Book. The context and the speaker are the same in each play.

1.1.251–52:   *Lady F.* Hast thou denied thyself a Faulconbridge?
              Bast. As faithfully as I deny the devil.

Probably an echo of the Catechism: "That I should forsake the deuil and all his workes."

1.1.256:   Heaven! lay not my transgression to my charge.

Compare Acts 7.60: "Lord, lay not this sinne to their charge."
The Rheims has, "Lord, lay not this sinne vnto them," and the first edition of Tyndale's New Testament (1526) has, "lorde impute not this synne vnto them." But Tyndale's revised New Testaments (1534, 1535) and all Protestant versions of the New Testament (Coverdale, Matthew, Taverner, Great, Geneva, Bishops') uniformly read "Lord, lay not this sinne to their charge" at Acts 7.60.
Compare Deut. 21.8: "O Lorde, be mercifull vnto thy people Israel, . . . and lay no innocent blood to the charge of thy people."
Compare 2 Tim. 4.16: "I pray God, that it may not be laid to their charge."

2.1.14:   Shadowing their right under your wings of war.

"Under the shadow of thy wings" is a frequent biblical expression, especially in the Psalms.
Ps. 17.8: "Hide me vnder the shadowe of thy wings."
Ps. 36.7: "Shall put their trust vnder the shadow of thy wings."
Ps. 57.1: "Vnder the shadow of thy wings shal be my refuge."
Ps. 63.8 (63.7, Geneva): "Vnder the shadowe of thy wings will I reioyce."
Compare also Ps. 61.4; 91.1, 4; Ruth 2.12.
Compare *Henry VIII* 5.1.160–61.

2.1.87:   Whiles we, God's wrathful agent, do correct. . . .

Compare Rom. 13.4: "For hee is the minister of God: . . . for he beareth not the sword for nought: for he is the minister of God to take vengeance on him that doth euil."

The Tudors stressed the doctrine that secular rulers were God's duly-appointed deputies or agents. Romans 13 was frequently quoted in the homilies to support that claim. See the reference at *2 Henry VI* 3.2.285–86 where the homily "Concerning Good Order, and Obedience to Rulers and Magistrates" is quoted. See also all six parts of the homily "Against Disobedience and Wilfull Rebellion."

Compare *Richard III* 5.3.108, 113 and the comments thereon, where Richmond claims to be God's minister of chastisement, even as King John claims to be God's appointed agent in this passage. King Philip of France also claims that his commission is from God: "Under whose warrant I impeach thy wrong, / And by whose help I mean to chastise it" (2.1.110–17).

Compare also Hamlet's words, "but heaven hath pleas'd it so . . . / That I must be their scourge and minister" (3.4.173–75).

2.1.177–82:   This is thy eldest son's son,

> . . . .
>
> Thy sins are visited in this poor child,
> The canon of the law is laid on him,
> Being but the second generation
> Removed from thy sin-conceiving womb.

Based on the Second Commandment as it occurs in the Catechism and Communion Service: "For I the Lord thy God . . . visit the sinnes of the fathers vpon the children, vnto the thirde and fourth generation of them that hate me."

The Geneva has "visiting the iniquitie of the fathers vpon the children," at Ex. 20.5, the Second Commandment. All other Protestant Tudor translations (Tyndale, Coverdale, Matthew, Taverner, Great, Bishops') have "sinne" in the singular.

Shakespeare clearly has the Catechism in mind. He was required to memorize it in school, it being bound in the same pamphlet or booklet with the ABC and called *The ABC with the Catechism*. The ABC book is referred to at *King John* 1.1.196: "And then comes answer like an Absey book."

2.1.182:   Thy sin-conceiving womb.

Compare Ps. 51.5: "In sinne hath my mother conceiued me."
Compare also the opening words of the Baptism Service: "Dearely beloued, forasmuch as all men be conceiued and borne in sin. . . ."

[2.1.245–46: Ps. 10.20 (10.18, Geneva); 9.9. With strong overtones of the biblical commands to defend the rights of the fatherless and oppressed. See also 2.1.176–77. These references to the Psalms are clearer in the Psalter.]

[2.1.283–84: Luke 11.4; 16.9.]

[2.1.329: see above at 1.1.19.]

[2.1.566: see above at 2.1.87. See also the reference at *Richard II* 4.1.99–100.]

3.1.7–8:   I trust I may not trust thee, for thy word
            Is but the vain breath of a common man.

Compare Ps. 146.2–3 (146.3–4, Geneva): "Put not your trust in princes, nor in any childe of man: . . . For when the breath of man goeth forth, he shal turne againe to his earth."
Compare also Isa. 2.22: "Cease you from the man whose breath is in his nostrels."
Perhaps an analogy rather than a reference, since the "breath of a common man" is set in contrast to the "king's oath" of line 10.

[3.1.53: Matt. 6.28–29.]

3.1.77–78:   To solemnize this day the glorious sun
              Stays in his course.

Joshua 10.12–14: "Sunne, staie thou in Gibeon, and thou moone, in the valley of Aialon. And the sunne abode, and the moone stood still, . . . so the sunne abode in the middes of the heauen, and hasted not to go downe for a whole day. And there was no day like that before it, nor after it."
Ecclus. 46.4: "Stoode not the sunne still by his meanes, and one day was as long as two?"
See 5.5.1–4, below.

3.1.83–86:   A wicked day, and not a holy day!
              What hath this day deserv'd? what hath it done,
              That it in golden letters should be set
              Among the high tides in the calendar?

The reference is to the officially designated holy days in the Anglican Church. These were printed in red letters in the church calendars that prefaced the Prayer Book. "Golden letters" has the sense of "red letters," as at 2.1.316.

Noble suggests that the "golden letters" of line 85 refer instead to "The Golden number" in both the almanac and the table "To finde Easter for euer" that also preceded the Prayer Book. But the sense of the passage strongly favors the former explanation: holy days that were typeset in red letters. The golden numbers were never referred to as letters, but as numbers.

A third explanation is that the reference is to the high tides of the sea that were marked in secular almanacs. Shakespeare may well be mixing his metaphors, since 3.1.92 tells seamen not to fear shipwreck on that day. But the main import of 3.1.83–86 is to the officially designated holy days of the English Church that were printed in red letters in Prayer Book calendars. Moreover, "tide" could also mean "time, season," as in "eastertide." In that case, the "high tides in the calendar" would simply mean the church calendar's great festivals or holy days, which were printed in red letters.

3.1.87–88:   Nay, rather turn this day out of the week,
              This day of shame.

Reminiscent of Job 3.3, 6: "Let the day perish, wherein I was borne, . . . let it not be ioyned vnto the dayes of the yeere, nor let it come into the count of the moneths." But this may be an analogy rather than a reference.
Compare also Jer. 20.14.

3.1.89–90:   Let wives with child
              Pray that their burthens may not fall this day.

Evidently patterned on Jesus' words describing the tribulations that would occur at the end of the world.
Compare Matt. 24.19–20: "Wo shalbe to them that are with child, and to them that giue sucke in those dayes. But pray that your flight bee not in the winter."

[3.1.107: Judges 5.20.]

3.1.108:   A widow cries; be husband to me, heavens!

Another passage in the play that pleads for justice for widows and orphans, which has strong overtones of Scripture. Compare the following texts:

Ex. 22.22–23: "Ye shall not trouble any widow, nor fatherlesse childe. If thou vexe or trouble such, and so he call and cry vnto me, I will surely heare his cry."

Ps. 68.5: "He is a father of the fatherlesse, and defendeth the cause of the widowes: euen God in his holy habitation."

Judith 9.4: "O God, o my God, heare me also a widdow."

See also Deut. 10.18; Isa. 1.17; Ps. 146.9, as well as 2.1.245–46, above. Compare *2 Henry VI* 5.1.187–88 and the comments thereon.

Noble thinks that Constance's words "be husband to me, heavens!" were inspired by Isa. 54.4–5: "Thou . . . shalt not remember the reproch of thy widowhode any more. For he that made thee, is thine husband (whose Name is the Lord of hostes)." Isaiah's context, however, is much different.

3.1.136:   Hail, you anointed deputies of heaven!

Derived ultimately from Scripture where the kings of Israel were called "the Lords anointed," since they were anointed with oil when crowned king. See the references at *I Henry IV* 4.3.40, *3 Henry VI* 3.1.17, and *Richard III* 4.4.151, and the comments thereon.

For the expression "deputies of heaven," see above at 2.1.87.

3.1.153–60:   No Italian priest
              Shall tithe or toll in our dominions;
              But as we, under God, are supreme head,

              . . . .

              Where we do reign, we will alone uphold
              Without th' assistance of a mortal hand.
              So tell the Pope, all reverence set apart
              To him and his usurp'd authority.

Compare Article 37 of the Thirty-Nine Articles of Religion adopted by the Anglican Church in 1563: "The Queenes Maiestie hath the chiefe power in this Realme of England, and other her dominions, . . . and is not, nor ought to be, subiect to any foraine iurisdiction. . . . The Bishoppe of Rome hath no iurisdiction in this Realme of England" (*STC* 10046; 1593 ed.).

But Shakespeare's immediate source was *The Troublesome Raigne* that he followed closely: "Tell thy Maister so from me, and say, *John* of *England* said it, that never an Italian Priest of them all, shall either have tythe, tole, or poling penie out of *England*, but as I am King, so wil I raigne next under God, supreame head both over spirituall and temrall" (1.979–84).

The expressions "usurped power" and "usurped authority" applied to the

Pope were well known in Shakespeare's day. Part 3 of the homily "Concerning Good Order, and Obedience to Rulers and Magistrates" has: "And here let us take heede that we vnderstand not these . . . to bee meant in any condition of the pretended or coloured power of the Bishop of Rome. For truely the Scripture of GOD alloweth no such vsurped power, full of enormities, abusions, and blasphemies. . . . And concerning the vsurped power of the Bishop of Rome, . . . we may easily perceiue how false, fained, and forged it is."

The expression occurs neither in *The Troublesome Raigne* nor in Holinshed, but Usurped Power is one of the characters in Bale's *King Johan*, Usurped Power representing the Pope.

3.1.172–79:   Then, by the lawful power that I have,
              Thou shalt stand curs'd and excommunicate,
              And blessed shall he be that doth revolt
              From his allegiance to an heretic,
              And meritorious shall that hand be call'd,

          · · · · · · · · · · · ·

              That takes away by any secret course
              Thy hateful life.

This incident is specifically referred to in part 6 of the homily "Against Disobedience and Wilfull Rebellion": "And to vse one example of our owne countrey: The Bishoppe of Rome did picke a quarrell to King *Iohn* of England, about the election of *Steuen Langton* to the Bishopricke of Canterburie, wherein the King had ancient right, . . . the Bishops of Rome hauing no right, but had begunne then to vsurpe vpon the Kinges of Englande, and all other Christian Kinges, . . . and likewise cursing King *Iohn*, and discharginge his subiects of their oath of fidelitie vnto their Soueraigne Lord. Now had Englishmen at that time knowen their duetie to their prince set forth in GODS worde, would . . . Englishe subiects haue taken part against the King of England, and against Englishemen, with the French King and Frenchmen, beeing incensed against this Realme by the Bishoppe of Rome?"

The homily elaborates at length on the events of King John's reign and how he was forced to submit as a vassal to this "false vsurper the Bishop of Rome."

But here also, as in the previous reference, Shakespeare's primary source is *The Troublesome Raigne:* "Then I *Pandulph* of *Padoa*, Legate from the Apostolick See, doo in the name of S. *Peter* and his successor our holy Father Pope *Innocent*, pronounce thee accursed discharging every of thy subjects of all dutie and fealtie that they doo owe to thee, and pardon and forgiunes of sinne to those of them whatsoever, which shall carrie armes against thee, or murder thee: this I pronounce, and charge all good men to abhorre thee as an excommunicate person" (1.993–1000).

3.1.181–82:   Good father Cardinal, cry thou amen
              To my keen curses.

A reference to the Commination Service in the Prayer Book, patterned on Deuteronomy 27. It consisted of ten curses recited by the minister (as, "Cursed is he that letteth in Iudgement the right of the stranger, of them that be fatherlesse, and of widowes"), to which the congregation answered "Amen."

The word "commination" means a denunciation or threat of punishment against sinners. This service was to be said principally on Ash Wednesday and "diuers times in the yeere."

3.1.208–9:   O Lewis, stand fast! the devil tempts thee here
             In likeness of a new untrimmed bride.

Probably an echo of 2 Cor. 11.14, which Shakespeare refers to several times in his plays: "Satan him selfe is transformed into an Angel of light."

3.1.265–66:   O, let thy vow
              First made to heaven, first be to heaven perform'd.

Compare Deut. 23.21, 23: "When thou shalt vowe a vowe vnto the Lorde thy God, thou shalt not be slacke to paye it. . . . That . . . thou shalt keepe and performe."

Compare also Ps. 61.8 and Nahum 1.15 where "perform" is also used with "vows," but the expression was probably common, although not recorded by Tilley as a proverb.

3.1.283–87:   The truth thou art unsure
              To swear, swears only not to be forsworn,

              . . . .

              But thou dost swear only to be forsworn,
              And most forsworn, to keep what thou dost swear.

Cardinal Pandulph's speech in which he urges King Philip to renounce what he had sworn probably reflects the homily "Against Swearing and

Perjury." Part 1 of that homily warns "what perill and danger it is vainely to sweare, or to be forsworne." Part 2 of the same homily reiterates "how damnable a thing it is, either to forsweare ourselues, or to keepe an vnlawfull, and an vnaduised oath." There is no parallel to these words in any of Shakespeare's sources.

The syntax of the Cardinal's speech is difficult, as is its punctuation in the First Folio, when the play was first printed, but when Pandulph tells Philip that you swear only not to be forsworn, he means that to be valid, Philip's oath must not be contrary to some greater oath.

3.1.344–45:   Thy rage shall burn thee up, and thou shalt turn
               To ashes.

Compare Wisdom 2.3, Bishops': "Our body shalbe turned into ashes."
Compare the Burial Service: "We therefore commit his body to the ground, earth to earth, ashes to ashes."
At best an analogy rather than a reference as the contexts are considerably different.

3.3.61:   He is a very serpent in my way.

Gen. 49.17, all versions except Geneva (Tyndale, Coverdale, Matthew, Taverner, Great, Bishops'): "Dan shal be a serpent in the way."
Geneva: "Dan shall be a serpent by the way."

3.3.64:   Thou art his keeper.
           Hub.   And I'll keep him so.

Gen. 4.9: "Am I my brothers keeper?"
Closest parallel in Shakespeare's sources: Hubert's words in *The Troublesome Raigne:* "Frolick yong Prince, though I your keeper bee, / Yet shall your keeper live at your commaund" (1.1124–25).
Of themselves, these words in *The Troublesome Raigne* do not readily suggest a biblical reference. But the word "keeper" in these lines apparently reminded Shakespeare of Cain's words, and he seems to have transformed Hubert's words into a more explicit biblical reference. In his play, Shakespeare has King John borrow Cain's words ("Thou art his keeper") as John strongly suggests to Hubert that he slay Arthur. In reply, Hubert paraphrases Cain's words to indicate that he understands what he has to do.
Later in *The Troublesome Raigne,* Prince Arthur calls Hubert "curteous

keeper" and "gentle keeper" when Hubert is about to blind him (1.1333, 1338). Here also no biblical references seem apparent, but the word "keeper" evidently reminded Shakespeare of Cain's words.

3.4.25, 28: Death, death. . . .

. . . .

Thou hate and terror to prosperity.

Ecclus. 41.1: "O death, how bitter is the remembrance of thee to a man that liueth at reste in his possessions . . . and that hath prosperitie."

3.4.25–36: Death, death. O amiable lovely death!

. . . .

Arise forth from the couch of lasting night,

. . . .

And I will kiss thy detestable bones,

. . . .

Come, grin on me, and I will think thou smil'st,
And buss thee as thy wife. Misery's love,
O, come to me!

Ecclus. 41.2: "O death, how acceptable is thy iudgemente vnto the needeful, and vnto him whose strength fayleth, . . . and is vexed with all things, and to him that despaireth, and hath lost patience!"

3.4.79: For since the birth of Cain, the first male child.

A reference to Cain, the first child born to Adam and Eve. Gen. 4.1–17.

3.4.108: Life is as tedious as a twice-told tale.

Compare Wisdom 2.1: "Our life is short and tedious."
Compare Ps. 90.9: "We bring our yeeres to an ende, as it were a tale that is tolde."
Compare Ecclus. 20.18: "A man without grace is as a foolish tale which is ofte tolde."
While Shakespeare may be echoing Scripture in this passage, there were also many parallel proverbs. Tilley has:

T38: "A good tale ill told is marred in the telling."
T39: "A good tale is none the worse to be twice told."
T42: "One tale is good until another be told."

Compare also the passage at 4.2.18: "This act is as an ancient tale new told."

See *Macbeth* 5.5.26–27 and *Romeo and Juliet* 5.3.229–30 and the comments thereon in the volume *Biblical References in Shakespeare's Tragedies.*

[3.4.137: Ps. 73.17 (73.18, Geneva).]

[4.1.68–70: Gal. 1.8.]

4.1.90–91:   None, but to lose your eyes.
         Arth. O heaven! that there were but a mote in yours.

Matt. 7.3: "Why seest thou the mote, that is in thy brothers eye?" (Also Luke 6.41.)

Though Shakespeare's context differs considerably from Jesus' words at Matt. 7.3, it is likely that he drew on these well-known words in the Sermon on the Mount.

4.1.110:   And strew'd repentant ashes on his head.

The use of sackcloth and ashes as symbols of sorrow and repentance is biblical. Strewing ashes or dust on the head and tearing one's garments are signs of extreme sorrow.

2 Sam. 13.19: "Tamar put ashes on her head and rent the garment of diuers colours which was on her . . . and went her way crying."

2 Sam. 1.2: "A man came . . . from Saul with his clothes rent, and earth vpon his head."

Job. 2.12: "Euery one of them rent his garment, and sprinkled dust vpon their heads."

Matt. 11.21: "They had repented long agone in sackecloth and ashes."
See also Joshua 7.6; Dan. 9.3; Jonah 3.6; and 2 Esdras 9.38.

[4.2.32–34: Matt. 9.16; Mark 2.21.]

[4.2.104: Hab. 2.12.]

4.3.10:   Heaven take my soul, and England keep my bones!

While this passage is not a direct reference to Scripture, it is based on the language with which wills were opened. Shakespeare's own will began: "I Comend my Soule into the handes of god my Creator . . . And my bodye to the Earth whereof yt ys made." This language of wills comes from Scripture:

Luke 23.46: "Father, into thine hands I commend my spirit."

Ps. 31.6 (31.5, Geneva): "Into thy handes I commend my spirit."

Burial Service: "We therefore commit his body to the ground, earth to earth, ashes to ashes, dust to dust."

Gen. 3.19: "Till thou returne to the earth: for out of it wast thou taken."

In *The Troublesome Raigne* Arthur says: "I dye I dye, heaven take my fleeting soule" (2.25). There are no parallel words in Holinshed.

4.3.122:   Thou art more deep damn'd than Prince Lucifer.

Based on Isa. 14.12: "How art thou fallen from heauen, O Lucifer."

In Isaiah, Nebuchadnezzar, king of Babylon, is the one addressed under the figure of "Lucifer," which means "light-bearer," and refers to the planet Venus in its appearance as the morning star before sunrise. But in Christian circles that text was often applied to Satan, perhaps from associating Isaiah 14.12 with Luke 10.18: "I sawe Satan, like lightening, fall downe from heauen." Even Saint Jerome (d. 420) interpreted Isaiah 14.12 as a reference to the devil.

See the references in *Henry VIII* 3.2.371–72 and 3.2.440–41 and the comments thereon for a fuller discussion of Isaiah 14.12.

For the title "Prince Lucifer," compare such texts as Matthew 9.34, 12.24, and Mark 3.22 where Satan is called "the prince of deuils."

4.3.135–36:   If I in act, consent, or sin of thought
               Be guilty. . . .

Probably an echo of the General Confession in the Communion Service wherein acknowledgement is made of sins and wickednesses which have been committed "by thought, word, and deede," which Shakespeare refers to elsewhere in his plays. See the comments on *Othello* 4.2.152–53 in the volume *Biblical References in Shakespeare's Tragedies*.

4.3.138:   Let hell want pains enough to torture me.

Compare Ps. 18.4 (18.5, Geneva): "The paines of hell came about me."

Compare Ps. 116.3: "The paynes of hell gat holde vpon me."

A reference to the Psalter. The Geneva has "sorowes of the graue" in the former passage, and "griefes of the graue" at Ps. 116.3.

4.3.140–41:   And lose my way
              Among the thorns and dangers of this world.

The idea of losing one's way in life among the thorns of this world is probably borrowed from Jesus' parable of the sower.

Matt. 13.22: "He that receiueth the seede among thornes, is he that heareth the word: but the care of this worlde . . . choke the worde."

See also Luke 8.14.

[5.2.154–58: Joel 3.10. But this was typical of 1588 Armada exhortations.]

5.5.1–4:   The sun of heaven, methought, was loath to set,
           But stay'd and made the western welkin blush,
           When English measure backward their own ground
           In faint retire. O, bravely came we off.

These lines contain a suggestion of Joshua's making the sun stand still until victory was attained.

Compare Josh. 10.13: "And the sunne abode, and the moone stood still, vntill the people auenged themselues vpon their enemies: . . . so the sunne abode in the middes of the heauen, and hasted not to go downe for a whole day."

See 3.1.77–78, above.

The closest parallel in Shakespeare's sources occurs in *The Troublesome Raigne*. That passage contains no biblical references, but may have suggested Shakespeare's apparent reference to Joshua 10.13:

> Why shines the Sunne to favour this consort?
> Why doo the windes not breake their brazen gates?
>
> . . . .
>
> But see the welkin rolleth gently on,
> Theres not a lowring clowde to frowne on them;
> The heaven, the earth, the sunne, the moone and all
> Conspire with those confederates my decay.
>
>   (2.199–206)

5.6.29–30:   A monk, I tell you, a resolved villain,
             Whose bowels suddenly burst out.

Compare the death of Judas after betraying Christ at Acts 1.18: "He braste a sunder in the middes, and all his bowels gushed out."

Compare Foxe, who likewise says of the monk who served as the king's taster and was willing to poison himself so he could kill the king: "his guts gushing out of his belly. . . ." (4.53).

Holinshed gives three differing versions of how John died. He favors the version that the king died "through anguish of mind, rather than through force of sicknesse" (4.47). Both alternate accounts involve poison (poisoned ale in one account and poisoned pears in the other), but neither speak of bowels bursting (4.47).

The closest parallel in *The Troublesome Raigne* is when the Bastard says of John's anguish after he was poisoned: "Whose bowells are devided in themselves" (2.1092). But this is said of the king, not of the monk as in Shakespeare and Foxe.

By Shakespeare's time it was widely believed that John had been poisoned, and Shakespeare followed this tradition in his play. His source, either directly or indirectly, was probably Foxe, and he followed Foxe who says that it was the monk whose bowels burst, rather than the king whom the monk poisoned. *The Book of Martyrs* has very few woodcuts, but in the edition that Shakespeare probably used, Foxe's account of King John contains a composite woodcut with six scenes relating to the poisoning. The caption for one of the scenes is: "The monke lyeth here burst of the poyson that he dranke to the king" (1583 ed.; *STC* 11225). In the first edition (1563; *STC* 11222) the caption for that scene reads: "The Monk dead of the poyson he drank to the king." But in all later editions published before *King John* appeared (1570, 1576, 1583, 1596; *STC* 11223–26), the caption has "burst." (There are no woodcuts in the *Abridgement* that was published in 1589, *STC* 11229.)

5.6.37–38:   Withhold thine indignation, mighty heaven,
             And tempt us not to bear above our power!

1 Cor. 10.13: "God is faithfull, which will not suffer you to bee tempted aboue that you be able, but . . . that ye may be able to beare it."

I Henry IV

As soon as *The History of Henry the Fourth* appeared in 1596–97, it became one of Shakespeare's most popular plays. Unlike its sequel, *The Second Part of Henry the Fourth*, a much less popular play that was printed only once prior to the Folio of 1623, part 1 was printed twice in 1598, and reprinted five more times before it appeared in the First Folio.

Shakespeare's two principal sources for the play were the second edition of Holinshed's *Chronicles* (1587), and a lost play or plays about Henry V of which the anonymous play, *The Famous Victories of Henry the Fifth*, published in 1598, is a condensed and corrupt version. Shakespeare seems to have relied mainly on Holinshed for the historical material and on the lost Henry V play (or plays) for most of what is in the comic scenes. Secondary sources include Samuel Daniel's *Civil Wars* (1595), John Stow's *Chronicles of England* (1580) and *Annals of England* (1592), *A Mirror for Magistrates* (1559), and the anonymous play *Thomas of Woodstock* (ca. 1591–95; not printed until 1870). Shakespeare also seems to have read Thomas Nashe prior to writing *I Henry IV*, for his play contains some twenty verbal parallels and echoes from several works written by Nashe.

Of lesser importance would be the many interludes, plays, and various works that contain characters parallel to Falstaff, or that are in the madcap prince tradition. These include Nicholas Udall's *Ralph Roister Doister* (1566–67), the interlude *Thersites* (printed ca. 1560), John Lyly's play *Endimion* (1591), and others. Shakespeare, however, could have found all the "wild prince" material that he needed in Holinshed or in the original *Famous Victories* play.

Shakespeare found few biblical references in most of these works. There are no biblical references in either Holinshed's or Daniel's accounts of Henry IV. The anonymous *Famous Victories* has only three probable references to Scripture: "curst be the day wherin I was borne" (624), most likely borrowed from Jeremiah 20.14; "God is my witnesse" (654) from Romans 1.9; and "I am borne new againe" (581) that resembles John 3.3. Shakespeare borrowed none of these, and it is probably safe to conclude that he likewise borrowed no references from the original Henry V play(s), of which the *Famous Victories* is a corrupt version. Nor did he make use of the few biblical references that he found in Stow's *Chronicles*, *The Mirror for Magistrates*, *Thomas of Woodstock*, and the possible sources of lesser importance. Some of the latter, as the interlude *Thersites*, have a number of biblical references, but it is not certain that Shakespeare had these works in mind when he wrote his play. If he did, he made no use of the references that can be found in them. The reference to the homilies at 1.2.104–5 may have been suggested to Shakespeare by Nashe, but for the most part, the many biblical references in the play are his own.

The popularity of *I Henry IV* rests in large part on the character of Falstaff, and it is he who utters many of the biblical and liturgical references in the play. Of the fifty-four references in the following list, twenty-six come from the mouth of Falstaff. In Shakespeare's play he was originally called Oldcastle (that is also his name in *The Famous Victories*), who in real history was Sir John Oldcastle (d. 1417), high sheriff of Herefordshire. In Holinshed, Oldcastle is a valiant captain in the French wars, highly favored of the king, who was later charged with Wycliffite heresy and condemned. A second tradition depicts him as a scholar, hero, and Protestant martyr. The many biblical references that Falstaff makes were probably suggested by Oldcastle's religious background. Shakespeare makes him a fallen knight who rejects his religious background, facetiously paraphrases Scripture, and frequently mimics Puritan idiom.

In the list that follows, page numbers preceded by the number 4 (as 4.328), refer to volume 4 of Bullough. Line numbers for *The Famous Victories* are for the text that appears in Bullough, pages 299–343 of volume 4.

[1.1.5–6: Gen. 4.11.]

1.1.19–21:   The sepulchre of Christ—
             Whose soldier now, under whose blessed cross
             We are impressed and engag'd to fight.

Compare 2 Tim. 2.3–4: "As a good souldiour of Iesus Christ. . . . him that hath chosen him to be a souldier."
Compare also the reference at *Richard II* 4.1.99–100.

1.1.25–27:   Those blessed feet
             Which fourteen hundred years ago were nail'd
             For our advantage on the bitter cross.

A general reference to the crucifixion.
Compare the Prayer of Consecration in the Communion Service: "Christ to suffer death vpon the Crosse for our redemption."

1.1.78–79:   Thou . . . mak'st me sin
             In envy.

Compare Rom. 1.29: "Being . . . full of enuie."
Compare the Litany: "From enuie, hatred, and malice, and all
vncharitablenesse. Good Lord deliuer vs."
Compare also Titus 3.3.
Probably a statement reflecting the standard Christian view of envy rather
than a conscious reference to Scripture or the Prayer Book. Envy was one of
the Seven Deadly Sins.

[1.2.83: Prov. 22.1; Eccl. 7.3 (7.1, AV); Ecclus. 41.12.]

1.2.88–89:   Wisdom cries out in the streets, and no man regards it.

Prov. 1.20, 24, Great Bible: "Wisdome cryeth without, and putteth forth
her voyce in the stretes. . . . I haue called, and ye refused it: I haue stretched
out my hande, and no man regarded it." (Also Coverdale, Matthew, Taverner.)
The Bishops' is identical in verse 20, but omits "it" in verse 24 after
"refused" and after "regarded": "Because I haue called, and yee refused, I
haue stretched out my hande, and no man regarded."
Geneva: "Wisdome cryeth without: she vttereth her voyce in the
streets. . . . Because I haue called, and yee refused: I have stretched out mine
hande, and none would regarde."
In this passage, Shakespeare appears to be closest to the Great Bible and to
the translations that preceded it (Coverdale, Matthew, Taverner), and is least
like the Geneva.
This reference to Prov. 1.20, 24 seems to have been considered objectionable since in the First Folio the words "wisdom cries out in the streets, and"
were omitted at 1.2.88–89. Thus in the Folio the Prince answers Falstaff:
"Thou didst well: for no man regards it." Yet the Prince's clear reference to
Prov. 1.20, 24 appears in all quarto editions of the play that appeared prior to
the 1623 Folio. The deletions and the softening of oaths in the play, however,
were not uniform and seem to be principally associated with either the
literary editor of Q5 (1613), which served as copy-text for the Folio, or with
Folio Compositor B.

1.2.92–95:   Before I knew thee, Hal, I knew nothing, and now am I, if a
             man should speak truly, little better than one of the wicked.

Falstaff appears to compare himself to Adam in a state of innocence, corrupted by Prince Hal who caused him to sin. Genesis 3.

Compare the reference at *2 Henry IV* 2.4.327–29 where the phrase "of the wicked" also occurs. Falstaff is mimicking Puritan idiom in both passages.

1.2.102: I see a good amendment of life in thee.

Luke 15.7: "Which neede none amendement of life."
Matt. 3.8, 11: "Amendement of life."
Acts 26.20: "Amendement of life."
Acts 3.19: "Amend your liues therefore."
Only the Geneva has "amendement of life" and "amend your liues" in the above texts. Other versions have such terms as "repent," "repentance," and "penance."

But the expression occurs several times in the Prayer Book, and the Prayer Book was probably Shakespeare's more immediate source.

Opening sentences, Morning and Evening Prayer: "Amend your liues, for the kingdome of God is at hand."

The Litany: "To amend our liues according to thy holy Word."

Exhortation in Communion Service: "With full purpose of amendement of life."

Communion Service, the following Exhortation: "Amend your liues, and bee in perfect charity with all men."

The expression also occurs in all three parts of the homily "Of Repentance."

1.2.104–5: Why, Hal, 'tis my vocation, Hal, 'tis no sin for a man to labor in his vocation.

Compare 1 Cor. 7.20: "Let euery man abide in the same vocation wherein he was called."

That every man should labor at his vocation or calling was a well-known proverb in Shakespeare's day. See Tilley C23, C480, M104, M854. That theme was also stressed in the homilies and in the Prayer Book.

Compare the homily "Against Idlenesse": "Euery one ought, in his lawfull vocation and calling, to giue himself to labour." "Earnestly apply your selues, euery man in his vocation, to honest labour." "Euery one . . . ought . . . in some kind of labour to exercise himselfe, according as the vocation whereunto GOD hath called him shall require." The words "labour" and "vocation" are used in combination with each other several more times throughout the homily.

Homily "Concerning Good Order, and Obedience to Rulers and Magistrates": "Euery degree of people in their vocation, calling and office, hath appointed to them their duty and order."

Compare the Catechism: "To learne and labour truely to get mine owne liuing."

Compare the Commination Service: "Seeking alwayes his glory, and seruing him duely in our vocation."

Compare the Geneva (not the Tomson) note on 2 Thess. 3:10: "None ought to liue idely, but ought to giue himselfe to some vocation, to get his liuing by."

See also Eph. 4.1.

In *Christs Teares ouer Ierusalem*, Thomas Nashe uses the same expression in the same context as Falstaff, that of acquiring wealth by robbery: "He held it as lawful for hym (since al labouring in a mans vocation is but getting) to gette wealth as wel with his sword by the High-way side, as the Laborer with his Spade" (McKerrow 2.64).

Compare also the "Prayer to be sayd before a man begin his worke": "Moreouer (O Lord) we beseech thee that thou wouldest strengthen vs with thy holy spirite, that we may faythfully trauayle in our estate and vocation without fraud or deceit. . . ." This prayer was one of several prayers "to be vsed in priuate houses," which were often appended to Geneva Bibles in Shakespeare's day, particularly at the end of Sternhold and Hopkins' metrical version of the Psalms.

1.2.107:   O, if men were to be sav'd by merit.

A reference to the religious controversy of whether men are justified by faith or by works, a key point of contention during the Reformation.

Rom. 3.20, 28: "Therfore by the workes of the Lawe shal no flesh be iustified in his sight. . . . Therefore we conclude, that a man is iustified by faith without the workes of the Lawe."

Shakespeare refers to the same controversy in *Love's Labor's Lost* when the Princess says: "See, see, my beauty will be sav'd by merit. / O heresy in fair, fit for these days!" (4.1.21–22)

The homily "Of Fasting," part 1, denounces salvation by merit of works when it warns us not "to put any confidence in our workes, as by the merite and deseruing of them to purchase to our selues and others remission of sin, . . . for that were mere blasphemie. . . . For it is of the free grace and mercie of GOD, . . . without merite or deseruing on our part, that our sinnes are forgiuen vs."

1.2.152–54:   Well, God give thee the spirit of persuasion and him the ears of
              profiting, that what thou speakest may move and what he
              hears may be believ'd.

Compare the collect in the Communion Service to be said after the
offertory and at the close of other services: "Graunt wee beseech thee
Almightie God, that the wordes which wee haue heard this day with our
outward eares, may through thy grace be so grafted inwardly in our hearts,
that they may bring forth in vs the fruit of good liuing."
    Compare Rom. 10.14: "How shall they beleeue in him, of whome they
haue not heard?"
    Compare 2 Chron. 18.20–21: "There came foorth a spirit . . . and said, I
will perswade him. . . . Thou shalt perswade, and shalt also preuaile."
    At best analogies rather than references, yet there are no similar passages
in Shakespeare's secular sources. Here, also, Falstaff is probably parodying
Puritan idiom.

1.2.217:   Redeeming time.

    Eph. 5.16: "Redeeming the time."
    Col. 4.5: "Redeeme the time."
    Except for the Great Bible, Taverner, and Tomson's New Testament, most
Tudor English Bibles have either "redeeming the time" or "redeem the time"
at Eph. 5.16 and Col. 4.5. The Great Bible has "winnyng occasion" in the
former and "lose no oportunitie" in the latter. Taverner has "purchasynge
opportunitie" and "redeme the tyme." Tomson has "redeeming the season"
in Ephesians and "redeeme the season" in Colossians.
    Tomson's New Testament first appeared in 1576 and became so popular
that thirty-six editions appeared between 1576 and 1612, when Shakespeare's
dramatic career ended. Starting in 1587, Tomson's New Testament also
began to be bound up with numerous editions of the Geneva Old Testament
to form a Geneva-Tomson Bible. Shakespeare's acquaintance with Tomson's
New Testament is a matter of debate. It is clear, however, that in this passage,
Shakespeare's reference is not to the Tomson New Testament.

1.3.33–34:   Came there a certain lord, neat, and trimly dress'd,
             Fresh as a bridegroom.

    Compare Isa. 61.10: "He hath decked mee like a bridegrome."
    Compare Ps. 19.5: "Which commeth forth as a bridegrome out of his
chamber."

Most likely an analogy rather than a reference to either text.

1.3.125:   And if the devil come and roar for them.

1 Peter 5.8: "Your aduersarie the deuil as a roaring lyon walketh about."
Compare the homily "Against Disobedience and Wilfull Rebellion," part
1: "The anger and displeasure of the Prince, is as the roaring of a Lyon."

[1.3.201–5: Rom. 10.6–7; Deut. 30.12–13.]

1.3.239:   Why, look you, I am whipt and scourg'd with rods.

Compare the scourging and beating of Christ:
Mark 15:15: "When he had scourged him."
Mark 14.65 and Matt. 26.67: "Smote him with their rods."
Compare also 2 Cor. 11.25: "I was thrise beaten with roddes."
Compare 1 Kings 12.11, 14: "My father hath chastised you with rods, but
I will correct you with scourges."
Compare Ps. 89.32: "I will visite their offences with the rod, and their
sinne with scourges."

2.2.26:   Stony-hearted.

In this context, the phrase "stony-hearted" is probably not a reference to
Scripture, since this was a common expression, and is listed in both Tilley
and Dent (H311) as a proverb. But compare the reference at *2 Henry IV*
4.5.107, and the comments thereon.

2.2.86:   O, we are undone.

A common expression. But compare Isa. 6.5: "Wo is me: for I am
vndone."
See also 5.2.3, below.

2.4.93–94:   Since the old days of goodman Adam.

A reference to Adam. Gen. 2.15–20.

2.4.133:   I would I were a weaver, I could sing psalms.

A reference to the Psalms of the Bible. Many Puritans and dissenters were weavers, and sang Psalms at their work.

Instead of "I could sing psalms, or any thing," as in all quarto editions, the Folio has, "I could sing all manner of songs." See the comment about the Folio's textual variants at 1.2.88–89, above.

2.4.165–68:   I have scap'd by miracle. I am eight times thrust through the doublet, four through the hose, my buckler cut through and through.

Are there echoes here of Paul's words at 2 Cor. 11.24–25: "Fiue times receiued I fourtie stripes saue one. I was thrise beaten with roddes: I was once stoned: I suffred thrise shipwracke"?

2.4.172:   Sons of darkness.

Compare 1 Thess. 5.5: "Yee are all the children of light, and the children of the daye: wee are not of the night, neither of darkenes."

Contrast John 12.36: "That ye may be the children of the light."

Compare Eph. 5.8: "For ye were once darkenes, but are nowe light: . . . walke as children of light."

2.4.225–26:   These lies are like their father that begets them.

John 8.44: "Ye are of your father the deuil, and the lusts of your father ye wil do: he hath bin a murtherer from the beginning, and abode not in the trueth, because there is no trueth in him. When he speaketh a lie, then speaketh hee of his owne: for he is a liar, and the father thereof."

2.4.277:   Watch to-night, pray to-morrow.

Compare Matt. 26.41: "Watch, and pray."

See also Mark 13.33; 14.38; Eph. 6.18; Col. 4.2.

Various editions of the Geneva Bible have "Watch and praye" as a page heading at Luke 22.

2.4.337:   Lucifer.

Derived ultimately from Isa. 14.12: "How art thou fallen from heauen, O Lucifer."

Homily "Against Disobedience and Wilfull Rebellion," part 1: "The first authour of which rebellion . . . was *Lucifer.*"

2.4.412–14:   This pitch (as ancient writers do report) doth defile, so doth the company thou keepest.

Ecclus. 13.1: "He that toucheth pitche, shalbe defiled with it."

2.4.428–29:   If then the tree may be known by the fruit, as the fruit by the tree.

Luke 6.44: "Euery tree is knowen by his owne fruite."
See also Matt. 12.33.
This text is also referred to in Lyly's *Euphues* (1.207); Shakespeare parodies Lyly's ornate style in this passage.

2.4.446–47:   Thou art violently carried away from grace.

Compare Gal. 5.4: "Ye are fallen from grace."
But Shakespeare is probably using a common expression that derives from Scripture, rather than making a conscious reference to Gal. 5.4.

2.4.463:   That old white-bearded Sathan.

"Satan" or "adversary." Derived ultimately from Scripture. The term is first used in Scripture at 1 Chron. 21.1 and occurs most frequently in Job, the synoptic Gospels, and Revelation.
Rev. 12.9: "That olde serpent, called the deuill and Satan."

2.4.473–74:   Then Pharaoh's lean kine are to be lov'd.

A reference to Pharoah's dream in Gen. 41.
Gen. 41.1, 3: "Pharaoh also dreamed. . . . And loe, seuen other kine came vp after them out of the riuer, euill fauoured and leane fleshed." Also 41.19–21.

[3.1.57–58: See 2.4.225–26, above.]

3.1.131: That would set my teeth nothing an edge.

  Compare Jer. 31.29: "The childrens teeth are set on edge."

3.1.157–62: O, he is as tedious
                As . . . a railing wife.
                . . . I had rather live
                With cheese and garlic in a windmill, far,
                Than feed on cates and have him talk to me
                In any summer house in Christendom.

  Compare Prov. 25.24: "It is better to dwell in a corner of the house toppe,
then with a contentious woman in a wide house."
  See also Prov. 21.19; 27.15.

3.1.165: Valiant as a lion.

  Compare Prov. 28.1: "The righteous are bolde as a lyon."
  Perhaps an analogy rather than a reference.
  Closest parallel in Shakespeare's sources: "He is as fierce as a Lyon." Said
of Prince Hal in the anonymous play, *The Famous Victories of Henry the
Fifth* (1000).

3.2.10–11: For the hot vengeance, and the rod of heaven,
                To punish my mistreadings.

  With strong overtones of biblical phrases and ideas.
  Compare Ps. 89.32: "I will visite their offences with the rod, and their
sinne with scourges."
  Compare Ps. 2.9: "Bruise them with a rod of iron."
  Compare Job 21.9: "The rod of God is not vpon them."
  Compare Lam. 3.1: "The rod of his indignation."
  Compare Jude 7: "Suffer the vengeance of eternall fire." (Also Tyndale,
Coverdale, Matthew.) Taverner: "The vengeaunce of euerlasting fyre." Great
Bishops', Rheims: "The paine of eternal fire."

3.2.50–54: And then I stole all courtesy from heaven,
               And dress'd myself in such humility
               That I did pluck allegiance from men's hearts,

    . . . .

               Even in the presence of the crowned King.

Compare 2 Sam. 15.5–6: "And when any man came neere to him, and did him obeisance, hee put forth his hande, and tooke him, and kissed him. And on this maner did Absalom to all Israel, that came to the King for iudgement: so Absalom stale the heartes of the men of Israel."
See 4.3.82–84, below.

[3.2.51: 1 Peter 5.5, AV only, but no Tudor version.]

[3.2.70, 74–77, 84: Prov. 25.17.]

3.2.71–73: They surfeited with honey and began
               To loathe the taste of sweetness, whereof a little
               More than a little is by much too much.

Prov. 25.16: "If thou haue found honie, eate that is sufficient for thee, least thou be ouerful, and vomit it."
See also Prov. 27.7.

[3.2.112: Luke 2.12, Great Bible.]

3.2.135–36: When I will wear a garment all of blood,
                And stain my favors in a bloody mask.

Prince Hal promises his father that he will redeem his former wayward conduct when he defeats Percy's forces and returns from the war stained with their blood. A similar thought occurs at Isa. 63.1–3: "Who is this that commeth from Edom, with red garments . . . ? Wherefore is thine apparel red? . . . Their bloud shalbe sprinkled vpon my garments, and I will staine all my raiment."
See also Rev. 19.13.

3.3.11–12: Sir John, you are so fretful you cannot live long.

Compare Ecclus. 30.23–24: "Driue sorowe farre from thee: for sorow hath slayne many. . . . Enuie and wrath shorten the life, and carefulnes bringeth age before the time."

At best an analogy rather than a reference, since the thought is common.

3.3.24–25:   I'll amend my life.

See above at 1.2.102.

3.3.31–33:   I think upon hell-fire and Dives that liv'd in purple; for there he
is in his robes, burning, burning.

A reference to the parable of the rich man ("Dives" in Latin) and Lazarus in Luke 16.19–31: "There was a certeine rich man, which was clothed in purple and fine linnen. . . . The riche man also dyed and was buried. And being in hell in torments. . . ."

3.3.35:   By this fire, that's God's angel.

Ex. 3.2: "The Angell of the Lord appeared vnto him in a flame of fire."

Acts 7.30: "An Angell of the Lord in a flame of fire."

Heb. 1.7: "Of the Angels he saith, He maketh the Spirits his messengers, and his ministers a flame of fire" (Geneva).

All other Tudor versions have "angels" for "Spirits" at Hebrews 1.7, parallel to the Bishops': "Vnto the angels he saieth, He maketh his angels spirits, and his ministers a flame of fire." Thus, these versions are closer to 3.3.35 at this text than is the Geneva Bible.

Ps. 104.4: "He maketh his angels spirits: and his ministers a flaming fire."

This oath also occurs in the anonymous play *Misogonus* 3.1.240: "By this fier that bournez thats gods aungell I sweare a great oth." Written about 1565, *Misogonus* was one of the better comedies of its time on the prodigal son theme. Whether Shakespeare knew the play or was simply using a common oath, is unknown.

The Folio omits "that's God's angel" at 3.3.35: "My Oath should bee, *By this Fire*." See the comment at 1.2.88–89, above, regarding the Folio's deletions of certain objectionable passages. Since 3.3.35 seems to have been set by Folio Compositor A, however, it would appear that the literary editor of Q5, from which the First Folio was set, was responsible for excising the words "that's God's angel."

3.3.37:   The son of utter darkness.

Compare Matt. 22.13: "Cast him into vtter darkenes."
Compare Matt. 25.30: "Into vtter darkenes."
See also Matt. 8.12.

3.3.79–80:   Will you make a younker of me?

Evidently a reference to the parable of the Prodigal Son at Luke 15.11–31 (15.11–32, AV). In the parable, an alternate designation for the prodigal son is "the yonger" (15.12–13), just as the obedient son is also called "the elder" (15.25). Falstaff's words mean, "Am I to be robbed, like the prodigal son, by strumpets?" He had just accused the Hostess of picking his pocket: "This house is turn'd bawdy-house, they pick pockets" (3.3.98–99). The prodigal son had wasted his money in "riotous liuing" and "with harlots" (15.13, 30).
Compare *The Merchant of Venice* 2.6.14–17:

> How like a younger or a prodigal
> . . . .
> Hugg'd and embraced by the strumpet wind!
> How like the prodigal doth she return.

See 4.2.33–35, below.

3.3.147:   The lion's whelp.

Compare Gen. 49.9: "A Lions whelpe."

3.3.149:   The King himself is to be fear'd as the lion.

Prov. 20.2: "The feare of the King is like the roaring of a lyon."
Prov. 19.12: "The Kinges wrath is like the roaring of a lyon."

3.3.164–65:   Thou knowest in the state of innocency Adam fell.

A reference to the fall of Adam in Genesis 3.
Gen. 3.22: "God said, Behold, the man is become as one of vs, to know good and euil."
Gen. 3.7: "The eyes of them both were opened."

Marriage Service: "An honourable estate, instituted of God in Paradise, in the time of mans innocencie."

Homily "Against Disobedience and Wilfull Rebellion": "Assoone as hee had created man, . . . being yet in the state of innocency."

See 1.2.92–95, above.

3.3.166–68:   Thou seest I have more flesh than another man, and therefore more frailty.

Compare Matt. 26.41 and Mark 14.38: "The flesh is weake."

Compare the preliminary rubric of the Confirmation Service: "Partly by the frailty of their owne flesh."

The expression, "Flesh is frail," had become proverbial. See Tilley F363.

[3.3.171: Marriage Service.]

[3.3.184: Matt. 27.24.]

[4.1.81: Dan. 11.40; 8.4.]

[4.1.108: Gal. 1.8; Acts 1.9–10.]

[4.1.117: Rev. 14.20. But the idea may have come from Holinshed (4.184), where it appears in a different context.]

4.2.25–26:   As ragged as Lazarus, . . . where the glutton's dogs lick'd his sores.

Luke 16.20–21: "There was a certeine begger named Lazarus, which was laied at his gate full of sores, and desired to be refreshed with the crommes that fel from the rich mans table: yea, and the dogs came and licked his sores."

See 3.3.31–33, above.

4.2.33–35:   You would think that I had a hundred and fifty totter'd prodigals lately come from swine-keeping, from eating draff and husks.

Luke 15.15–16: "Hee sent him to his farme, to feede swine. And he would faine haue filled his belly with the huskes, that the swine ate."

A clear reference to the Geneva Bible. The Geneva was the first English version to use "huskes." All other versions, except the Rheims New Testament, have "cods." The Rheims followed the Geneva, as did the Authorized King James Bible.

See 3.3.79–80, above.

Thomas Nashe refers to the same parable in *The Vnfortvnate Traveller:* "The onely thing they did well was the prodigall childs hunger, most of their schollers being hungerly kept; & surely you would haue sayd they had bin brought vp in hogs academie to learne to eate acornes. . . . Not a ieast had they to keepe their auditors from sleeping but of swill and draffe" (McKerrow 2.250). But Shakespeare's reference may not have been borrowed from Nashe, since Shakespeare frequently refers to the parable of the Prodigal Son, and the context in Nashe is completely different from Shakespeare's.

[4.2.38: 1 Cor. 2.9, Bishops'.]

4.3.40:   You stand against anointed majesty.

Derived from the biblical title for kings, "the Lords anointed." David several times said that he could not raise his hand against "the Lords anointed." 1 Sam. 26.9, 11, 16; 24.7, 11 (24.6, 10, AV); 2 Sam. 1.14, 16. The phrase is also used in the homilies. See part 2 of the homily "Against Disobedience and Wilfull Rebellion."

See also *3 Henry VI* 3.1.17 and the comments thereon.

4.3.82–84:   By this face,
                    This seeming brow of justice, did he win
                    The hearts of all that he did angle for.

2 Sam. 15.4–6: "Absalom sayd moreouer, Oh that I were made iudge in the lande, that euery man which hath any matter or controuersie, might come to mee, that I might doe him iustice. . . . So Absalom stale the heartes of the men of Israel."

In 2 Sam. 15.4–6, Absalom lays the groundwork for his rebellion against King David, his father. But in this passage, as well as at 3.2.50–54, above, Shakespeare applies these words not to Prince Hal, but to Bolingbroke's usurpation of the throne from Richard II. Compare the reference at *Richard II* 1.4.23–28, and the comments thereon.

5.1.72–80:   These things indeed you have articulate,

                    .   .   .   .

To face the garment of rebellion
With some fine color that may please the eye

. . . .

And never yet did insurrection want
Such water-colors to impaint his cause.

Compare the homily "Against Disobedience and Wilfull Rebellion," part 3: "It is wonderous to see what false colors and fained causes, by slanderous lies . . . rebels will deuise to cloke their rebellion withall."

Part 4: "Though it haue the image of the plough painted therein. . . . And though some rebels beare the picture of the fiue wounds paynted, . . . not those wounds which are painted in a clout by some lewd paynter."

Shakespeare's words, "With some fine color," and "Such water-colors to impaint his cause," seem to be borrowed from parts 3 and 4 of the homily. In the passage from part 4 quoted above, the painting refers to the banners borne by rebel leaders painted with symbols intended to justify their rebellion and attract followers.

Part 4: Though rebels "pretend sundry causes, as the redresse of the common wealth . . . or reformation of religion, . . . though they haue made a great shew of holy meaning by beginning their rebellions, . . . by such false pretences and shewes they doe deceiue."

5.2.3:   Then are we all undone.

See 2.2.86, above.

5.2.20:   All his offenses live upon my head.

Compare Ps. 7.17 (7.16, Geneva): "For his trauel shal come vpon his own head; and his wickednes shall fall on his own pate."

Compare Josh. 2.19: "His blood shall be vpon his head, . . . his blood shall be on our head."

Compare 1 Sam. 25.39: "The Lord hath recompensed the wickednesse of Nabal vpon his owne head."

See also 2 Sam. 1.16; 2 Chron. 6.23; Joel 3.4; etc.

[5.2.85: Josh. 10.24; Ps. 60.12.]

5.3.33:   Here's no vanity!

Probably said with Eccl. 1.2 in mind: "Vanitie of vanities, saith the Preacher: vanitie of vanities, all is vanitie." See also Eccl. 12.8.

The message of Ecclesiastes is that all in life is vanity. Falstaff says these words when he sees the corpse of Sir Walter Blunt, for death puts an end to life's vanities.

5.4.85–86:   Thou art dust,
            And food for . . . worms.

Compare Job 21.26: "They shall sleepe both in the dust, and the wormes shall couer them."

Compare Isa. 51.8: "The worme shall eate them."

Only the Authorized Version has "the worme shall feede sweetly on him" at Job 24.20, parallel to 5.4.85–86. The Geneva has: "The worme shall feele his sweetnes." None of the other versions of Shakespeare's day employ "food" or "feed" at that text. The Bishops' has: "He shall be sweete to the wormes." The Coverdale, Matthew, Taverner, and Great Bibles have "Their dainties wer wormes." Those who claim that this passage is closest to Job 24.20 are using the Authorized Version of 1611 rather than a Bible of Shakespeare's day.

5.4.150:   Bear the sin upon their own heads.

See 5.2.20, above.

2 Henry IV

The relationship between the two parts of *Henry IV* is a matter of dispute. At least four views prevail: (1) Shakespeare did not originally intend to write a second part, for the two parts are independent; each play is complete within itself and stands on its own. (2) Although Shakespeare intended to write only one play, part 2 took shape in his mind as he composed part 1. (3) Part 2 was written because part 1 was such a success, but part 2 proved to be much less popular. (4) The two parts were originally conceived as a single play, and neither is complete without the other. The only reason that we have two plays is because they are too long to be one. Like part 1, part 2 also has a large number of biblical references (60 vs. 54 in part 1), although considerably fewer are spoken by Falstaff (15 vs. 26).[1]

Shakespeare's two principal sources for the play were the second edition of Holinshed's *Chronicles* (1587), which contains no biblical references in its life of Henry IV, and a lost play or plays about Henry V crudely preserved in *The Famous Victories of Henry the Fifth*, a boisterous comedy that was published anonymously and corruptly in 1598. *The Famous Victories* covers the same period of time as all three of Shakespeare's plays about Prince Hal, who became Henry V. The play calls him Henry V from the outset, even during the time of his youthful escapades. From the old play Shakespeare took the basic outlines for the comic scenes in parts 1 and 2, and the battles in *Henry V.* The political scenes are not stressed in *The Famous Victories;* Shakespeare turned principally to Holinshed for the latter, although he altered history whenever it suited his purpose. There were Henry V plays being performed in London in the 1580s. Tarlton acted in one of them, and he died in 1588. Henslowe's *Diary* records that a new *harey the v* was acted by the Lord Admiral's men at the Rose Theater on 28 November 1595, and twelve more times by 15 July 1596. How closely *The Famous Victories* resembles those earlier plays we do not know. The play that has come down to us, evidently a memorial reconstruction of an earlier play, has at most three biblical references (listed in the introductory comments on *1 Henry IV*), and Shakespeare used none of them.

Secondary sources include Samuel Daniel's *Civil Wars* (1595), Edward Hall's *Union of the Two . . . Families of Lancaster and York* (1548), John Stow's *Chronicles of England* (1580) and his *Annals of England* (1592), *The Mirror for Magistrates* (1559), and Thomas Elyot's *The Governor* (1531).

Finally, Shakespeare may have reviewed or still have had in mind all the secondary works that he consulted when he wrote part 1: the anonymous play *Thomas of Woodstock* (ca. 1591–95; not printed until 1870), Thomas Nashe, and the many works in the madcap prince tradition. If so, then Shakespeare borrowed none of the few biblical references that can be found in them. It is not even certain that Shakespeare read some of these secondary sources, including Hall. Holinshed often followed Hall closely, and all of Shakespeare's alleged borrowings from Hall could have come from Holinshed or from some other source.

The reasons why part 2 is less popular than its predecessor are not hard to see. The political scenes in the play are less effective. Old Percy is much less interesting than his dead son, Hotspur, and unlike Hotspur, he lets himself be persuaded not to fight. Archbishop Scroop is not as theatrically effective as Glendower, and he is defeated by deceit rather than in warfare. Even the comic scenes involving Falstaff are not on a par with those in part 1. Shakespeare's use of Scripture in both plays is much the same, but the historical material he had to work with was less interesting.

In the list that follows, page numbers preceded by the number 4 (as 4.279), refer to volume 4 of Bullough.

Induction, line 32:   Stoop'd his anointed head.

In ancient Israel, the king was called "the Lords anointed." David several times said that he could not raise his hand against King Saul, "the Lords anointed." 1 Sam. 26.9, 11, 16; 24.7, 11 (24.6, 10, AV); 2 Sam. 1.14, 16. The phrase also occurs in the homilies. See part 2 of the homily "Against Disobedience and Wilfull Rebellion."

See the reference at *3 Henry VI* 3.1.17, and the comments thereon.

1.1.47:   He seem'd in running to devour the way.

Compare Job 39.27 (39.24, AV): "He swalloweth the ground for fearcenes."

Both passages relate to the speed of horses. If Shakespeare had Job in mind in this passage, then he is closer to the Geneva Bible. The Bishops' has: "Yet rusheth hee in fiercely, beating the grounde." The Coverdale, Matthew, Taverner, and Great Bibles have: "Yet russheth he in fearcely, and beateth vpon the grounde."

But the expression also occurs in Catullus (35.7): *Viam vorabit*, "He will devour the way with haste," and in Ben Jonson's play *Sejanus* (5.764–65).

Jonson says that the fickle Romans who hastened to tear down Sejanus's statues when he fell, ran with the same speed "with which they greedily deuoure the way / To some great sports, or a new theatre" (Ed. Herford and Simpson, 4.466).

Sejanus was first acted in 1603 and printed by Thomas Thorpe in 1605. When it appeared in the first folio edition of Jonson's works, 1616, Jonson announced: "This Tragoedie was first acted, in the yeere 1603. By the Kings Maiesties Servants." Shakespeare was listed as one of the "principall Tragoedians." But *2 Henry IV* had preceded *Sejanus* by about five years, and although Shakespeare must have known the play well, he did not borrow the expression from Jonson.

1.1.67:   How doth my son and brother?

See 2 Sam. 18.29, 32: "Is the yong man Absalom safe?"
Some have compared the arrival of the messengers to Northumberland, informing him about the outcome of the battle of Shrewsbury and of the welfare of his son Hotspur, to the two messengers that Joab sent to King David to inform him of the outcome of the rebellion and of the welfare of Absalom, David's son. Compare the play 1.1.7–160 with 2 Sam. 18.5–33. But the comparison is tenuous and the differences in the two accounts seem to outweigh the similarities.

1.1.157–58:   Let one spirit of the first-born Cain
                    Reign in all bosoms.

A reference to Cain, the firstborn of Adam and Eve, who slew his brother. Gen. 4.1–8.

[1.1.203: Matt. 22.37.]

1.2.7:   This foolish-compounded clay, man.

Job 13.12: "Your memories may be compared vnto ashes, and your bodies to bodies of clay."
Job 33.6: "I am also formed of the clay."
Isa. 64.8: "We are the clay, and thou art our potter."
Job 10.9: "Thou hast made me as the clay."
Geneva note on Job 10.9: "As brittle as a pot of clay."
On the basis of Job 33.6, Richmond Noble thinks that Shakespeare had

the Geneva Bible in mind in this passage. The Bishops' has "moulde" instead of "clay" at Job 33.6. But the evidence is not conclusive since the Bishops', like the Geneva, has "clay" at both Job 13.12 and Isa. 64.8, although it has "moulde" at Job 10.9 and 33.6.

1.2.34–35:   Let him be damn'd like the glutton! Pray God his tongue be hotter!

A reference to the parable of the rich man and Lazarus at Luke 16.19–31. At death the rich man went to hell and requested that Lazarus "dippe the tip of his finger in water, and coole my tongue: for I am tormented in this flame" (16.24).

1.2.35:   A whoreson Achitophel!

A reference to David's trusted counselor (2 Sam. 15.12) who sided with Absalom when Absalom attempted to usurp his father's throne. When he foresaw defeat, he hanged himself: "Nowe when Ahithophel sawe that his counsel was not followed, . . . he went home vnto his citie, . . . and hanged him selfe" (2 Sam. 17.23).

The Geneva spelling is "Ahithophel," parallel to that of the Authorized King James Bible. Coverdale (1535 and 1553) has "Achitophel," as does Taverner (1539). The Bishops' has both spellings. In the five editions that I have checked, the first and second folio editions (1568 and 1572) have "Ahithophel," while the editions of 1577, 1584, and 1585 have "Achitophel." The Great Bible of 1553 has "Ahithophel" as does Matthew's Bible of 1549.

In Shakespeare's play, the spelling in both the Quarto (1600) and the First Folio appears as "Achitophel." The Quarto was almost certainly printed from Shakespeare's "foul papers." Shakespeare probably used the spelling "Achitophel," although it is possible that he may have written "Ahithophel" and the typesetter changed it to the form he was familiar with, "Achitophel." Thus, it is not possible to determine from the spelling "Achitophel" which version of the Bible Shakespeare followed, although the evidence favors the conclusion that it was not the Geneva Bible.

The story of Ahithophel was well known in the sixteenth century. He appears in George Peele's play, *The Love of King David and Fair Bethsabe* (printed in 1599), as "Achitophel." Shakespeare's play was written ca. 1597–98 and first printed in 1600.

[1.2.45: Prov. 3.24: Ps. 4.9 (4.8, AV).]

[1.2.98–99: Matt. 5.13.]

1.2.126–27:   I am as poor as Job, . . . but not so patient.

A reference to Job after he had been reduced to poverty.
Job 1.21: "Naked came I out of my mothers wombe, and naked shall I
returne thither."
James 5.11: "Ye haue heard of the patience of Iob."

1.2.156–57:   You are as a candle, the better part burnt out.

Compare Job 18.6: "His candle shalbe put out with him."
Compare Job 21.17: "How oft shall the candle of the wicked bee put out?"
Perhaps an analogy rather than a reference.

1.2.164:   Like his ill angel.

Compare Acts 12.15: "Then said they, it is his Angell."
Compare also the medieval religious tradition of the good and bad guard-
ian angels (Shakespeare's metaphor in sonnet 144), based ultimately on Jesus'
words at Matt. 18.10: "See that ye despise not one of these litle ones: for I
say vnto you, that in heauen their Angels always behold the face of my
Father which is in heauen."
See also Heb. 1.14; Ps. 34.7.

1.2.165–67:   Your ill angel is light, but I hope he that looks upon me will
            take me without weighing.

Evidently a pun on 2 Cor. 11.14 and on the *angel*, a gold coin bearing the
figure of the archangel Michael. Satan is called an "Angel of light" at 2 Cor.
11.14, and a defective *angel*, if weighed, would be light in weight. The pun
on Falstaff's excessive weight is also clear. See 2.1.194, below.

[1.2.178–80: Rev. 17.8; 3.5; Phil. 4.3; Rev. 21.27; Luke 10.20.]

1.2.191–92:   I am only old in judgment and understanding.

Compare Job 12.12: "Among the ancient is wisedome, and in the length of
dayes is vnderstanding."

Bishops': "Among old persons there is wisedome, and in age is vnderstanding."

Compare 1 Cor. 14.20: "In vnderstanding be of a ripe age."

1.2.197–98:   The young lion repents, . . . not in ashes and sackcloth.

Matt. 11.21: "They had repented long agone in sackecloth and ashes."
Luke 10.13: "Repented, sitting in sackecloth and ashes."

1.2.225–26:   Not a penny, you are too impatient to bear crosses.

A reference to Luke 14.27, as well as a pun on the silver coins stamped with a cross. Falstaff had just asked for a loan of one thousand pounds.
Luke 14.27: "Whosoeuer beareth not his crosse."
Luke 9.23: "Let him . . . take vp his crosse daily, and follow me."
See 3.1.55, below.

1.3.15–17:   The question then, Lord Hastings, standeth thus:
             Whether our present five and twenty thousand
             May hold up head without Northumberland?

Compare Luke 14.31–32: "What King going to make warre against another King, sitteth not downe first, and taketh counsell, whether he be able with ten thousand, to meete him that commeth against him with twentie thousand? Or els while he is yet a great way of, he sendeth an ambassage, and desireth conditions of peace."
See the following reference where Shakespeare refers to the parable of the builder in the same chapter in Luke:

1.3.41–61:   When we mean to build,

             .   .   .   .
             Then must we rate the cost of the erection,
             Which if we find outweighs ability,
             What do we then but draw anew the model
             In fewer offices, or at least desist
             To build at all? Much more, in this great work [should we]

             .   .   .   .
             Consent upon a sure foundation, [lest]

             .   .   .   .

Like one that draws the model of an house
Beyond his power to build it, who, half thorough,
Gives o'er, and leaves his part-created cost
A naked subject.

Luke 14.28–30: "For which of you mynding to builde a towre, sitteth not downe before, and counteth the cost, whether he haue sufficient to performe it, lest that after he hath laid the foundation, and is not able to performe it, all that behold it, beginne to mocke him, saying, This man began to builde, and was not able to make an end?"

Most of this passage was deleted by the censor when Shakespeare's "foul papers" were sent to the printer for publication in 1600. The censor was the deputy of the Bishop of London. Upon reading the manuscript of *2 Henry IV*, he ordered that eight brief passages be deleted since they seemed to compare Queen Elizabeth to Richard II or might otherwise tend to rebellion. In this instance, the lines excised were 1.3.36–55. As the bishop's deputy, the censor probably recognized the similarity of the lines he ordered struck out to Luke 14, but the political implications of the passage came first.

The next passage that the censor struck out was 1.3.85–108; these lines included the following three references. None of the other six deletions involved biblical references. All eight deletions are preserved in the Folio.

1.3.89–90: An habitation giddy and unsure
            Hath he that buildeth on the vulgar heart.

Compare Luke 6.49: "Like a man that built an house vpon the earth without foundation, against which the flood did beat, and it fel by and by: and the fall of that house was great."
Compare also Matt. 7.26–27.

1.3.95–99: Thou, beastly feeder, art so full of him,
            That thou provok'st thyself to cast him up.
            So, so, thou common dog, didst thou disgorge
            Thy glutton bosom of the royal Richard,
            And now thou wouldst eat thy dead vomit up.

2 Peter 2.22: "The dogge is returned to his own vomit."
Prov. 26.11: "As a dogge turneth againe to his owne vomit."
See *Henry V* 3.7.64–65 where 2 Peter 2.22 is quoted in French.

1.3.103–4:   Thou, that threw'st dust upon his goodly head
             When through proud London he came sighing on.

Compare 2 Sam. 16.13: "And as Dauid and his men went by the way, Shimei went by the side of the mountaine ouer agaynst him, and cursed as he went, and threw stones against him, and cast dust."

Compare *Richard II* 5.2.30: "But dust was thrown upon his sacred head."

2.1.51:   Wilt thou kill God's officers and the King's?

Based on Romans 13.3–6: "For Princes ["rulers," all other Tudor versions except Rheims] are not to be feared for good workes, but for euil. . . . For hee is the minister of God. . . . For they are Gods ministers."

That rulers are God's officers or representatives was a well-rehearsed theme in Elizabethan England. Romans 13 was quoted in the homily "Concerning Good Order, and Obedience to Rulers and Magistrates," as well as the homily "Against Disobedience and Wilfull Rebellion." Part 1 of the former homily calls government officials "GODS Officers": "Submission, and subiection to the high powers, which bee set in authority by GOD, for as much as they bee GODS Lieuetenants, GODS Presidentes, GODS Officers, . . . ordained of GOD himselfe."

See 4.2.28, below.

2.1.102–3:   I put thee now to thy book-oath.

An oath made on the Bible.

2.1.109–11:   Sir John, I am well acquainted with your manner of wrenching
              the true cause the false way.

Compare Ecclus. 19.24: "There is a certeine subtiltie that is fine, but it is vnrighteous: and there is that wresteth the open and manifest Law."

Ecclus. 19.25 describes a certain type of evildoer who "fayneth himselfe deafe" as he commits his evil, and at 1.2.66–67 Falstaff tells the Chief Justice, "I am deaf."

2.1.144–45:   The story of the Prodigal.

A reference to the parable of the Prodigal Son in Luke 15.11–31 (15.11–32, AV). The word "prodigal" occurs nowhere in the text of the Bible, but Jesus' parable was known as the parable of the Prodigal Son. Caption headings in both the Geneva and Bishops' Bibles refer to the account as being that of "the prodigal sonne." The chapter heading in the Great Bible calls it the parable "of the sonne that was lost."

2.1.194:   The Lord lighten thee!

Evening Prayer: "Lighten our darknes we beseech thee, O Lord."
2 Sam. 22.29: "Thou art my light, O Lorde: and the Lord will lighten my darkenes."
Ps. 13.3: "Consider and heare me, O Lord my God: lighten mine eyes."
Prov. 29.13: "The Lord lighteneth both theyr eyes."
Ezra 9.8: "That our God may lyght our eyes."
Ps. 19.8: "The commandement of the Lord is pure, and giueth light vnto the eyes."
The pun on Falstaff's excessive weight is obvious. See 1.2.165–67, above.

2.2.23–24:   And God knows whether those that bawl out the ruins of thy
             linen shall inherit his kingdom.

Matt. 25.34: "Inherit ye the kingdome prepared for you."
Tomson's New Testament has, "Take the inheritance of the kingdome prepared for you."
Evidently Shakespeare did not have the popular Tomson New Testament in mind in this passage.
The Folio omits 2.2.23–27. The person responsible for removing these lines was not a censor, as is the case with the eight passages deleted from the quarto (see 1.3.41–61, above), but a literary editor who sought to tidy up the copy from which the Folio was set, and purge it of indecencies and profanities. In seeking to expunge the Folio text of anything profane, the reference to Matt. 25.34 was removed.

2.2.47:   Let the end try the man.

A proverb. See Tilley E116: "The end crowns (tries) all."
But compare also Ecclus. 11.27: "In a mans ende, his workes are discouered."
Compare also Job 34.36: "I desire that Iob may bee tryed, vnto the ende."

2.2.101–5:   *Poins.* . . .And how doth the martlemas, your master?
             Bard. In bodily health, sir.
             Poins. Marry, the immortal part needs a physician, but that
                moves him not; though that be sick, it dies not.

A humorous application of Matt. 9.12: "The whole neede not a physition,
but they that are sicke."
See also Mark 2.17.

2.2.117–18:   They will be kin to us, or they will fetch it from Japhet.

Japheth was the third son of Noah, considered the ancestor of the Europeans.
    Gen. 10.2–5: "The sonnes of Iapheth. . . . Of these were the yles of the
Gentiles deuided in their landes, . . . after their families in their nations."
    Prince Hal says that some will try to prove they are related to the King
even if they have to go back to Japheth, the father of all Europeans.

2.2.131:   Thine, by yea and no.

A common Puritan oath based on Matt. 5.37: "Let your communication
be, Yea, yea: Nay, nay. For whatsoeuer is more then these, commeth of
euil."
See 3.2.9, below.

2.2.142:   Thus we play the fools with the time.

Compare Eph. 5.15–16: "Walke circumspectly, not as fooles, but as wise,
redeeming the time."
    The passage at 2.2.149–50 is probably also a reference to Ephesians 5.
Compare the reference to Eph. 5.16 in *1 Henry IV* 1.2.217.

2.2.143:   The spirits of the wise sit in the clouds and mock us.

Compare Ps. 2.4: "He that dwelleth in heauen shal laugh them to scorne:
the Lorde shall haue them in derision."
Compare Ps. 2.4, Sternhold and Hopkins:

                    But he that in the heauen dwelleth,
                       their doings wil deride:

And make them al a mocking stocke,
throughout the world so wide.

Compare Ps. 59.8, Sternhold and Hopkins:

But lord thou hast their waies espide
and laught thereat apace
The heathen folke thou shalt deride
and mock them to their face.

2.2.149–50:   *Prince.* What company?
              Page. Ephesians, my lord, of the old church.

The reference is probably to the evil habits and company that Paul told the church at Ephesus to put away.

Eph. 5.3–4: "But fornication, and al vncleannes, or couetousnes, let it not bee once named among you, as it becommeth Saints, neither filthines, neither foolish talking, neither iesting, which are thinges not comely."

Eph. 5.7: "Bee not therefore companions with them."

Eph. 5.18: "And bee not drunke with wine."

The Page refers to the type of company Falstaff keeps with. In the previous chapter Paul wrote the Ephesians to cast off their old wayward personality and put on a new way of life. Eph. 4.22–24: "That yee cast of . . . the olde man, which is corrupt . . . and put on the newe man, which after God is created in righteousnes."

Other plays of the period make similar references. In *Sir John Oldcastle* (printed 1600), Harpool, the servant of Sir John Oldcastle, jests (4.1.138–40): "I am neither heretike nor puritane, but of the old church: ile sweare, drinke ale, kisse a wench, . . ." (*The Shakespeare Apocrypha*, ed. C. F. Tucker Brooke, p. 153). Likewise in Thomas Middleton's play *The Family of Love* (printed 1608), Mistress Purge says (1.3.111–13): "This playing is not lawful, for I cannot find that either plays or players were allowed in the prime church of Ephesus by the elders" (*The Works of Thomas Middleton*, ed. A. H. Bullen, 3.27).

2.4.57–59:   You cannot one bear with another's confirmities. . . . one must
             bear, and that must be you.

Rom. 15.1: "We which are strong, ought to beare the infirmities of the weake, and not to please our selues."

A clear reference to the Geneva Bible. Most other Tudor translations have "beare the frailenes." Taverner has "beare the fraylite." Only the Geneva has "beare the infirmities." The Rheims has "susteine the infirmities."

One of the Hostess's many malapropisms. Shakespeare facetiously makes her say "confirmities" rather than "infirmities."

2.4.60:   You are the weaker vessel.

1 Peter 3.7: "Giuing honour vnto the woman, as vnto the weaker vessell."

2.4.88:   Master Dumbe, our minister.

Probably a reference to Isa. 56.10 that was applied especially by Puritans to negligent, greedy preachers: "Their ᵏ watchmen are all blinde: they haue no knowledge: they are all domme dogges: they can not barke: they lie and sleepe and delite in sleeping."

Note "k" in the Geneva Bible reads: "Hee sheweth that this affliction shall come through the faulte of the gouernours, Prophets and pastours, whose ignorance, negligence, auarice and obstinacie prouoked Gods wrath against them."

In Bishop Joseph Hall's *A Plaine and Familiar Explication . . . of All the Hard Texts of . . . the Old and New Testament,* 1633 (*STC* 12702), appears this comment on Isa. 56.10: "Alas, the watchmen of my people, their spirituall overseers, are altogether blinde, and ignorant, and not so only, but as they are blind, so they are dumb also, not opening their mouthes, to give warning of the dangers of my people, and the judgements which are imminent over them; even like unprofitable dogges, which being set to keepe the house, have no tongue to barke."

2.4.221:   The Nine Worthies.

A group of renowned champions that included three biblical characters: Joshua, David, and Judas Maccabaeus.

[2.4.235: Ecclus. 28.6; Ps. 39.5 (39.4, Geneva).]

2.4.327–29:   Is she of the wicked? is thine hostess here of the wicked? or is thy boy of the wicked?

The expression "of the wicked" occurs many times in Scripture, particularly in the book of Proverbs. The Puritans picked up the phrase and applied it to nonbelievers. Prince Hal appears to be making fun of a cant religious phrase.

Prov. 3.33: "The curse of the Lorde is in the house of the wicked."
Prov. 4.14: "Enter not into the way of the wicked."
Prov. 4.19: "The waye of the wicked is as the darkenesse."
Prov. 10.6: "Iniquitie shall couer the mouth of the wicked."
Prov. 10.7: "The name of the wicked shall rotte."
Prov. 10.20: "The heart of the wicked is little worth."
See also Prov. 10:27, 28, 32; 11.11, 23; 12.5, 6, 10, 26; 14.11; etc.

2.4.333:   Lucifer.

Isa. 14.12: "How art thou fallen from heauen, O Lucifer."
Homily "Against Disobedience and Wilfull Rebellion," part 1: "The first authour of which rebellion . . . was *Lucifer.*"
The name "Lucifer" occurs just once in Scripture, at Isa. 14.12. There it is applied to Nebuchadnezzar, the king of Babylon, who is compared to Venus or Lucifer, the morning star. But in Shakespeare's day the title "Lucifer" was mistakenly applied to Satan. Even Saint Jerome (d. 420) had associated Lucifer with Satan.

2.4.335:   For the boy, there is a good angel about him.

See above at 1.2.164. Derived ultimately from Matt. 18.10.

2.4.335–36:   But the devil blinds him too.

Compare 2 Cor. 4.4: "The God of this worlde hath blinded the minds . . . of the infidels."
Whereas the Quarto reads "the diuel blinds him too," the Folio has "the Deuill outbids him too." Based on the context and the cluster of biblical references that follow one another in rapid succession within the space of ten lines, it would seem that the Quarto reading (a clear biblical reference) is the correct one. That Satan pretends to be an angel of light to blind and mislead the unwary was a common belief.

[2.4.338–39: Prov. 5.5; 7.27 (of the prostitute and those who visit her).]

[2.4.350–51: Gal. 5.17.]

2.4.362:   So idly to prophane the precious time.

Contrast Hal's words in this passage with his words at 2.2.142, above, which seem to echo Eph. 5.15–16: "Walke circumspectly, not as fooles, but as wise, redeeming the time: for the dayes are euill."

3.1.18–19:   Wilt thou upon the high and giddy mast
             Seal up the ship-boy's eyes, and rock his brains?

Compare Prov. 23.34, although from a different context: "And thou shalt be as one that sleepeth in the middes of the sea, and as he that sleepeth in the toppe of the mast."
    Prov. 23.34 is quoted in the homily "Against Gluttony and Drunken-nesse." See also *Richard III* 3.4.99–101 where the reference to Prov. 23.34 is clear.

[3.1.45: Rev. 20.12; Dan. 7.10; 12.1; Phil. 4.3; Ps. 69.29 (69.28, Geneva).]

[3.1.47–49: Amos 9.5; Ps. 46.2–3. But there are similar passages elsewhere. See Ovid's *Metamorphoses* 15.262–67 (Loeb Classical Library 2.382–83).]

3.1.55:   What crosses to ensue.

Derived ultimately from Jesus' words about bearing one's cross.
Matt. 16.24: "Let him forsake him selfe, and take vp his crosse."
See also Matt. 10.38; Mark 8.34; 10.21; Luke 9.23; 14.27.
See above at 1.2.225–26.

[3.1.76–77: James 1.15. See also *Richard II* 5.1.58–59 where Shakespeare uses the same expression.]

3.2.9:   By yea and no.

See 2.2.131, above.

3.2.37–38:   Death, as the Psalmist saith, is certain to all, all shall die.

While there is no text in the Psalms that says "death is certain," there are many texts that comment on the brevity of man's life. Perhaps the closest passage in the Psalms to the thought that "death is certain" is Ps. 89.47 (89.48, Geneva): "What man is he that liueth, and shal not see death?"

See also Ps. 49.7–10, 14.

Compare Tilley D142: "Death is common to all," and M505: "All men must die."

3.2.257–60:   Will you tell me, Master Shallow, how to choose a man? Care I
              for the limb, the thews, the stature, bulk, and big assemblance
              of a man? Give me the spirit.

Compare 1 Sam. 16.7: "The Lord saide vnto Samuel, Looke not on his countenance, nor on the height of his stature, because I haue refused him: for God seeth not as man seeth: for man looketh on the outwarde appearance, but the Lorde beholdeth the heart."

Compare John 6.63: "It is the Spirit that quickneth: the flesh profiteth nothing."

Most likely analogies rather than references.

[3.2.315: Gen. 30.14–16.]

[4.1.46: Matt. 3.16; John 1.32.]

[4.1.192–94: Matt. 3.12; Luke 22.31.]

4.1.203–7:   He cannot so precisely weed this land

             . . . .

             His foes are so enrooted with his friends
             That, plucking to unfix an enemy,
             He doth unfasten so and shake a friend.

Matt. 13.25–30: "Sowed tares among the wheat. . . . Lest while ye go about to gather the tares, ye plucke vp also with them the wheat. Let both growe together."

Only the Bishops' and Rheims have "root vp" rather than "plucke vp" at Matt. 13.29. All other versions have "plucke vp," as does the Prayer Book Gospel reading for the fifth and sixth Sundays after Epiphany.

The closest parallel in Shakespeare's sources occurs in Holinshed. By usurping the crowne and punishing those who rebelled against him, Holinshed says, Henry "wan himselfe more hatred, than in all his life time . . . had beene possible for him to have weeded out & remooved" (4.279). This passage may have suggested to Shakespeare the account in Matthew 13.

4.1.213–14:   The King hath wasted all his rods
               On late offenders.

Ps. 89.32: "I will visite their offences with the rod."
The Geneva version of the Psalms has "transgression" rather than "offences."
See also 2 Chron. 10.11.

[4.1.215: 1 Kings 12.11, 14; 2 Chron. 10.11, 14.]

4.2.10:   Turning the word to sword and life to death.

Are these words a pun on Eph. 6.17: "The sword of the Spirit, which is the worde of God"? Prince John tells the Archbishop of York that it was better when he preached the word to his flock, than for him to exchange his preaching of the word for the sword.
Compare also Phil. 2.16: "Holding forth the worde of life."
A similar statement occurs in *The Merry Wives* 3.1.44–45: "What? the sword and the word? Do you study them both, Master Parson?"

[4.2.19: Acts 12.22.]

4.2.27:   Under the counterfeited zeal of God.

Rom. 10.2: "They haue the zeale of God, but not according to knowledge."
The Geneva Bible was the first version to use "zeale of God" at Rom. 10.2, which was followed by the Bishops', Rheims, and the Authorized Version. The Tyndale, Matthew, and Great Bibles have "a feruent minde to god warde." Coverdale has, "are zelous Gods cause." Taverner: "a feruent mynde towardes God."

4.2.28:   The subjects of his substitute, my father.

Based on Rom. 13.3–6 where earthly rulers are called "God's ministers." See especially 13.4: "For hee is the minister of God."

See 2.1.51, above, with its reference to the homily "Concerning Good Order, and Obedience to Rulers and Magistrates," in which kings and rulers are called "GODS Lieuetenants, GODS Presidentes, GODS Officers."

4.3.14:   Fear and trembling.

Eph. 6.5: "With feare and trembling."
While "fear and trembling" may have been a common expression in Shakespeare's day, its origin was probably Scripture. Falstaff's use of the phrase in this passage is probably intended to be another instance in which he facetiously quotes Scripture and mimics Puritan idiom.

[4.3.88–89: Ecclus. 31.28.]

4.4.79–80:   'Tis seldom when the bee doth leave her comb
              In the dead carrion.

This comparison may have been suggested by the account in Judges 14.8: "He went aside to see the karkeis of the lion: and behold, there was a swarme of bees, and hony in the body of the Lyon."

4.5.8:   I am here, brother, full of heaviness.

Compare Ps. 69.21 (69.20, Geneva): "I am full of heauinesse."
Compare Phil. 2.26: "And was full of heauines."
But the expression was probably common.

4.5.107:   Whom thou hast whetted on thy stony heart.

Compare Ezek. 11.19: "I will take the stonie heart out of their bodies, and will giue them an heart of flesh."
Compare Ezek. 36.26: "I will take away the stonie heart out of your body."
But the expression was proverbial. See Tilley H311: "A heart as hard as a stone."
The expression also occurs in the concluding prayer to all six parts of the homily "Against Disobedience and Wilfull Rebellion": "O most mercifull Father, (if it be thy holy will) make soft and tender the stonie hearts of all

those that exalt themselues against thy Trueth, and seeke either to trouble the quiet of this Realme of England, or to oppresse the Crowne of the same."

4.5.115–16:   Only compound me with forgotten dust;
              Give that which gave thee life unto the worms.

Compare Job 21.26: "They shall sleepe both in the dust, and the wormes shall couer them."
Compare Isa. 51.8: "The worme shall eate them."

[4.5.142–44: Rev. 11.15; 17.14; 1 Tim. 6.15–16; 1 Peter 5.4.]

[4.5.149: Rom. 1.9; Gen. 31.50. But Shakespeare's source may have been *The Famous Victories*, 654 (4.318), where a similar expression occurs. See also the anonymous play *Thomas of Woodstock*, 1635 (Bullough 3.477).]

[4.5.181–83: Gen. 49.1–2. Compare *The Famous Victories*, 666 (4.318).]

4.5.183–85:   God knows, my son,
              By what by-paths and indirect crook'd ways
              I met this crown.

Compare Prov. 2.15: "Whose wayes are crooked."
Compare Isa. 59.8: "They haue made them crooked paths."
Compare Ps. 125.5, Geneva: "These that turne aside by their crooked wayes." ("Turne backe vnto their owne wickednesse," Psalter.)
Although "crooked ways" was no doubt a common expression, it does not occur in Shakespeare's sources. The closest parallel to these words of King Henry occurs in *The Famous Victories* 674–75:

> For God knowes my sonne, how hardly I came by it,
> And how hardly I have maintained it.
>
> (4.318)

Holinshed has: "Well faire sonne (said the king with a great sigh) what right I had to it, God knoweth" (4.277–78). Shakespeare may have had Scripture in mind when he added "crook'd ways" to his sources.

[5.1.75–77: Prov. 13.20; Ecclus. 9.16–17. But this was a proverbial saying. See Tilley M248, M535.]

[5.2.103: Rom. 13.4.]

5.3.101:   O base Assyrian knight, what is thy news?

When Shakespeare mentions Assyrians, the associations are probably biblical, as in *Henry V* 4.7.62, where "Assyrian slings" is no doubt based on Judith 9.7: "Behold, the Assyrians: . . . they trust in shield, speare and bow, and sling." Why Falstaff calls Pistol a "base Assyrian knight" is uncertain, but it is probably a humorous description of Pistol's antics as the braggart soldier. The title page of the Quarto calls him "swaggering Pistoll." The Assyrians were thought of as cruel, bloody plunderers, eager for booty, that theme being stressed in the book of Nahum.

5.3.111–12:   I am, sir, under the King, in some authority.

Luke 7.8: "For I likewise am a man set vnder authoritie, and haue vnder me souldiers, and I say vnto one, Goe, and hee goeth."
If Shakespeare had Luke 7.8 in mind in this passage, then his reference is probably to the Geneva Bible. Tyndale, Matthew, Taverner, Great, and the Bishops' Bibles have "vnder power." Coverdale has: "subiecte to the hygher auctorite," but it is more likely that Shakespeare followed the Geneva rather than the Coverdale Bible.

5.3.137–38:   Blessed are they that have been my friends.

Are these words patterned on the Beatitudes? If so, Falstaff would again be paraphrasing Scripture.
Matt. 5.4: "Blessed are they that mourne."
Matt. 5.6: "Blessed are they which hunger."
Matt. 5.10: "Blessed are they which suffer persecution."
Falstaff's next words, "woe to my Lord Chief Justice!" (5.3.138), could also be facetiously patterned on the woes Jesus pronounced at Matt. 23.13–29. See also Matt. 11.21.

5.4.12–13:   But I pray God the fruit of her womb miscarry.

Compare Ps. 127.4 (127.3, Geneva): "The fruite of the wombe."
Compare Luke 1.42: "Blessed art thou among women, because the fruite of the wombe is blessed."
See also Deut. 7.13; Isa. 13.18.
Compare the context of Ex. 21.22, Bishops': "If men striue, and hurt a woman with child, so that her fruite depart from her, . . . then he shall be sore punished." The Geneva has: "So that her childe depart from her."

[5.5.47: Matt. 7.23; 25.12.]

5.5.53–54:   The grave doth gape
                For thee.

Compare Isa. 5.14, Bishops': "Therefore gapeth hell, and openeth her mouth marueilous wide that [they] . . . may descende into it."
Geneva: "Hell hath inlarged it selfe."
Shakespeare is least like the Geneva Bible in this reference and closer to the other versions of the day, all of which are parallel to the Bishops'.
See *Henry V* 2.1.61, and the comments thereon.

Epilogue.13–14:   And here I commit my body to your mercies.

Compare the Burial Service: "We therefore commit his body to the ground."

NOTE

1. The count of sixty biblical and liturgical references in *2 Henry IV* excludes the passages at 1.1.67, 2.1.102–3, and 2.4.221.

Henry V

When Shakespeare's *Henry V* appeared on the London stage in 1599, plays about England's epic hero who had conquered France were not new. *Tarlton's Jests,* a collection of anecdotes about the actor Richard Tarlton who died in 1588, mentions his comic role in a "Henry the fift" play. In *Pierce Penilesse* (1592), Thomas Nashe mentions a play on Henry V in which Henry leads the French king prisoner and forces him and the Dauphin to swear fealty, although no surviving play has that scene. Henslowe's *Diary* records thirteen performances of a Henry V play at the Rose Theater between 28 November 1595 and 15 July 1596. Finally, we have the anonymous *Famous Victories of Henry the Fifth* entered in the Stationers' Register on 14 May 1594, and published in 1598 in a corrupt text.

How all these plays, which appeared before Shakespeare's play, are related to each other is not clear. What is clear is that there are more parallels between Shakespeare's *Henry V* and the *Famous Victories* than there are between the *Famous Victories* and *Henry IV* parts 1 and 2. Some of these parallels are significant, and there would no doubt be more of them were not the text of the *Famous Victories* so mutilated. The *Famous Victories* covers the same historical period as Shakespeare's three plays on Henry V, with the first half of the play parallel to the two *Henry IV* plays, while the last half corresponds to *Henry V.*

As is true of *1* and *2 Henry IV,* the principal sources for *Henry V* were the second edition of Holinshed's *Chronicles* (1587), and the lost play or plays about Henry V of which the *Famous Victories* is a corrupt and condensed version. But whereas there are no biblical references in those portions of Holinshed's *Chronicles* that Shakespeare used for *1* and *2 Henry IV,* Holinshed's account of Henry V has at least seven clear biblical references, of which Shakespeare borrowed three (1.2.98–100, 2.4.102, and 4.8.123). Even in its corrupt state, the *Famous Victories* has three biblical references, but Shakespeare borrowed none of them.

Of Shakespeare's secondary sources, Hall's chronicle is probably the most important. In fact, much of Holinshed's account of Henry V is taken from Hall, often word for word. Most of the biblical references in Holinshed's account were borrowed from Hall, including two of the outstanding references that Shakespeare makes in his play: that to the book of Numbers at 1.2.98 (Numbers being the only book of the Bible that Shakespeare mentions by name in any of his plays), and the reference to Psalm 115 at 4.8.123. So clear is Hall's influence on Shakespeare in *Henry V* that it appears Shakespeare had both Holinshed and Hall open before him as he wrote some parts of the play. However, there is nothing in any of Shakespeare's sources that is parallel to Henry's discussion on the responsibility for war and the fate of the soldiers who die therein (4.1.124–91), or to Henry's musings on kingship (4.1.230–84), which contain a large number of biblical and liturgical references. These passages with their references are original with Shakespeare.

Other secondary sources include Robert Fabyan's *Chronicle*, which appeared in several editions between 1516 and 1559; John Stow's *Chronicles* (1580), as well as his *Annals* (1592); Samuel Daniel's *Civil Wars* (1595); Caxton's version of the Brut Chronicle; and several lives of Henry V written in the fifteenth century, most of which were still unpublished in the sixteenth. These include the *Gesta Henrici Quinti*, written by the chaplain of Henry's army who accompanied him on the first compaign, the anonymous *Vita et Gesta Henrici Quinti*, and the *Vita Henrici Quinti* by Titus Livius in both Latin and English. But Shakespeare's debt to most of these works is minor, and it is unlikely that he borrowed any biblical references from them. It is not even certain which of these lives of Henry, if any, Shakespeare may have read. His acquaintance with any of them may have been indirect.

Henry's visit to his soldiers on the eve of the battle may have been suggested by an English translation of the *Annals* of Tacitus published in 1598, since neither Hall nor Holinshed mention his visit. But Shakespeare might have borrowed it from *The First English Life of King Henry the Fifth*, the English translation of Titus Livius's Latin life of Henry. Shakespeare may have read the anonymous poem *The Battle of Agincourt*, printed in 1530. The archbishop's example of the order that prevails among bees could have been from any of several sources, including Virgil, Pliny, Elyot, and Lyly. Other possible sources are negligible, and the resemblances in them to *Henry V* are mostly generic rather than specific; it is unlikely that they influenced the biblical references that Shakespeare makes in his play.

In the list that follows, page numbers preceded by the number 4, as in (4.384), refer to volume 4 of Bullough. References to Hall's *Chronicle* are to the 1550 edition, *STC* 12723.

1.1.15:   Lazars

Derived ultimately from the parable of the rich man and Lazarus.

Luke 16.20: "A certeine begger named Lazarus, which was laied at his gate full of sores."

Compare also *The Faerie Queene* 1.4.3.(6).

The parable of Lazarus was the source of the word "lazar," a person afflicted with a loathsome disease, especially leprosy.

1.1.22:   The King is full of grace and fair regard.

John 1.14: "Ful of grace and trueth."

Communion Service, Gospel reading for the Annunciation of the Virgin Mary, Luke 1.28: "Haile ful of grace."

While all Tudor English Bibles have "ful of grace and trueth (verite)" at John 1.14, neither the Geneva nor the Bishops' have "ful of grace" at Luke 1.28. The Geneva has: "Haile thou that are freely beloued," while the Bishops' reads: "Hayle thou that art in hygh fauour." All other versions (Tyndale, Coverdale, Matthew, Taverner, Great, Rheims) have "full of grace," parallel to the Prayer Book.

1.1.26–27:   But that his wildness, mortified in him,
            Seem'd to die too.

Compare Col. 3.5: "Mortifie therefore your members which are on the earth."

Compare Nowell's *Catechism:*

Ma. How many partes be there of Repentance?
Sch. Two cheife partes. The mortifying of the olde man or the fleshe: and
    the quickening of the new man or the spirite.
Ma. I woulde haue these more largely and plainly set out.
Sch. The mortifying of the olde man is vnfayned and syncere acknowl-
    edging and confession of sinne. . . ." (p. 48; 1570 ed.; *STC* 18708).

Compare the hymn "The Complaint of a Sinner," attached to Sternhold and Hopkins' metrical Psalms:

> That I with sin repleat,
> May liue and sin may die:
> That being mortified,
> This sin of mine in me . . .

"Mortify" is the accepted religious term, drawn from Scripture, used to denote the death of the old sinful self before the onset of grace. One of the many theological terms used by the archbishop.

1.1.29:   And whipt th' offending Adam out of him.

That is, drove original, inherited, Adamic sin out of him. Probably a reference to the old Adam that was to die at baptism.

Baptismal Service: "Graunt, that he being dead vnto sinne, and liuing vnto righteousnesse . . . may crucifie the olde man, and vtterly abolish the whole body of sinne." Also: "Mercifull God, grant that the old Adam in these children may be so buried, that the new man may be raised vp in them."

The archbishop had just said that Henry's former wildness "seem'd to die too." Compare Rom. 6.6; 2 Cor. 5.17; Eph. 4.22–24; and Col. 3.9–10, on which these passages in the Baptismal Service are based. In these texts the Apostle Paul urges believers to cast off the "olde man," the offending Adam, and put on a new personality.

1.1.29–30:   And whipt th' offending Adam out of him,
               Leaving his body as a paradise.

In contrast to Adam who was driven out of paradise because of sin, Hal's transformation was as if an angel had whipped sin out of him, leaving his body a paradise.

Gen. 3.23–24: "Therefore the Lorde God sent him foorth from the garden of Eden. . . . Thus he cast out man, and at the East side of the garden of Eden he set the Cherubims."

The imagery and ideas are from the Genesis account.

[1.1.30–31: 1 Cor. 3.16.]

1.1.67:   It must be so; for miracles are ceas'd.

Protestants believed that miracles ceased after New Testament times. Compare 1 Cor. 13.8: "Loue doeth neuer fall away, though that prophesyings be abolished, or the tongues cease, or knowledge vanish away."

Compare *All's Well That Ends Well* 2.3.1: "They say miracles are past."

Bishop Joseph Hall's *Explication . . . of All the Hard Texts,* 1633 (*STC* 12702), comments thus on 1 Cor. 13.8: "Charity [love] is a during and perpetuall grace; and where it is truly rooted in the heart, never faileth; whereas other gifts, and tongues, and prophesie, and knowledge, at last vanish away."

Were it doctrinally admissable, the archbishop would prefer to credit Hal's conversion to a miracle. As it is, he must accept the Bishop of Ely's explanation.

[1.2.7: Ps. 91.11; Matt. 4.6; Luke 4.10.]

1.2.23:   We charge you, in the name of God.

Compare the wording of 1 Tim. 6.13: "I charge thee in the sight of God."
Compare 1 Tim. 5.21: "I charge thee before God."
Compare 2 Tim 4.1: "I charge thee therefore before God."
See also 1 Thess. 5.27.

1.2.31–32:   That what you speak is in your conscience wash'd
             As pure as sin with baptism.

Acts 22.16: "Arise, and be baptized, and washe awaye thy sinnes."
Baptismal Service: "By the Baptisme of thy welbeloued Son Iesus
Christ, . . . to the mystical washing away of sinne."
Compare also Heb. 10.22: "Sprinkled in our hearts from an euill con-
science, and washed in our bodies with pure water."
See also Acts 2.38.

1.2.97:   The sin upon my head.

A variation of the frequent biblical expression that if one sins, "his blood
shall be vpon his head" (Joshua 2.19).
See also 2 Sam. 1.16; 3.29; 1 Kings 2.32–33; 2.37; 2 Chron. 6.23; Esther
9.25; Ps. 7.17 (7.16, Geneva); Jer. 23.19.
See 4.1.186–87, below.

1.2.98–100:   For in the book of Numbers it is writ,
              When the man dies, let the inheritance
              Descend unto the daughter.

Num. 27.8: "Also thou shalt speake vnto the children of Israel, saying, If a
man dye and haue no sonne, then ye shall turne his inheritaunce vnto his
daughter."
See also Joshua 17.3–4.
Numbers is the only book of the Bible specifically named by Shakespeare.
His source was both Hall and Holinshed. Holinshed has: "The archbishop
further alledged out of the booke of Numbers this saieng: When a man dieth
without a sonne, let the inheritance descend to his daughter" (4.379). Shakespeare omits "without a sonne," which occurs in both Hall and Holinshed,
evidently assuming it would be understood that there were no male heirs.

1.2.109:   Lion's whelp.

Compare Gen. 49.9: "As a Lions whelpe shalt thou come vp from the spoyle."

1.2.183–90:   Therefore doth heaven divide
                 The state of man in divers functions,

                 . . . .

                 To which is fixed, as an aim or butt,
                 Obedience; for so work the honey-bees,
                 Creatures that by a rule in nature teach
                 The act of order to a peopled kingdom.
                 They have a king, and officers of sorts.

The archbishop's words echo a familiar theme in Elizabethan England: the need for order and the observance of degree. Compare the homily "Concerning Good Order, and Obedience to Rulers and Magistrates": "Almighty GOD hath created and appointed all things in heauen, earth, and waters, in a most excellent and perfect order. . . . In earth hee hath assigned and appointed Kings, Princes, with other gouernours vnder them, in all good and necessary order. . . . And man himselfe also hath all his parts both within and without . . . in a profitable, necessarie, and pleasant order: euery degree of people in their vocation, calling and office, hath appoined to them their duty and order."

Compare also all six parts of the homily "Against Disobedience and Wilfull Rebellion." While the archbishop's words about order and obedience reflect the homilies, Shakespeare's source for the illustration of the bees is uncertain. The most likely candidates are Virgil's *Georgics*, Pliny's *Natural History*, Elyot's *Governor*, and Lyly's *Euphues*, although a number of other sources are also possible.

1.2.287–88:   And some are yet ungotten and unborn
                 That shall have cause to curse the Dolphin's scorn.

Evidently another echo from the homilies. Compare part 4 of the homily "Against Disobedience and Wilfull Rebellion": "That the childe yet vnborne may rue it, and shall many yeeres hereafter curse them."

Compare *Richard II* 4.1.322–23 where the same passage in the homily is referred to.

1.2.303:   God, that run before our business.

1.2.307–8:   For, God before, / We'll chide. . . .

Compare Deut. 31.3: "The Lord thy God hee wil go ouer before thee."
Compare also 3.6.156, below.

2.1.61:   The grave doth gape, and doting death is near.

Compare Isa. 5.14, Bishops': "Therefore gapeth hell, and openeth her
mouth marueilous wide, that [they] . . . may descende into it."
Geneva: "Hell hath inlarged it selfe."
The Coverdale, Matthew, Taverner, and Great Bibles all have "therefore
gapeth hell." Shakespeare is least like the Geneva Bible in this reference, and
probably echoes the Bishops' Bible, the version that was ordered to be read
in the churches after it was published in 1568.
See 3.3.13, below, and the parallel passage in *Hamlet* 1.2.244, "though
hell itself should gape."

2.1.76:   Lazar.

See above at 1.1.15.

[2.1.117: Job 14.1; Burial Service.]

2.2.33–34:   And shall forget the office of our hand
              Sooner than quittance of desert and merit.

Compare Ps. 137.5: "If I forget thee, O Hierusalem: let my right hand
forget her cunning."
Geneva: "If I forget thee, O Ierusalem, let my right hand forget to play."

2.2.42:   It was excess of wine that set him on.

Compare 1 Peter 4.3, Great, Bishops': "In excesse of wines."
Rheims: "Excesse of wine."
Tyndale, Coverdale, Matthew, Taverner, Geneva: "drunkennes."
Shakespeare probably had the Bishops' Bible in mind in this passage,
although he also could have become acquainted with the expression "excesse
of wines" from the Great Bible, the first authorized Bible of the Anglican
Church, or from sermons based upon either version. Although he is actually

closest to the Rheims New Testament, it is unlikely that his reference was to the Rheims.

2.2.79–81:   The mercy that was quick in us but late,
             By your own counsel is suppress'd and kill'd.
             You must not dare, for shame, to talk of mercy.

Compare Ecclus. 28.4, Bishops': "Hee that sheweth no mercie to a man which is like himselfe, howe dare he aske forgiuenes of his sinnes?"

The Coverdale, Matthew, Taverner, and Great Bibles are parallel to the Bishops'. The Geneva has "will" instead of "dare": "Hee will shew no mercie to a man, which is like him selfe: and will he aske forgiuenes of his owne sinnes?"

Compare also James 2.13, Great, Bishops': "For he shal haue iudgement without mercie, that hath shewed no mercie."

See also *The Faerie Queene* 6.1.42.(1–2).

[2.2.96–99: Ps. 55.12–15 (55.12–14, Geneva).But Shakespeare's source was probably Holinshed, 4.384. Compare especially Holinshed's "privat or publike councell" with 2.2.96.]

[2.2.114–17: Matt. 4.1 –10; Luke 4.1–12; 2 Cor. 11.14.]

2.2.121–22:   If that same demon that hath gull'd thee thus
              Should with his lion gait walk the whole world.

1 Peter 5.8: "Your aduersarie the deuil as a roaring lyon walketh about seeking whom he may deuoure."

2.2.123:   He might return to vasty Tartar back.

Compare 2 Peter 2.4: "God spared not the Angels, that had sinned, but cast them downe into hel [Greek, *tartarus*]."

After Shakespeare refers to 1 Peter 5.8, the devil walking throughout the world seeking victims to devour, he next speaks of the devil returning to tartarus. The Greek word *tartarus* occurs only once in the New Testament, at 2 Peter 2.4, where it was borrowed from classical literature. In Homer's *Iliad*, it refers to an underground prison as far below hades as the earth was below heaven. Those confined in it were Cronos and the Titans who had rebelled against Zeus. Later poets use "tartarus" as synonymous with hades. "Tartarus" occurs frequently in Ovid's *Metamorphoses*, as well as in the works of Horace and Virgil, since the Greek word had been borrowed by Latin poets and writers. Whether Shakespeare was aware that the word "hel" at 2 Peter 2.4 was translated from the Greek word *tartarus*, or whether his reference was entirely to classical sources, cannot be determined, although this passage is both preceded and followed by biblical references.

2.2.123–24:   He might return to vasty Tartar back,
                    And tell the legions.

   Mark 5.9: "And he [the "vncleane spirit"] answered, saying, My name is Legion: for we are many."

2.2.141–42:   For this revolt of thine, methinks, is like
                    Another fall of man.

A reference to the fall of man in the garden of Eden. Genesis 3.

[2.2.178–79: Matt. 16.28; Mark 9.1; Luke 9.27; Heb. 2.9. Compare Holinshed 4.386.]

[2.2.190: Ps. 31.17 (31.15, Geneva).]

2.3.9–10:   He's in Arthur's bosom, if ever man went to Arthur's bosom.

   Luke 16.22–23: "Was caryed by the Angels into Abrahams bosome. . . . He lift vp his eyes, and sawe Abraham afarre of, and Lazarus in his bosome."
   "Arthur" is Hostess Quickly's malapropism for "Abraham." See *Richard III* 4.3.38.

2.3.38–39:   And talk'd of the whore of Babylon.

   Rev. 17.5: "And in her forehead was a name written, A Mysterie, great Babylon, the mother of whoredomes."
   Geneva note "f" on Rev. 17.4: "This woman is the Antichrist that is, the Pope."
   Geneva Bibles with Junius's notes on Revelation have the following note on Rev. 17.4: "That harlot, the spirituall Babylon, which is Rome."

2.3.55–56:   Let us to France, like horse-leeches, my boys,
                    To suck, to suck, the very blood to suck!

Compare Prov. 30.15: "The horse leache hath two [h] daughters which crye, Giue, giue."

Geneva note "h" on Prov. 30.15: "The leache hath two forkes in her tongue . . . where by she sucketh the blood."

2.4.99–100:   Therefore in fierce tempest is he coming,
             In thunder and in earthquake, like a Jove.

Compare Isa. 29.7, Bishops': "Thou shalt be visited of the Lord of hostes, with thunder, earthquake, and with a great noyse, with storme and tempest." (The Geneva (29.6) has "shaking" instead of "earthquake.")

Compare Ex. 19.16, 18: "There was thunders and lightninges, and a thick cloud vpon the mount. . . . And mount Sinay was all on smoke, because the Lorde came downe vpon it in fire, . . . and all the mount trembled exceedingly."

2.4.102:   And bids you, in the bowels of the Lord.

Philem. 20: "Comfort my bowels in the Lord."

Phil. 1.8, Bishops': "In the bowels of Iesus Christ."

The Rheims New Testament is parallel to the Bishops' at Phil. 1.8. All other versions have "from the verie heart roote."

But Shakespeare borrowed this reference from either Hall or Holinshed. Holinshed has: "Neuerthelesse exhorted the French king in the bowels of Jesu Christ, to render him that which was his owne" (4.384).

Hall: "We exhort you in the bowelles of our sauiour Jesu Christe . . . that you ought to render to al men that whiche you ought to do" (sig. b.v[v]).

3.2.22:   Be merciful, great duke, to men of mould.

Compare Job 33.6, all versions except Geneva: "I am fashioned and made euen of the same moulde."

Geneva: "I am also formed of the clay."

Compare Tobit 8.8, all versions except Geneva: "Thou madest Adam of the moulde of the earth."

Geneva (8.6): "Thou madest Adam." (The Geneva omits "of the moulde of the earth.")

If Shakespeare had Scripture in mind in this passage, then his reference could be to any English Bible except the Geneva.

3.2.36–37:   He hath heard that men of few words are the best men.

Compare Eccles. 5.1 (5.2, AV): "Let thy wordes be fewe."
But the saying was proverbial. Tilley records the following proverbs:

W796: "Few words among friends are best."
W797: "Few words and many deeds."
W798: "Few words are best."
W799: "Few words show men wise."

Compare *Love's Labor's Lost* 4.2.80: "*Vir sapit qui pauca loquitur.*" (That man is wise who speaks little.)
See also Prov. 17.27–28; 10.19.

3.2.114–15:   By the mess, ere theise eyes of mine take themselves to slomber.

Compare Ps. 132.4: "I will not suffer mine eyes to sleepe, nor mine eye lids to slumber." (Compare also Prov. 6.4.)
Perhaps an unconscious echo rather than a reference.

3.3.1–43:   Some have compared Henry's speech at 3.3.1–43, demanding the surrender of Harfleur, to the terms of surrender for a besieged city set out in Deut. 20.10–14. Although the terms of surrender in Deuteronomy and in Henry's speech are much the same, there are no verbal parallels in the two accounts, and similar terms of surrender occur in both Holinshed (4.388) and Hall (sig. c.i[r]). Shakespeare had probably seen the reference to Deuteronomy in an earlier passage in Hall, where it appeared in a letter written to the French king by Henry while he was still in England at Southampton. In his letter, Henry said that he preferred peace to war, just as the book of Deuteronomy said "fyrste to offre peace" to a city that was about to be besieged (sig. b.v[v]). But Hall makes no mention of Deuteronomy during the siege itself. To grant mercy to a besieged city that surrendered was a standard policy in warfare, frequently mentioned by writers on military discipline. Compare also Marlowe's *1 Tamburlaine* 4.1

3.3.10:   The gates of mercy shall be all shut up.

Compare Ps. 77.9, Geneva: "Hath God forgotten to be mercifull? hath he shut vp his tender mercies in displeasure?"

Psalter: "Hath God forgotten to bee gracious: and will he shut vp his louing kindnesse in displeasure?"

Compare also Matt. 25.10, Tyndale, Coverdale, Matthew, Taverner, Great: "The gate was shut vp."

Geneva, Rheims: "The gate was shut."

Bishops': "The doore was shut vp."

Compare also the reference at *3 Henry VI* 1.4.177, and the comments thereon.

3.3.13: Wide as hell.

Compare 2.1.61, above.

3.3.16: The prince of fiends.

In Scripture one of Satan's designations is "the prince of deuils." See Matt. 9.34; 12.24; Mark 3.22.

3.3.26–27: As send precepts to the leviathan
            To come ashore.

Job 40.20 (41.1, AV): "Canst thou drawe out Liuiathan with an hooke?"

Ps. 104.26: "There goe the ships, and there is that Leuiathan: whom thou hast made to take his pastime therein."

See also Ps. 74.15 (74.14, Geneva) and Isa. 27.1 where leviathan is again mentioned. Shakespeare's reference would be primarily to Job.

[3.3.37–38: Ps. 137.9.]

3.3.39–41: Whiles the mad mothers with their howls confus'd
            Do break the clouds, as did the wives of Jewry
            At Herod's bloody-hunting slaughter-men.

Matt. 2.16, 18: "Then Herode . . . sent forth, and slew all the male children that were in Beth-lehem. . . . In Rama was a voice heard, mourning, and weeping, and great lamentation: Rachel weeping for her children, and would not be comforted."

[3.5.15: See 4.1.289, below.]

3.6.7–9: A man that I love and honor with my soul, and my heart, and my duty, and my live, and my living, and my uttermost power.

Luke 10.27: "Thou shalt loue thy Lord God with all thine heart, and with all thy soule, and with all thy strength, and with all thy thought."
See also Mark 12.30; Deut. 6.5.

[3.6.119: Mark 5.39; John 11.11–13.]

[3.6.130: See *1 Henry VI* 5.1.9.]

3.6.156: Yet, God before, tell him we will come on.

Compare Deut. 31.3: "The Lord thy God hee wil go ouer before thee."
Compare Deut. 31.8: "The Lord him selfe doeth goe before thee: he will be with thee."
Compare Isa. 52.12: "The Lord will go before you."
Holinshed has: "The king of England did expresse and signifie to him, that with the aid of God, and helpe of his people, he would recover his right and inheritance" (4.381). Also: ". . . by the aid of God, in whome is my whole trust and confidence" (4.383). Shakespeare seems to have transformed these parallels in Holinshed into a more explicit biblical reference.
See 1.2.303 and 1.2.307–8, above.

[3.6.169: See 2.2.190, above. Compare *Macbeth* 2.3.130.]

3.7.11–40: J. H. Walter, editor of the Arden Shakespeare, claims that the Dauphin's description of his horse "has an obvious relationship to the war horse of *Job* xxxix. 19–25" (39.22–28, Geneva), but the two accounts have little in common. "Ça, ha!" ("that one, ha!") of line 13 is not parallel to "Ha, ha" of Job 39.28 (39.25, AV). The former is spoken by the Dauphin, while in Job, "Ha, ha" is what the horse figuratively says "among the trumpets." Even less convincing is the alleged parallel between *"chez les narines de feu!"* ("with fiery nostrils," 3.7.14–15), and Job 39.20, "the glory of his nostrils is terrible." Walter is using the Authorized Version. The Geneva has (39.23), "his strong neying is fearefull." The Bishops' has (39.20), "his stoute neying is fearefull." All other English Bibles of Shakespeare's day (Coverdale, Matthew, Taverner, Great) likewise have "neying" rather than "nostrils."

3.7.64–65: *"Le chien est retourné à son propre vomissement, et la truie lavée au bourbier."*

2 Peter 2.22: "The dogge is returned to his own vomit: and, The sow that was washed, to the wallowing in the myer."

In the Folio, the first authoritative text of the play, this passage reads: "*Le chien est retourne a son propre vemissement est la leuye lauee au bourbier.*" Richmond Noble claims that when the typesetter's errors in this passage are corrected, the French Bible being quoted is Olivetan's translation, the first French Protestant Bible, and the version that preceded the "French Geneva Bible" of 1560. It reads: "Le chien est retourné a son propre vomissement: & la truie lauee est retournee au bourbier" (Noble 86–87). But only a few editions of the Olivetan Bible had that reading at 2 Peter 2.22.

The Olivetan Bible appeared in 1535 and remained the standard French Protestant Bible till 1560, when it was superseded by newer Protestant versions. But Olivetan's translation was repeatedly revised after it appeared in 1535, and different editions had substantially different readings at 2 Peter 2.22. This includes the very first edition which rendered 2 Peter 2.22 as: "Le chien est retourne a son propre vomissement: et la truye lauee *est retournee* au veaultrement de la fange." Olivetan Bibles and New Testaments published in 1538, 1539, 1544, and 1546 are the same as the first edition at this text, except for spelling variations and the use of accent marks. Editions of Olivetan published in 1540, 1551, and 1556 render 2 Peter 2.22 as Noble quotes it; Noble specifically had the 1551 edition in mind, published in Lyons by Jean de Tournes. He considered this 1551 edition the "exact source" of *Henry V* 3.7.64–65. But editions of Olivetan revised by John Calvin and published in 1551 and 1554 also read differently.

When the Olivetan Bible was revised in 1560 under the direction of the ministers of Geneva ("par l'aduis des ministres de Geneue") and became the Bible of the Reformed Church in Geneva (the "French Geneva Bible"), it rendered 2 Peter 2.22 as: "Le chien est retourne a son propre vomissement: & la truye lauee *est retournee* a se veautrer au bourbier." That "French Geneva Bible" was again revised in 1588 "par les Pasteurs & Professeurs de l'Eglise de Geneue," and this 1588 edition also became a standard text. Its reading of 2 Peter 2.22 was the same as that of the 1560 edition, except that some of the accent marks characteristic of French are supplied. In both of these versions, 2 Peter 2.22 is the same as in the Olivetan Bible Noble quotes, except that the words "a se veauter" are added: "la truye lauee *est retournee* a se veautrer au bourbier." It is much more likely that Shakespeare's acquaintance with a French Bible or New Testament was with one of these popular versions that were repeatedly published during his lifetime, rather than with the older Olivetan Bible that was the accepted Protestant French Bible from 1535–60, before he was born.

It is true that Shakespeare's reference in French to 2 Peter 2.22 at *Henry V* 3.7.64–65 is closest to a few editions of the Olivetan Bible and to two known editions of the New Testament that follow Olivetan and render 2 Peter 2.22

with the fewest number of words. But that can best be accounted for by the fact that Shakespeare frequently transforms and condenses his sources—omitting words that are understood, when necessary—to suit his context and meter. In this passage, it is probably safest to conclude that Shakespeare used one of the standard versions of his day and omitted all the words that he felt were understood: "*est retournee a se veautrer.*" See the passages at 1.2.98–100, above, and at *2 Henry VI* 2.1.51–52, and the comments thereon for other examples where Shakespeare followed this practice of omitting words from Scripture that he felt would be understood by his audience. Compare also 4.8.123, below, where Shakespeare seems to have simplified his sources to achieve the required meter.

See also *2 Henry IV* 1.3.95–99, where the Archbishop refers to 2 Peter 2.22.

[4.chorus.4, "womb of night": Contrast Ps. 110.3, "wombe of the morning."]

4.chorus.43–44:   Like the sun,
                His liberal eye doth give to every one.

Compare Ecclus. 42.16: "The sunne that shineth, looketh vpon all thinges."

Compare Matt. 5.45: "He maketh his sunne to arise on the euill, and the good."

Perhaps an unconscious echo rather than a reference.

4.1.131–33, 145–56:   We know we are the King's subjects. If his cause be
                    wrong, our obedience to the King wipes the crime of
                    it out of us. . . . who to disobey were against all
                    proportion of subjection.

A clear echo of that familiar theme in the homilies that obedience and subjection to the king are God-ordained duties, even if the king abuses his authority.

Homily "Concerning Good Order, and Obedience to Rulers and Magistrates," part 3: "It is the will of GOD, GOD will that you be in subiection to your head and king. This is GODS ordinance, GODS commandement, and GODS holy will, that the whole body of euery Realme, and all the members and parts of the same, shall be subiect to their head, their king. . . . Thus we learne by the word of GOD, to yeeld to our king, that is due to our king: that is, honour, obedience. . . ."

Part 2 of the same homily: "Whereby Christ taught vs plainely, that euen the wicked rulers haue their power and authoritie from GOD, and therefore it is not lawfull for their Subiects to withstand them, although they abuse their power: much lesse then is it lawfull for subiects, to withstand their godly and Christian Princes."

Catechism: "To honour and obey the King and his ministers."

4.1.135–37:   When all those legs, and arms, and heads, chopp'd off in a battle, shall join together at the latter day.

Based on popular conceptions of the resurrection on the day of judgment. Ezekiel's vision of the field of dry bones contributed to that conception.

Compare Ezek. 37.7–8: "There was a noyse, and behold, there was a shaking, and the bones came together, bone to his bone. And when I behelde, loe, the sinewes, and the flesh grewe vpon them, and aboue, the skin couered them."

4.1.137:   Shall join together at the latter day.

Compare Job 19.25, Bishops': "I shall rise out of the earth in the latter day." (Also Coverdale, Matthew, Taverner, Great.)

Geneva: "He shall stand the last on the earth."

If Shakespeare had Job 19.25 in mind in this passage, then his reference could have been to any English Bible except the Geneva.

4.1.167–69:   Though they can outstrip men, they have no wings to fly from God.

Compare Ps. 139.6–9 (139.7–10, Geneva): "Whither shall I goe then from thy presence? If I clime vp into heauen, thou art there: if I go downe to hell, thou art there also. If I take the wings of the morning: and remaine in the vttermost parts of the sea. Euen there also shall thy hand leade me: and thy right hand shal holde me."

Compare also Amos 9.2–3; Jer. 23.23–24.

[4.1.169: Jer. 51.20; Ezek. 5.12–13; 14.21.]

[4.1.171–73: Matt. 16.25; Mark 8.35; Luke 9.24; 17.33.]

[4.1.179–80: Matt. 7.4; Luke 6.42; see also 1.2.31–32, above.]

4.1.180:   And dying so, death is to him advantage.

Phil. 1.21, all versions except Geneva and Rheims: "For Christ is to mee life, and death is to me aduauntage."
Geneva: "For Christ is to me both in life, and in death aduantage."
Rheims: "For vnto me, to liue is Christ; and to die is gaine."
Shakespeare appears to be closer to the standard English Bibles of his day that were in the Tyndale tradition (Tyndale, Coverdale, Matthew, Taverner, Great, and Bishops'), less like the Geneva, and least like the Rheims. All six Bibles have identical readings, with variations only in the spellings, and Shakespeare's reference could be to any of them.

4.1.186–87:   Every man that dies ill, the ill upon his own head.

Compare 1 Sam. 25.39: "The Lord hath recompensed the wickednesse of Nabal vpon his owne head."
Compare 1 Kings 2.32: "The Lorde shal bring his blood vpon his owne head."
Compare Ps. 7.17 (7.16, Geneva): "His trauel shal come vpon his own head: and his wickednes shall fall on his own pate."
See 1.2.97, above.

4.1.267–70:   Not all these, laid in bed majestical,
              Can sleep so soundly as the wretched slave;
              Who, with a body fill'd and vacant mind,
              Gets him to rest, cramm'd with distressful bread.

Compare Eccl. 5.11 (5.12, AV): "The sleepe of him that traueileth, is sweete, whether he eate litle or much: but the sacietie [satiety] of the riche will not suffer him to sleepe."

4.1.270–73:   Cramm'd with distressful bread,
              .   .   .   .
              Sweats in the eye of Phoebus.

Compare Gen. 3.19: "In the sweate of thy face shalt thou eate bread."

[4.1.271: Matt. 23.15.]

[4.1.289: Compare the frequent biblical phrase "the Lorde of hostes." It occurs over sixty times in the book of Isaiah alone, from Isa. 1.9 onward. Compare 3.5.15, above.]

4.1.292–94:   Not to-day, O Lord,
              O, not to-day, think not upon the fault
              My father made in compassing the crown!

King Henry's prayer seems to be patterned on Ps. 115.1: "Not vnto vs,
O Lord, not vnto vs, but vnto thy Name giue the prayse."
See 4.8.123, below, where the same Psalm is referred to.

[4.2.23: Isa. 40.24, "blowe vpon them." But a similar expression occurs in Holinshed
(4.394).]

[4.3.5, "God's arm": Isa. 51.9; 52.10; Ps. 44.3–4 (44.3, Geneva).]

[4.3.28: Ex. 20.17.]

4.3.34–36:   Rather proclaim it, Westmerland, through my host,
             That he which hath no stomach to this fight,
             Let him depart.

Compare Gideon's words to his army before the battle at Judges 7.3:
"Nowe therefore proclaime in the audience of the people, and say, Who so is
timerous or fearefull, let him returne, and depart."
  Compare 1 Macc. 5.49: "Wherefore Iudas commaunded a proclamation to
be made throughout the host."
  Compare 2 Macc. 14.18: "The manlines of them that were with Iudas, and
the bolde stomackes that they had for their countrey."
  See also Deut. 20.8; 1 Macc. 3.56.
  Compare Fabyan's *Chronicle:* "Made proclamacions through his host, that
every man should slee his prisoner" (4.398).

[4.3.117, "fresher robes": Rev. 6.11; 7.13–14.]

[4.4.71: 1 Peter 5.8.]

[4.6.26–27: Matt. 26.28.]

4.7.34–39:   Alexander, God knows, and you know, in his rages, and his
             furies, and his wraths, and his cholers, and his moods, and his
             displeasures, and his indignations, and also being a little intoxi-
             cates in his prains, did, in his ales and his angers, look you, kill
             his best friend, Clytus.

This incident is mentioned in the homily "Against Gluttony and Drunkennesse": "The great *Alexander* after that hee had conquered the whole world, was himselfe ouercome by drunkennesse, insomuch that being drunken, hee slew his faithfull friend *Clitus*."

4.7.61–62:   As swift as stones
                   Enforced from the old Assyrian slings.

Compare Judith 9.7: "Behold, the Assyrians are multyplied by their power: . . . they trust in shield, speare and bow, and sling."

Shakespeare is closest to the Geneva Bible in this passage. The texts of the other versions—Coverdale, Matthew, Taverner, Great, Bishops' (9.6 in the Bishops')—differ substantially from the Geneva and contain no reference to slings.

4.7.137–38:   Though he be as good a gentleman as the devil is, as Lucifer
                   and Belzebub himself. . . .

The name "Lucifer," misapplied to the devil, is taken from Isa. 14.12. See the reference at *2 Henry IV* 2.4.333.

Beelzebub, meaning "lord of flies," was a title mockingly applied to Satan. Matt. 12.24 identifies Beelzebub as "the prince of deuils." See also Mark 3.22; Luke 11.15.

4.8.46:   All offenses, my lord, come from the heart.

Compare Matt. 15.19: "For out of the hearte come euill thoughtes, murders, adulteries, fornications, theftes, false testimonies, slanders."
Compare also Mark 7.21.

4.8.106–108:   O God, thy arm was here;
                   And not to us, but to thy arm alone,
                   Ascribe we all!

Ps. 44.3–4 (44.3, Geneva): "For they gate not the lande in possession through their owne sworde: neyther was it their owne arme that helped them. But thy right hand and thine arme."

Ps. 98.2 (98.1, Geneva): "With his owne right hand, and with his holy arme: hath he gotten himself the victorie."

See also Ps. 115.1, quoted above at 4.1.292–94.

4.8.123:   Let there be sung *Non nobis* and *Te Deum*.

Non nobis Domine is the Latin title in the Bishops' Bible of Psalm 115, which may be echoed in the play at 4.1.292–94 and 4.8.106–8, above. The text of the Latin Vulgate reads: "NON NOBIS DOMINE, NON NOBIS: sed nomini tuo da gloriam" ("Not vnto vs, O Lord, not vnto vs, but vnto thy Name giue the prayse," Psalter). But in the Latin Vulgate Bible this psalm is joined to the previous one, *In exitu Israel*, and both psalms are numbered Psalm 113. In all Protestant English Bibles, as well as in the Psalter of the Anglican church, *In exitu Israel* is Psalm 114, while *Non nobis Domine* is Psalm 115.

The *Te Deum* is a hymn of thanksgiving in the Prayer Book that was sung or said in Morning Prayer after the reading of the first lesson.

Shakespeare's sources for this passage included both Hall and Holinshed. Holinshed relates that after Henry's victory at Agincourt, Henry "gave thanks to almightie God for so happie a victorie, causing his prelats and chapleins to sing this psalme: *In exitu Israel de Aegypto*, and commanded everie man to kneele downe on the ground at this verse: *Non nobis Domine, non nobis, sed nomini tuo da gloriam*. Which doone, he caused *Te Deum*, with certeine anthems to be soong, giving laud and praise to God, without boasting of his owne force or anie humane power" (4.398).

Holinshed followed Hall closely in this passage. Hall's account reads: "And fyrst to geue thankes to almightie God geuer & tributor of this glorious victory, he caused his prelates & chapelaines fyrst to sing this psalme *In exitu Israel de Egipto*. &c. commaundyng euery man to knele doune on the ground at this verse. *Non nobis domine, non nobis, sed nomine tuo da gloriam*, which is to say in Englishe, Not to vs lord, not to vs, but to thy name let the glory be geuen: whiche done he caused *Te deum* with certaine anthemes to be song geuyng laudes and praisynges to God, and not boastyng nor braggynge of him selfe nor his humaine power" (sig. c.vi^v).

Hall's narrative reflects the Vulgate's arrangement of the Psalms. For when Hall says "at this verse" of the psalm (singular) the soldiers were to kneel, it is apparent that what in the English Bible are two psalms, were to Hall only one.

In the Catholic Church, *In exitu Israel* was an important psalm, for it was repeatedly recited at Vespers. But to Shakespeare, the *Non nobis* was a separate psalm, and not part of the previous psalm, *In exitu Israel*. Shakespeare may have been uncertain whether one or both psalms were sung along with the *Te Deum*, or he may have concluded that his sources were not accurate in speaking of both psalms as one. Richmond Noble thinks that Shakespeare knew the Latin titles of the psalms and went out of his way to correct what he thought was Holinshed's error (81). Elsewhere, however, Shakespeare followed Holinshed closely and copied his mistakes. It is more likely that Shakespeare simply chose to simplify his sources and, to achieve the required meter, wrote, "Let there be sung *Non nobis* and *Te Deum*." See 1.2.98–100, above, where Shakespeare probably omitted the phrase "without a sonne" in order to achieve the required meter.

Stow refers to the same Psalm in a different context. He records that when Henry IV was dying, he gave this farewell advice to Prince Hal: "And in thy selfe eschew al vaineglorie and elation of heart, following the holesome counsell of the Psalmist, (which sayeth) *Non nobis Domine, non nobis, sed nomini tuo da gloriam* (which Not unto us Lord, not unto us, but to thy holy Name be given laude and praise)" (4.219).

5.2.41: Her vine, the merry cheerer of the heart.

Ps. 104.15: "Wine that maketh glad the heart of man."
Compare also Judges 9.13: "The Vine sayde vnto them, Should I leaue my wyne, whereby I cheare God and man"?
See also Ecclus. 31.28.

5.2.117–18: The tongues of men are full of deceits.

Compare Ps. 50.19: "With thy tongue thou hast set forth deceite."
Compare Rom. 3.13: "They haue vsed their tongues to deceite."
Compare also Micah 6.12.

[5.2.203–4: Luke 7.50; 1 Peter 1.9; Eph. 2.8.]

5.2.359–61: God, the best maker of all marriages,
Combine your hearts in one, your realms in one!
As man and wife, being two, are one in love.

Gen. 2.24: "Therefore shal man leaue his father and his mother, and shall cleaue to his wife, and they shalbe one flesh."
Matt. 19.6: "Wherefore they are no more twaine, but one flesh."
See also the Marriage Service.

Henry VIII

The Globe Theater was destroyed by fire on 29 June 1613 during a performance of *Henry VIII*. In describing the event three days later, Sir Henry Wotton (who was not present on that occasion) wrote: "The King's players had a new play, called *All Is True*, representing some principal pieces of the reign of Henry VIII, which was set forth with many extraordinary circumstances of pomp and majesty . . . sufficient . . . to make greatness very familiar, if not ridiculous." He goes on to explain that at the point in the play when Henry came as a masquer to Cardinal Wolsey's house (1.4.49), certain chambers, or short cannon, were discharged setting fire to the thatched roof, so that the entire playhouse burned to the ground within an hour. Thus the theater that had been the home of Shakespeare's company since 1599 came to its end, although John Stow's *Annals* (1631) tell us that it was rebuilt the next spring "in far fairer manner than before."

There had been several plays dealing with the reign of Henry VIII prior to Shakespeare's. Henslowe's *Diary* records that in an inventory taken on 10 March 1598, one of the costumes owned by The Admiral's Men was a suit for the actor who played the part of "Will. Sommers," Henry VIII's fool. In June and July of 1601, Henslowe made several payments to Henry Chettle for "the Boocke of carnalle wolseye lyfe." This play was so successful that later that year he paid four dramatists (Chettle, Drayton, Munday, and Smith) for "A Boocke called the Rissynge of carnowlle wollsey" which became "the firste pt of carnowll wollsey," this first part to be performed before its sister play, which now became part 2.

None of these plays have survived. A play about Henry VIII that has survived is Samuel Rowley's *When You See Me You Know Me*, first published in 1605 and republished in 1613, 1621, and 1632. A rather unhistorical play with much clowning (walking about at night in disguise, Henry is thrown in jail where he carouses with the other prisoners), it also has a strong Protestant bias. Prince Edward is depicted as the champion of true religion, unlike his sister Mary who constantly invokes the virgin, angels, and saints as intercessors. Wolsey's intrigues and his attempts to bribe his way to the papal throne are portrayed. Bishops Bonner and Gardiner hate Cranmer and Queen Katherine Parr as Lutheran heretics, and plot to have Henry execute the queen. Despite the play's Protestant bias, Henry is depicted as having a running battle with Luther throughout the play.

The parallels between Shakespeare's play and Rowley's make it clear that Shakespeare knew *When You See Me*. It contains at most some twenty biblical references, seven of which occur on a single page (sig. H1ᵛ) in a discussion praising music. It makes a clear reference to the Sermon on the Mount (sig. G2ʳ) and compares Wolsey to Caiaphas (sig. L2ᵛ; 4.508 of Bullough). But with the possible exception of the passage at 1.1.209–10, 215, discussed in the list of references, Shakespeare did not borrow any references from Rowley's play, and it is unlikely that any of the lost plays about Henry VIII influenced his biblical references.

Shakespeare's main source for *Henry VIII* was Holinshed's *Chronicles* (1587), which he followed closely. Other sources include Foxe's *Book of Martyrs (Acts and Monuments)* from which Shakespeare borrowed the account of Cranmer's trial in act 5. At times certain phrases and ideas are closer to Hall than to Holinshed, indicating that Shakespeare also read Hall's *Union of the Two Noble . . . Families of Lancaster and York*. The play also contains minor influences from John Speed's recently published *History of Great Britain* (1611). There is little likelihood that Shakespeare had read the manuscript of George Cavendish, *The Life and Death of Cardinal Wolsey*, which was not published until 1641, but Cavendish's account influenced Shakespeare by means of Holinshed, who found large portions of it reproduced, often word for word, in Stow's *Chronicles*. An outstanding example of the influence of Cavendish borrowed from Holinshed is pointed out at 3.2.455–57.

Shakespeare found few biblical references in Holinshed, Hall, and Foxe. Holinshed seldom refers to Scripture in his narrative, even when expressing religious ideas. None of the many biblical references that Shakespeare makes in the play are from Holinshed, although phrases and expressions in Holinshed occasionally suggested a biblical or liturgical reference to Shakespeare, as at 2.1.32–33 and 2.1.64–65. At 5.1.135–38 Shakespeare borrows a reference from Foxe, but that is an exception rather than the rule. Almost all the biblical references that Shakespeare makes in the play are his own, even when closely following his sources.

Several outstanding references in the play seem to have been inspired by sermons that were delivered around the time that *Henry VIII* was written, early in 1613. During the previous autumn Prince Henry, the heir to the throne, had died, and the following February, Henry's sister, Princess Elizabeth, was married to Prince Frederick, the Elector Palatine. The biblical references at 5.4.33–35, 5.4.51–52, and 5.4.52–54 seem to have been made as Shakespeare followed the convention of complimenting the royal family by applying those texts to them.

Henry VIII first appeared in print in the First Folio in 1623. Heminges and Condell included it in the Folio as having been written by Shakespeare, although they excluded plays of doubtful authorship, including *Pericles*.

Shakespeare's authorship of the play was not seriously questioned until 1850 when various critics began to see two different styles and an uneven, episodic design in the play. They explained these peculiarities by the collaborative theory, that Fletcher collaborated with Shakespeare in writing the play, and went so far as to divide the play into scenes written by Shakespeare and those written by Fletcher. The question of authorship has gone on unabated with equally competent critics on each side of the question strongly arguing for and against collaboration.

An analysis of the biblical references in the play as compared with the biblical references in Shakespeare's other plays would seem to indicate that the play is substantially Shakespeare's. The biblical references throughout the play cannot be differentiated from those that Shakespeare makes in plays that are undisputedly his, nor can it be said that the references in scenes generally assigned to Fletcher are in any way different or less typical of Shakespeare than the references in the scenes assigned to him. Moreover, many of the biblical references in scenes assigned to Fletcher (as in 1.3; 2.1; 3.2.204–459; 4.2; 5.2; 5.3; and 5.4) are references typical of Shakespeare that Shakespeare made in other plays that are known to be his. Finally, the main sources used in the play—Holinshed, Hall, and Foxe—were also Shakespeare's favorite sources. Fletcher may have considerably edited the manuscript after it arrived from Stratford and thus left his style and imprint on the play. But although the problem of authorship is not likely to be resolved anytime soon, I would favor the position that Shakespeare wrote most if not all of the play, and that Fletcher made changes in the play to suit his tastes and style while preparing the manuscript for the stage.

In the list that follows, page numbers preceded by the number 4, as in (4.462), refer to volume 4 of Bullough. References to *When You See Me You Know Me* are from the Tudor Facsimile text of that play listed in the bibliography.

1.1.6:   Those suns of glory, those two lights of men.

Shakespeare's words, "those two lights of men," are suggestive of the creation account in Genesis 1.16–17, "God then made two great lights . . . to shine vpon the earth," but the similarity may be accidental.

1.1.23:   As cherubins, all gilt.

Derived ultimately from Scripture, where cherubim are frequently mentioned. The word first appears at Genesis 3.24, and occurs many times thereafter. The lid of the ark (the mercy seat) had two cherubim of wrought gold on it, and various curtains in both the tabernacle and the temple were embroidered with cherubim. See Ex. 25.18–22; 37.7–9; 26.1, 31; Ezek. 10.4–7; Heb. 9.5.

See *Macbeth* 1.7.22 in the volume *Biblical References in Shakespeare's Tragedies* for a more detailed discussion of Shakespeare's references to cherubim.

[1.1.65: Eph. 4.7.]

1.1.140–41:   Heat not a furnace for your foe so hot
              That it do singe yourself.

Dan. 3.19, 22: "He charged and commanded that they shoulde heate the fornace at once seuen times more then it was wont to be heate. . . . Therefore, because . . . the fornace shoulde bee exceeding hote, the flame of the fire slewe those men that brought forth Shadrach, Meshach and Abednego."

1.1.158–60:   This holy fox,
              Or wolf, or both (for he is equal rav'nous
              As he is subtile . . .).

Compare Matt. 7.15: "Beware of false Prophets, which come to you in sheepes clothing, but inwardely they are raueing wolues."

Shakespeare's use of "rav'nous" with "wolf" was probably borrowed from Scripture. See *2 Henry VI* 3.1.77–78 where the reference to Matt. 7.15 is more obvious. Shakespeare seems to be closer to Scripture than to the parallel proverbs recorded by Tilley:

        F629: "As wily (crafty) as a fox."
        W601: "As hungry as a wolf."

1.1.209–10, 215:   The will of heav'n
                   Be done in this.

                   .   .   .   .   .   .

                   The will of heaven be done.

With overtones of the Lord's Prayer: "Thy wil be done euen in earth, as it is in heauen." Matt. 6.10. See also Matt. 26.39, 42; Luke 11.2.

The related expression "God's will be done" occurs twice in *When You See Me* (sig. B3ʳ; H3ʳ⁻ᵛ), but it had no doubt become so embedded in popular speech that it had become more of a common expression than a conscious biblical reference.

1.1.223–24: My life is spann'd already.
I am the shadow of poor Buckingham.

Ps. 39.6–7 (39.5–6, Geneva): "Behold, thou hast made my dayes as it were a span long. . . . For man walketh in a vayne shadowe."
Shakespeare's reference is to the Psalter. The Geneva and even the Bishops' versions of the Psalms have "hand breadth" instead of "span."

1.2.10–12: Half your suit
Never name to us; you have half our power.
The other moi'ty ere you ask is given.

Compare Mark 6.22–23: "The King said vnto the maide, Aske of me what thou wilt, and I will giue it thee. . . . Whatsoeuer thou shalt aske of mee, I will giue it thee, euen vnto the halfe of my kingdome."
See page 8 of the Introduction where this reference is discussed.

1.2.12: Ere you ask is given.

Compare Matt. 6.8: "Your Father knoweth whereof ye haue neede, before ye aske."
Compare Matt. 7.7; Luke 11.9: "Aske, and it shalbe giuen."
Compare also John 15.16: "Whatsoeuer ye shall aske . . . he may giue it you."
Perhaps an analogy rather than a conscious reference to Scripture.
Compare also 1.1.186–87: "His suit was granted / Ere it was ask'd."

[1.2.178–79: 2 Cor. 11.3, 14. But compare Holinshed: "The moonke maie be deceived through the divels illusion" (4.460).]

1.3.57: His dews fall every where.

Compare Ps. 133.3, Geneva: "As the dewe of Hermon, which falleth vpon the mountaynes of Zion."
Psalter: "As the dewe of Hermon: which fell vpon the hill of Sion."
The image of falling dew is common, but its origin is probably biblical.

The expression "God's dew" occurs at 2.4.80.

Compare *Cymbeline* 5.5.350–51: "The benediction of these covering heavens / Fall on their heads like dew!"

See also 4.2.133, below, and the comments thereon.

1.3.61:   Men of his way should be most liberal.

Probably an indirect reference to the qualifications for bishops as set out in the New Testament. At 1 Timothy 3.2 and Titus 1.8, Paul instructed that the bishop should be "a louer of hospitalitie" (Bishops'). The Geneva follows Tyndale and uses the older term "harberous" in these texts. (Harborous: affording harbor or shelter; given to hospitality.)

1.3.62:   They are set here for examples.

Compare the following texts concerning bishops and elders in the church:

1 Peter 5.3: "That ye may be ensamples to the flock."

1 Tim. 4.12: "Be vnto them that beleeue, an ensample."

2 Thess. 3.9: "That we might make our selues an ensample vnto you to followe vs."

Phil. 3.17: "As ye haue vs for an ensample."

2.1.32–33:   He was stirr'd
             With such an agony he sweat extremely.

Prayer Book, Litany: "By thine agonie and bloody Sweate, by thy Crosse and Passion, . . . Good Lord deliuer vs."

Luke 22.44: "Being in an agonie, he prayed more earnestly: and his sweat was like droppes of bloud."

Holinshed: "The duke was brought to the barre sore chafing, and swet marvellouslie" (4.462). Holinshed's text seems to have reminded Shakespeare of the Litany, and he borrowed the language of the Litany in this passage.

[2.1.59: Rom. 1.9; Gen. 31.50; compare *2 Henry VI* 1.3.188. In *Henry VIII*, these words ("heaven bear witness") are spoken by Buckingham when on trial. In Holinshed, Wolsey uses the parallel expression "tooke God to witnes" (4.465). Used for emphasis, these expressions had probably become so common that their biblical origins were forgotten.]

2.1.64–65:   But those that sought it [my death] I could wish more Chris-
             tians.
             Be what they will, I heartily forgive 'em.

Based on the Christian principle of loving one's enemies and freely forgiving even those that seek to hurt us.

Compare Matt. 5.44: "Loue your enemies: blesse them that cursse you: doe good to them that hate you, and pray for them which hurt you, and persecute you."

Compare Col. 3.13: "Forgiuing one another . . . euen as Christ forgaue you, euen so do ye."

Compare also Rom. 12.14, 21; Matt. 6.14–15; 18.35.

Holinshed: "But the eternall God forgive you my death, and I doo" (4.462). Shakespeare's more explicit echo of Scripture was probably inspired by Holinshed's text.

Compare 2.1.82–83, below.

2.1.66:   Yet let 'em look they glory not in mischief.

Compare Ps. 52.1: "Why boastest thou thy selfe . . . that thou canst do mischiefe?"

Perhaps an analogy rather than a reference. The Geneva has "wickednes" instead of "mischiefe" in this text.

2.1.68:   For then my guiltless blood must cry against 'em.

Gen. 4.10: "The voyce of thy brothers blood cryeth vnto me from the earth."

[2.1.75: Matt. 18.10; Heb. 1.14; Luke 16.22. See *Julius Caesar* 3.2.181 and the comments thereon in the volume *Biblical References in Shakespeare's Tragedies*.]

2.1.77–78:   Make of your prayers one sweet sacrifice,
             And lift my soul to heaven.

Compare Ps. 141.2: "Let my prayer be set forth in thy sight as the incense: and let the lifting vp of my handes be an euening sacrifice."

2.1.82–83:   I as free forgive you
             As I would be forgiven. I forgive all.

Compare Matt. 6.14–15: "For if ye do forgiue men their trespaces, your heauenly Father wil also forgiue you. But if ye do not forgiue men their trespaces, no more will your Father forgiue you your trespaces."

Compare also Matt. 18.35; Luke 6.37; Eph. 4.32.
See 2.1.64–65, above.

[2.1.122–23: Ps. 41.9. But compare Samuel Rowley's play, *When You See Me You Know Me*, sig. E3ʳ.]

2.1.128–30:   When they once perceive
               The least rub in your fortunes, fall away
               Like water from ye.

The expression "fall away like water" occurs in the Psalter at Ps. 58.6: "Let them fall away like water that runneth a pace."

Shakespeare makes a clear reference to Ps. 58.4–5 in *Troilus and Cressida* 2.2.172–73. He seems to have known this psalm well.

His reference is to the Psalter. The Geneva has, "Let them melt like the waters, let them passe away" (58.7 in the Geneva).

Compare Job 6.15: "My brethren haue deceiued mee as a brooke, and as the rising of the riuers they passe away."

Compare also the following passages that convey the same thought:

Prov. 19.7: "All the brethren of the poore doe hate him: how much more will his friendes depart far from him?"

Ecclus. 13.22: "If a riche man fall, his friendes set him vp againe: but when the poore falleth, his friends driue him away."

Compare also Prov. 14.20 and 19.4.

But these texts are analogies rather than references, since the thought is common, and there are many proverbs to this effect. See Tilley P468, R103. Shakespeare's reference is primarily to Psalm 58.6 according to the Psalter, from which he borrows the expression "fall away like water."

2.1.137–39:   It calls,
               I fear, too many curses on their heads
               That were the authors.

A common expression that finds many parallels in Scripture.

Compare Josh. 2.19: "His blood shall be vpon his head."

Compare 1 Sam. 25.39: "The Lord hath recompensed the wickednesse of Nabal vpon his owne head."

Compare Esther 9.25: "Let his wicked deuise . . . turne vpon his owne head."

Compare Ps. 7.17 (7.16, Geneva): "His trauel shal come vpon his own head." (The Geneva has "mischiefe" instead of "trauel.")

Compare Tilley C924: "Curses return upon the heads of those that curse."

Shakespeare may be closer to the proverb than to any of the biblical parallels.

Compare the anonymous play *Arden of Feversham*, first published in 1592: "For curses are like arrowes shot vpright, / Which falling doun light on the sutors [shooter's] head" (sig. G4ʳ).

Compare also *Hamlet* 5.2.385; *Richard III* 3.4.92–93; *2 Henry VI* 2.1.182–83.

[2.2.34: Luke 15.7, 10.]

[2.2.44–45: Matt. 6.13; Luke 11.4.]

2.2.47–49:   All men's honors
               Lie like one lump before him, to be fashion'd
               Into what pitch he please.

Compare Rom. 9.21: "Hath not the potter power of the clay to make of the same lumpe one vessell to honour, and another to dishonour?"

Compare also Wisdom 15.7 that contains the word "facioneth," although it lacks "lumpe": "The potter also tempereth soft earth, and facioneth euerie vessel with labour to our vse: but of the same clay he maketh both the vessels, that serue to cleane vses, and the contrarie likewise: but whereto euerie vessell serueth, the potter is the iudge."

[2.3.20–23: 1 Tim. 6.6; Ecclus. 40.18.]

[2.4.22: See 2.1.59, above, and the comments thereon.]

2.4.107–109:   Y' are meek and humble-mouthed,
                You sign your place and calling, in full seeming,
                With meekness and humility.

Speaking to Cardinal Wolsey, Queen Katherine points out the qualities that should be characteristic of Christians, particularly churchmen.

Compare Eph. 4.2: "With al humblenes of minde, and meeknes, with long suffering."

Compare Col. 3.12: "As the elect of God . . . put on tender mercy, kindnes, humblenes of minde, meekenes, long suffering."

Compare also Gal. 5.22–23; 2 Tim. 2.24–25.

At Eph. 4.2, the Bishops' Bible has "with all lowlinesse and meekenesse" instead of "with al humblenes of minde, and meeknes." Since the Bishops' lacks "humblenes" in that text, Richmond Noble considers Shakespeare's passage to be closer to the Geneva than to the Bishops'. But this evidence is not conclusive since at Col. 3.12, the Bishops' also has "humblenesse of minde, meekenesse, long suffering."

Closest parallel in Holinshed is his comment that Wolsey was more concerned about his honor than about his spirituality, "wherin should be shewed all meekenes, humilitie, and charitie" (4.477). Holinshed follows Cavendish in saying this about Wolsey at the time of Wolsey's death. Shakespeare's passage is spoken by Katherine to Wolsey.

3.1.100–101:   Heaven is above all yet; there sits a judge
               That no king can corrupt.

A common thought, but compare 2 Chron. 19.7: "Take heede, and do it: for there is no iniquitie with the Lorde our God, neither respect of persons, nor receiuing of reward."

Compare Rom. 2.11: "For there is no respect of persons with God."

Compare Ps. 50.6: "The heauens shal declare his righteousnesse: for God is iudge himselfe."

Compare also Ps. 7.8; 9.8; Isa. 11.3–4.

[3.1.107: Matt. 9.24; Mark 5.40; Luke 8.53; 2 Kings 19.21; 2 Chron. 30.10; Job 12.4; 22.19; Ps. 22.7; Isa. 37.22, etc. But the expression was probably common, although no parallels occur in Tilley or Dent. Compare Chaucer's "The Second Nun's Tale," 506.]

[3.1.114–15: Matt. 23.13–16, 23, 25, 27, 29; Luke 11.42–44, 46, 47, 52.]

3.1.145:   Ye have angels' faces, but heaven knows your hearts.

A common expression, and there were many proverbs to this effect. But compare the following texts:

1 Sam. 16.7: "Looke not on his countenance: . . . for man looketh on the outwarde appearance, but the Lorde beholdeth the heart."

1 Chron. 28.9: "The Lorde searcheth all heartes."

Acts 1.24: "Thou Lorde, which knowest the hearts of all men."

Tilley records the following proverbs:

F3: "Fair face foul heart."
F10: "He has one face to God and another to the devil."
F20: "He carries (bears) two faces under one hood."

3.1.151–52:   Like the lily,
              That once was mistress of the field, and flourish'd.

Matt. 6.28–29: "Learne, howe the lilies of the field do growe: they labour not, neither spinne: Yet I say vnto you, that euen Solomon in all his glory was not araied like one of these."

3.1.151–53:   Like the lily,
              That once was mistress of the field, and flourish'd,
              I'll hang my head and perish.

Matt. 6.30: "If God so clothe the grasse of the fielde which is to day, and to morowe is cast into the ouen. . . ."
Ps. 103.15–16: "Man . . . flourisheth as a flower of the field. For as soone as the winde goeth ouer it, it is gone: and the place thereof shall know it no more."

3.1.166–67:   Pray think us
              Those we profess, peacemakers, friends.

Compare Matt. 5.9: "Blessed are the peacemakers."
Like the previous passage, this one is also from the Sermon on the Mount.

3.2.100–101:   That she should lie i' th' bosom of
               Our hard-rul'd king.

Compare 1 Kings 1.2: "Let there be sought for my lorde the King a yong virgin, . . . and let her lie in thy bosome."

[3.2.144: Eccles. 3.1–8.]

3.2.197:   As doth a rock against the chiding flood.

Compare Matt. 7.24–25: "Hath builded his house on a rocke: And the raine fell, and the floods came, . . . and it fell not: for it was grounded on a rocke."
Perhaps an analogy rather than a reference since the context is different.

[3.2.243–44: Matt. 27.18; Mark 15.10; 1 Cor. 13.4.]

3.2.254–55:   Thy ambition,
              Thou scarlet sin.

Evidently a pun on the cardinal's scarlet robes as well as on sin.
Compare Isa. 1.18: "Though your sinnes were as crimsin, they shalbe
made white as snowe: though they were red like skarlet, they shalbe as
wool."

3.2.352–58:   This is the state of man: to-day he puts forth
              The tender leaves of hopes, to-morrow blossoms,
              And bears his blushing honors thick upon him;
              The third day comes a frost, a killing frost,

              .   .   .   .

              And then he falls as I do.

Compare Isa. 40.6–8: "All flesh is grasse, and all the grace thereof is as the
floure of the field. The grasse withereth, the floure fadeth, because the
Spirite of the Lord bloweth vpon it: surely the people is grasse. The grasse
withereth, the floure fadeth."
Compare 1 Peter 1.24: "Al flesh is as grasse, and al the glorie of man is as
the flower of grasse. The grasse withereth, and the flower falleth away."

3.2.365:   Vain pomp and glory of this world, I hate ye!

Prayer Book, Baptismal Service: "Doest thou forsake the deuill and all his
workes, the vaine pompe and glorie of the world?"
Compare 1 John 2.15–17.

3.2.366:   I feel my heart new open'd.

An indication of spiritual regeneration.
Compare Acts 16.14: "Lydia, . . . whose heart the Lord opened."

3.2.366–67:   O how wretched
              Is that poor man that hangs on princes' favors!

Compare Ps. 146.2 (146.3, Geneva): "Put not your trust in princes, nor in
any childe of man: for there is no helpe in them."
Compare Ps. 118.9: "It is better to trust in the Lorde: then to put any
confidence in princes."

Compare Jer. 17.5, 7: "Cursed be the man that trustest in man, and maketh flesh his arme, and withdraweth his heart from the Lord. . . . Blessed be the man, that trusteth in the Lord."

3.2.371–72:   And when he falls, he falls like Lucifer,
                Never to hope again.

Isa. 14.12: "How art thou fallen from heauen, O Lucifer, sonne of the morning?"

Compare Luke 10.18: "I sawe Satan, like lightening, fall downe from heauen."

Homily "Against Disobedience and Wilfull Rebellion," part 1: "Lucifer, . . . of the brightest and most glorious Angel, is become the blackest and most foulest fiend and deuill: and from the height of heauen, is fallen into the pit and bottome of hell."

See also Rev. 12.9.

[3.2.397, "for truth's sake": Ps. 115.1; 2 John 2.]

3.2.412–13:   Go get thee from me, Cromwell!
                I am a poor fall'n man.

Compare Prov. 19.7: "All the brethren of the poore doe hate him: how much more will his friendes depart far from him?"

Compare Ecclus. 13.22: "If a riche man fall, his friendes set him vp againe: but when the poore falleth, his friends driue him away."

Compare Prov. 14.20: "The poore is hated euen of his owne neyghbour: but the friendes of the riche are many."

At best an analogy rather than a reference. There were many proverbs to this effect. See 2.1.128–30, above, and the comments thereon.

3.2.440–41:   Cromwell, I charge thee, fling away ambition!
                By that sin fell the angels.

A general reference to the fall of both Lucifer and the legions of angels who fell with him. The cause of the fall was understood to be pride and ambition.

Compare the homily "Against Disobedience and Wilfull Rebellion," part 3: "For first, as ambition and desire to be aloft, which is the property of pride, stirreth vp many mens minds to rebellion, so commeth it of a Luciferian pride and presumption."

Part 5 of the same homily again mentions that the devil, "the authour of all euill," stirs up the "restlesse ambitious" to rebel.

Compare also *The Mirror for Magistrates*, The Tragedy of Cardinal Wolsey: "Your fault not halfe, so great as was my pryde, / For which offence, fell *Lucifer* from skyes" (358–59).

Isaiah 14.12–15 was the principal text behind this idea. Addressed to Nebuchadnezzar, king of Babylon, under the name of Lucifer, it was often applied to Satan, whose ambition made him seek to be equal to God: "How art thou fallen from heauen, O Lucifer, sonne of the morning? and cut downe to the ground, which didest cast lottes vpon the nations? Yet thou saydest in thine heart, I will ascend into heauen, and exalt my throne aboue beside the starres of God: I will sit also vpon the mount of the Congregation in the sides of the North. I will ascende aboue the height of the cloudes, and I will be like the most high. But thou shalt bee brought downe to the graue, to the sides of the pit."

Compare also the following texts concerning the fall of angels:

Jude 6: "The Angels also which kept not their first estate, but left their owne habitation, he hath reserued in euerlasting chaines vnder darkenes vnto the iudgement of the great day."

2 Peter 2.4: "God spared not the Angels, that had sinned, but cast them downe into hel and deliuered them into chaines of darknes, to be kept vnto damnation."

Rev. 12.9: "That olde serpent, called the deuill and Satan, was cast out, . . . and his Angels were cast out with him."

See also 1 Tim. 3.6.

Bishop Joseph Hall's *Explication . . . of All the Hard Texts* (STC 12702) comments thus on Jude 6, quoted above: "And the Angels, which not contented with that estate, wherein they were first created, but rebelling against God, and proudly affecting an higher glory; were thereupon cast downe from their heavenly habitations."

Compare *Paradise Lost* 1.36–40.

3.2.441–42:   How can man then
              (The image of his Maker) hope to win by it?

Gen. 1.26: "God said, Let vs make man in our image."

3.2.443:   Love thyself last.

Compare Phil. 2.3: "In meekenes of minde euery man esteeme other better then him selfe."

Compare 1 Cor. 10.24: "Let no man seeke his owne, but euerie man anothers wealth [well being]."

See also 1 Cor. 13.5.

While no direct biblical references are involved in much of what Wolsey says, his words contain strong overtones of Scripture and of Christian ideals based on Scripture.

3.2.443:   Cherish those hearts that hate thee.

Luke 6.27–28: "Loue your enemies: do wel to them which hate you. Blesse them that curse you."

See also Matt. 5.44; Rom. 12.14.

See 2.1.64–65, above.

3.2.445:   Still in thy right hand carry gentle peace.

Compare Rom. 12.18: "As much as in you is, haue peace with all men."

Compare Heb. 12.14: "Follow peace with all men."

Compare Ps. 34.13 (34.14, Geneva): "Seeke peace, and ensue it."

See the comment on 3.2.443 ("Love thyself last"), above.

3.2.455–57:   Had I but serv'd my God with half the zeal
               I serv'd my king, He would not in mine age
               Have left me naked to mine enemies.

Compare Ps. 71.8–9 (71.9–10, Geneva): "Cast me not away in the time of age. . . . For mine enemies speake against me."

Compare Ps. 71.16 (71.18, Geneva): "Forsake mee not, O God, in mine olde age, when I am gray headed."

Shakespeare's immediate source, however, was Holinshed: "If I had served God as diligentlie as I have doone the king, he would not have given me over in my greie haires" (4.476). George Cavendish, one of the Cardinal's gentlemen ushers, was the ultimate source for these words of Wolsey. In his *Life and Death of Cardinal Wolsey* (written ca. 1556–58 but not published until 1641), Wolsey says: "If I had serued god as dyligently as I haue don the kyng he wold not haue gevyn me ouer in my gray heares" (178–79).

Stow first printed large portions of Cavendish's manuscript in the 1580 edition of his *Chronicles of England* (STC 23333), and Stow was Holinshed's source. Cavendish's *Life* first appeared in the second edition of Holinshed, 1587, the edition Shakespeare used.

4.1.92:   Together sung *Te Deum.*

A reference to the *Te Deum laudamus* ("We praise thee, O Lord") sung daily during Morning Prayer.

Shakespeare's source was Holinshed: "All the queere [choir] soong *Te Deum*" at the coronation of Anne (4.483).

4.2.1:   Sick to death!

Compare 2 Kings 20.1; 2 Chron. 32.24; Isa. 38.1: "Sicke vnto death."

Compare also Phil. 2.27.

The expression "sick to (unto) death" may have originated with Scripture since it is simply a literal translation of the Hebrew in the above three Old Testament texts.

4.2.36:   Simony was fair play.

The buying or selling of ecclesiastical preferments. The term is based on Acts 8.18–20 where Simon the Samaritan offered money to the Apostles for the power of conferring the Holy Spirit by the laying on of hands.

Holinshed: "He forced little on simonie" (4.481). That is, he had no scruples about simony.

4.2.82, s.d.:   *Clad in white robes, . . . palm in their hands.*

Compare Rev. 7.9: "Clothed with long white robes, and palmes in their hands."

4.2.87–90:   Saw you not even now a blessed troop
                      Invite me to a banquet, . . .

                      . . . .
                      They promis'd me eternal happiness.

Compare Rev. 19.9: "Blessed are they which are called vnto the Lambes supper."

Compare Luke 14.15: "Blessed is he that eateth bread in the kingdome of God."

Queen Katherine's words, "Invite me to a banquet," are probably based on the biblical promises that at death faithful Christians will dine in the kingdom of God. There is, however, no hint of a banquet in the vision that appears to the Queen while she sleeps.

4.2.126–27:   When I shall dwell with worms, and my poor name
               Banish'd the kingdom!

Compare Job 24.20: "The worme shall feele his sweetnes: he shalbe no more remembred."
Compare Job 21.26: "They shall sleepe both in the dust, and the wormes shall couer them."
Compare Isa. 51.8: "The worme shall eate them like wool."
Compare also Job 17.14; 19.26; Isa. 14.11.

4.2.133:   The dews of heaven fall thick in blessings on her!

The image of falling dew to represent blessing and prosperity is probably biblical.
Compare Gen. 27.28: "God giue thee therefore of the dewe of heauen, and the fatnesse of the earth, and plentie of wheat and wine."
Deut. 33.28: "A land of wheat, and wine: also his heauens shal drop the dewe."
See also Ps. 133.3; Deut. 32.2; 33.13; Prov. 3.20; 19.12.
See 1.3.57, above.

5.1.110–11:   Most throughly to be winnowed, where my chaff
               And corn shall fly asunder.

Compare Luke 22.31: "Simon, Simon, behold Satan hath desired you, to winow you, as wheat."
Compare Matt. 3.12: "Which hath his fanne in his hande, and wil make cleane his floore, and gather his wheat into his garner, but will burne vp the chaffe with vnquencheable fire."
Compare also Amos 9.9.
Being a churchman, Cranmer is probably using biblical imagery when he says he desires to be winnowed so that his purity and innocence might be made manifest. If Shakespeare had Luke 22.31 in mind, then he is closest to the Geneva Bible. Only the Geneva has "winow" at that text. All other versions (Tyndale, Coverdale, Matthew, Taverner, Great, Bishops', Rheims) have "sift." The "fanne" of Matt. 3.12 is the winnowing fan.

5.1.135–38:   Ween you of better luck,
              I mean in perjur'd witness, than your Master,
              Whose minister you are, whiles here he liv'd
              Upon this naughty earth?

A reference to the perjured witnesses that the clergy sought to condemn
Jesus to death.

Matt. 26.59–60: "Now the chiefe Priests and the Elders, and al the whole
Counsel sought false witnes against Iesus, to put him to death. . . . Many
false witnesses came, yet found they none: but at the last came two false
witnesses."

See also Mark 14.55–57.

Shakespeare's source for these words was Foxe's *Book of Martyrs* (*Acts and
Monuments*): "Do you not consider what an easy thing it is, to procure three
or foure false knaves to witnesse agaynst you? Thinke you to have better
lucke that way, then your maister Christ had?" (4.486)

[5.1.159–60: Ps. 91.11; Matt. 4.6; Luke 4.10; Ps. 34.7; Heb. 1.14.]

[5.1.160–61: Ps. 57.1; 63.8 (63.7, Geneva); 17.8; 36.7. Compare *King John* 2.1.14.]

5.2.73:   I speak it with a single heart.

Compare Eph. 6.5: "In singlenes of your hearts."
Compare Col. 3.22: "In singlenes of heart."
Compare Gen. 20.5, Bishops': "With a single heart, and innocent
handes."
Only the Bishops' has "single heart" at Gen. 20.5. Most other translations—Tyndale, Coverdale, Matthew, Taverner, Great—have "with a pure
heart." The Geneva has "with an vpright minde."
Compare also Acts 2.46: "With gladnes and singlenes of heart."
The closest parallel in Shakespeare's sources occurs in Foxe's *Book of
Martyrs* where Cranmer tells the king that "with all my heart" I am ready to
go to the Tower if you so command me. (4.486). Shakespeare's passage at
5.2.73 is spoken by Cranmer to the Council that intended to put him on
trial. Shakespeare is considerably closer to Scripture.

5.2.139–40:   When we first put this dangerous stone a-rolling,
              'Twould fall upon ourselves.

Prov. 26.27: "He that diggeth a pit shall fall therein, and he that roleth a
stone, it shall returne vnto him."

There are many proverbs to this effect, but Shakespeare is closer to Prov. 26.27 than to any of them. See Tilley S889. See also Ecclus. 27.25; Ps. 7.16 (7.15, Geneva); 9.15–16.

Although Shakespeare follows Foxe's account closely in this scene, he adds the reference to Prov. 26.27 to what he found in Foxe. No similar words occur in Foxe. After adding the reference to Proverbs, Shakespeare returned to following Foxe's account: "Do you thinke that the King will suffer this mans finger to ake?" (4.488)

5.2.148:   Ye blew the fire that burns ye.

Compare Ecclus. 28.12: "If thou blow the sparke, it shal burne."
Compare also Dan. 3.19, 22 quoted above at 1.1.140–41.
But Shakespeare probably had a proverb in mind. Tilley records the following proverbs:

F251: "Do not blow the fire (coal) thou wouldst quench."
C465: "To blow the coals."

Variations on these proverbs were frequent in Shakespeare's day. Compare *The Paradise of Dainty Devices:* "And to my hope I reape no other hire, / But burne my self, and I to blowe the fire" (sig. L.iii^r).

[5.2.206–7: See above at 2.1.59 and 2.4.22.]

5.3.22–23:   I am not Sampson . . .
             To mow 'em down before me.

A reference to Samson's slaughter of a thousand Philistines with the jawbone of an ass.
Judges 15.15–16: "And he found a new iawebone of an asse, and put forth his hand, and caught it, and slew a thousand men therewith. Then Samson sayd, With the iaw of an asse are heapes vpon heapes: with the iawe of an asse haue I slayne a thousand men."
See also Judges 15.8.

5.3.64:   *Limbo Patrum.*

A reference to limbo, the underworld abode of just souls not entitled to go to heaven because of having died before Christ or because they lacked baptism. A teaching based on tradition rather than on Scripture. Compare the reference to purgatory at *Hamlet* 1.5.11–13.

[5.4.11: Luke 23.46; Ps. 31.6 (31.5, Geneva); Ps. 31.17 (31.15).]

5.4.23–24:   Saba was never
              More covetous of wisdom.

A reference to the Queen of Sheba who heard of King Solomon's great wisdom and came to test his wisdom with "hard questions."

1 Kings 10.3–4: "Salomon declared vnto her all her questions. . . . Then the Queene of Sheba sawe all Salomons wisedome."

Shakespeare used the spelling of the Latin Vulgate, *Saba*, the spelling adopted by most English Bibles (Matthew, Taverner, Great, Bishops', Douay). Coverdale has "ryche Arabia" instead of "Saba." The Geneva has "Sheba" in the text, but "Saba" in both the page and chapter headings at 1 Kings 10.

5.4.33–35:   In her days every man shall eat in safety
              Under his own vine what he plants, and sing
              The merry songs of peace to all his neighbors.

1 Kings 4.25: "Iudah and Israel dwelt without feare, euery man vnder his vine, and vnder his fig tree."

1 Kings 4.20: "Iudah and Israel were many, . . . eating, drinking, and making mery."

Micah 4.4: "They shall sit euery man vnder his vine, and vnder his fig tree, and none shall make them afraied."

Zech. 3.10: "In that day, sayeth the Lord of hostes, shall ye call euery man his neighbour vnder the vine, and vnder the figge tree."

See also 2 Kings 18.31; Isa. 36.16; 1 Macc. 14.11–12.

For a parallel to Shakespeare's "every man shall eat . . . what he plants," compare Isa. 65.21–22: "They shal plant vineyards, and eat the fruite of them. . . . They shal not plant, and another eate."

These biblical texts about every man sitting in security under his vine and fig tree were frequently applied to the peace of King James's reign. Shakespeare was following that convention in this passage. In *The Gallants Burden. A sermon preached at Pavles Crosse, the twentie nine of March, being the fift Sunday in Lent. 1612* (STC 117), Thomas Adams said: "Our feare of warre is lesse then theirs. . . . *Wee sitte vnder our owne Figge-trees, and eate the fruites of our owne Vineyards*" (10).

In the second of two sermons entitled *Lamentations for the Death of the Late Illustrious Prince Henry,* preached on 15 November 1612 in the king's chapel at St. James (STC 20294), Daniel Price said that the gentlemen who attended upon Prince Henry "liued vnder the *Branches* of our *Princely*

Cedar: . . . *you* onely returne to your owne *Families* to drinke of your owne *Vines,* and to eate vnder your owne *Figge-trees*" (sig. F4r).

5.4.51–52:   His honor and the greatness of his name
             Shall be, and make new nations.

Gen. 17.4–6: "Thou shalt be a father of many nations. . . . Thy name shalbe Abraham: for a father of many nations haue I made thee. Also I will make thee exceeding fruitfull, and will make nations of thee: yea, Kings shal proceede of thee." (See also verse 16.)

That Cranmer's words in this passage are a reference to Genesis 17 can be seen from the sermons given on the occasion of the marriage of Princess Elizabeth, the daughter of James I, to Prince Frederick, the Elector Palatine of Germany. The wedding took place on Saint Valentine's day, 14 February 1613. *Henry VIII* was first performed sometimes between that date and 29 June 1613, when the Globe Theater burned to the ground during a performance of the play. In *Vitis Palatina. A Sermon appointed to be preached at Whitehall vpon the Tuesday after the Mariage of the Ladie Elizabeth her Grace* (*STC* 14990), John King, the Bishop of London, applied Genesis 17 to Elizabeth:

> that shee may take roote in an Honorable people, . . . and be set vp as a Cedar in Libanus, . . . as a Palme tree in Cades, . . . and as a terebinth stretch forth her branches, and those branches may bee the branches of honour and grace. . . . that she may be *the mother of nations, and kings of the people may come of her* (31–32).

The margin gives Gen. 17.16 as the source.

George Webbe, pastor of Steeple Ashton, Wiltshire, preached a sermon entitled *The Bride Royall* (*STC* 25157) on the day of the marriage, and in the "Epistle Dedicatorie" of the printed sermon, he likewise applied Genesis 17 to the marriage: "*That your Highnesse (right worthie Prince) may be as* Abraham, *a Father of many Nations*" (sig. A5r). The margin gives Gen. 17.4, 5 as the source.

There may also be an allusion to the colonization of Virginia in these words. Jamestown had been founded in 1608.

5.4.52–54:   He shall flourish,
             And like a mountain cedar reach his branches
             To all the plains about him.

Compare Ps. 92.11–12 (92.12–13, Geneva): "The righteous shall florish like a palme tree: and shall spread abroad like a Cedar in Libanus. Such as be planted in the house of the Lord: shall florish."

Compare Ezek. 17.22–23: "I will also take off the toppe of this hie cedar . . . and I will plant it vpon an hie mountaine . . . and it shall bring foorth boughes . . . and be an excellent cedar, . . . and euery foule shall dwell in the shadow of the branches thereof."

Compare also Ezek. 31.3: "Beholde, Asshur was like a cedar in Lebanon with faire branches, and with thicke shadowing boughes, and shot vp very hye."

Ezek. 31.6–7: "Vnder his branches did all the beastes of the fielde bring foorth their yong, and vnder his shadowe dwelt all mighty nations. Thus was he faire in his greatnesse, and in the length of his branches." ·

Shakespeare's primary reference seems to be to Ps. 92.11–12. He makes a clear reference to Ps. 92.11 (92.12, Geneva) at *Hamlet* 5.2.40 and *Timon of Athens* 5.1.10–11.

But the inspiration for the reference to Psalm 92 in *Henry VIII* may have been the sermons of the day, as can be seen from the sermons of Daniel Price and Bishop John King, quoted above at 5.4.33–35 and 5.4.51–52. Both sermons mention cedars having stately branches.

Appendix A
Index to Shakespeare's Biblical References

The following index to biblical references in Shakespeare's history plays is arranged according to the books of the Bible from Genesis onward. To make the index as useful as possible, I have included not only the principal passages in Scripture to which Shakespeare refers, but also all of the secondary texts that parallel them. These secondary passages are sufficiently similar to Shakespeare's principal references to warrant their inclusion in this appendix. None of the items cited throughout the text in small type within brackets, however, are included in the appendix.

Whenever the chapter and verse numbers in the Geneva Bible and the Psalter differ from those in the Authorized Version of 1611, the numberings of the Authorized Version are given in parenthesis.

The Old Testament

Genesis

1.16–17	*H8* 1.1.16
1.26	*H8* 3.2.441–42
2.8	*R2* 2.1.42
2.15	*2H6* 4.2.134; *R2* 3.4.73
2.15–20	*1H4* 2.4.93–94
2.24	*H5* 5.2.359–61
Chap 3	*1H4* 1.2.92–95; 3.3.164–65; *H5* 2.2.141–42
3.7	*1H4* 3.3.164–65
3.13	*R2* 3.4.75–76
3.17	*R2* 3.4.75–76
3.19	*Jn.* 4.3.10; *H5* 4.1.270–73
3.22	*1H4* 3.3.164–65
3.23–24	*H5* 1.1.29–30
3.24	*H8* 1.1.23
4.1–8	*2H4* 1.1.157–58

216

4.1–17	*Jn.* 3.4.79
4.4	*R2* 1.1.104–6
4.8	*1H6* 1.3.39–40
4.9	*Jn.* 3.3.64
4.10	*1H6* 5.4.52–53; *R2* 1.1.104–6; *H8* 2.1.68
4.10–11	*3H6* 2.3.15
4.11	*R3* 1.2.63
4.12–14	*R2* 5.6.43
4.15	*R3* 4.4.140–42
9.6	*R3* 4.4.184
10.2–5	*2H4* 2.2.117–18
13.10	*R2* 2.1.42
14.17–20	*1H6* 5.5.92–93
Chap 17	*H8* 5.4.51–52
17.4–6	*H8* 5.4.51–52
17.16	*H8* 5.4.51–52
18.16	*R2* 1.3.304
19.24	*R2* 1.2.8
20.5	*H8* 5.2.73
27.1	*1H6* 2.5.8–9
27.28	*H8* 4.2.133
27.46	*1H6* 1.2.26
30.2	*1H6* 5.4.63
31.50	*2H6* 1.3.188
41.1, 3	*1H4* 2.4.473–74
42.38	*2H6* 2.3.18–19; *3H6* 2.5.40
48.10	*1H6* 2.5.8–9
49.9	*1H4* 3.3.147; *H5* 1.2.109
49.17	*Jn.* 3.3.61

Exodus

3.2	*1H4* 3.3.35
15.16	*R3* 1.4.217
19.16, 18	*H5* 2.4.99–100
Chap 20	*R3* 1.4.197
20.5	*R2* 4.1.322–23; *Jn.* 2.1.177–82
21.22	*2H4* 5.4.12–13
21.23	*R3* 4.4.184
22.18	*2H6* 2.3.2–7
22.22–23	*Jn.* 3.1.108
25.18–22	*H8* 1.1.23
26.1, 31	*H8* 1.1.23
31.18	*2H6* 1.3.141–42
32.15–16	*R3* 1.4.196
32.32–33	*R2* 1.3.202

34.28	*R3* 1.4.196
34.35	*R2* 4.1.283–84
37.7–9	*H8* 1.1.23

Leviticus

18.16–17	*R3* 4.4.345–46
20.6	*2H6* 2.3.2–7
24.17	*R3* 4.4.184
26.8	*2H6* 4.2.35
27.30–32	*1H6* 5.5.92–93

Numbers

| 16.32–33 | *3H6* 1.1.161; *R3* 1.2.65 |
| 27.8 | *H5* 1.2.98–100 |

Deuteronomy

4.29	*R2* 5.3.104
5.17	*R3* 1.4.197
6.5	*R2* 5.3.104; *H5* 3.6.7–9
7.13	*2H4* 5.4.12–13
9.10	*2H6* 1.3.141–42
10.12	*R2* 5.3.104
10.18	*Jn.* 3.1.108
11.6	*3H6* 1.1.161; *R3* 1.2.65
14.29	*2H6* 5.1.187–88
16.3	*R2* 3.1.21
16.11	*2H6* 5.1.187–88
18.10–12	*2H6* 2.3.2–7; 5.1.187–88
19.21	*R3* 4.4.184
20.8	*3H6* 5.4.44–49; *H5* 4.3.34–36
20.10–14	*H5* 3.3.1–43
20.17	*R2* 3.2.129
21.8	*Jn.* 1.1.256
21.9	*1H6* 5.4.44; 5.4.52–53
23.21	*R3* 1.4.201–6
23.21, 23	*Jn.* 3.1.265–66
24.19–21	*2H6* 5.1.187–88
26.12–13	*2H6* 5.1.187–88
Chap 27	*Jn.* 3.1.181–82
27.19	*2H6* 5.1.187–88
27.20	*R3* 1.4.136–37

30.6	*R2* 5.3.104
31.3	*H5* 1.2.303; 1.2.307–8; 3.6.156
31.8	*H5* 3.6.156
32.2	*H8* 4.2.133
32.35	*R3* 1.4.199–200
32.35, 43	*R3* 1.4.215–19
32.42	*3H6* 2.3.23
33.13	*H8* 4.2.133
33.28	*H8* 4.2.133
34.7	*1H6* 2.5.8–9

Joshua

2.19	*3H6* 1.4.168; *R3* 3.4.92–93; *1H4* 5.2.20; 5.4.150; *H5* 1.2.97; *H8* 2.1.137–39
7.6	*Jn.* 4.1.110
10.12–14	*Jn.* 3.1.77–78
10.13	*Jn.* 5.5.1–4
17.3–4	*H5* 1.2.98–100

Judges

Chaps 4–5	*1H6* 1.2.104–5
4.4	*1H6* 1.2.55; 1.2.104–5
7.3	*H5* 4.3.34–36
9.13	*H5* 5.2.41
11.30–39	*3H6* 5.1.90–91
Chaps 14–16	*1H6* 1.2.33
14.8	*2H4* 4.4.79–80
15.8	*H8* 5.3.22–23
15.15–16	*H8* 5.3.22–23

Ruth

2.12	*Jn.* 2.1.14

1 Samuel

1.3	*1H6* 1.1.31
3.2–3	*1H6* 2.5.8–9
4.15	*1H6* 2.5.8–9
7.9	*2H6* 3.1.69–71
10.1	*3H6* 3.1.17; *R2* 1.2.38–41[a]

12.5	*2H6* 1.3.188
14.9	*1H6* 1.6.16
16.6	*R3* 4.4.151
16.7	*R3* 3.1.9–11; *2H4* 3.2.257–60; *H8* 3.1.145
16.13	*3H6* 3.1.17
17.4, 10	*1H6* 1.2.33
18.17	*1H6* 1.1.31
24.7, 11 (24.6, 10)	*R3* 4.4.151; *R2* 1.2.38–41ª; *1H4* 4.3.40; *2H4* Induction 32
25.24	*1H6* 3.3.42
25.28	*1H6* 1.1.31
25.37	*2H6* 5.2.50–51
25.39	*R3* 3.4.92–93; *1H4* 5.2.20; 5.4.150; *H5* 4.1.186–87; *H8* 2.1.137–39
26.9, 11	*R2* 1.2.38–41ª; *1H4* 4.3.40; *2H4* Induction 32
26.9, 16	*R3* 4.4.151
28.7	*2H6* 4.7.107–8
28.8	*1H6* 5.3.10–12

2 Samuel

1.2	*Jn.* 4.1.110
1.14	*R3* 4.4.151; *1H4* 4.3.40
1.14, 16	*2H4* Induction 32
1.16	*3H6* 1.4.168; *R2* 5.1.69; *1H4* 5.2.20; 5.4.150; *H5* 1.2.97
3.28–29	*R2* 5.1.69
3.29	*3H6* 1.4.168; *H5* 1.2.97
5.10	*1H6* 1.1.31
13.19	*Jn.* 4.1.110
14.17	*R2* 2.2.76
15.4–6	*1H4* 4.3.82–84
15.5–6	*R2* 1.4.23–28; *1H4* 3.2.50–54
15.12	*2H4* 1.2.35
16.13	*R3* 5.2.6, 30; *2H4* 1.3.103–4
16.23	*R3* 2.2.151–52
17.23	*2H4* 1.2.35
18.29, 32	*2H4* 1.1.67
19.21	*R3* 4.4.151
22.2–3	*1H6* 2.1.26–27
22.5	*2H6* 3.3.24; *3H6* 2.3.17
22.19	*2H6* 2.3.24–25
22.29	*2H6* 2.1.64–65; *2H4* 2.1.194

1 Kings

1.2	*H8* 3.2.100–101
1.33–39	*3H6* 3.1.17
2.32	*3H6* 1.4.168; *H5* 4.1.186–87
2.32–33	*R3* 5.1.23–24; *H5* 1.2.97
2.37	*R2* 5.1.69; *H5* 1.2.97
4.20	*H8* 5.4.33–35
4.25	*H8* 5.4.33–35
10.3–4	*H8* 5.4.23–24
10.7	*1H6* 2.3.7–10
12.11, 14	*1H4* 1.3.239
22.27	*R2* 3.1.21

2 Kings

18.31	*H8* 5.4.33–35
20.1	*H8* 4.2.1

1 Chronicles

17.24	*1H6* 1.1.31
21.1	*1H4* 2.4.463
28.9	*H8* 3.1.145

2 Chronicles

6.23	*1H4* 5.2.20; 5.4.150; *H5* 1.2.97
9.6	*1H6* 2.3.7–10; 2.3.68
10.11	*2H4* 4.1.213–14
13.15	*1H6* 3.2.106
18.20–21	*1H4* 1.2.152–54
18.26	*R2* 3.1.21
19.7	*H8* 3.1.100–101
32.24	*H8* 4.2.1.

Ezra

9.8	*2H4* 2.1.194

Esther

4.3	*R2* 5.1.49
9.25	*H5* 1.2.97; *H8* 2.1.137–39

Job

1.21	*2H4* 1.2.126–27
2.12	*Jn.* 4.1.110
3.3, 6	*Jn.* 3.1.87–88
3.5	*1H6* 5.4.89
6.12	*R2* 3.2.167–68
6.15	*H8* 2.1.128–30
10.1	*R3* 1.3.178
10.9	*1H6* 2.5.14; *2H4* 1.2.7
10.21–22	*1H6* 5.4.89
12.12	*2H4* 1.2.191–92
12.22	*1H6* 5.4.89
13.12	*1H6* 2.5.14; *2H4* 1.2.7
14.15	*R3* 4.4.51
16.16	*1H6* 5.4.89
17.6	*3H6* 1.1.42
17.7	*1H6* 2.5.8–9
17.11–12	*R3* 1.4.76–77
17.14	*R3* 4.4.385–86; *H8* 4.2.126–27
18.4	*R2* 3.3.82–83
18.6	*3H6* 2.6.1; *2H4* 1.2.156–57
19.25	*H5* 4.1.137
19.26	*H8* 4.2.126–27
21.9	*1H4* 3.2.10–11
21.17	*3H6* 2.6.1; *2H4* 1.2.156–57
21.25	*R3* 1.3.178
21.26	*R3* 4.4.385–86; *1H4* 5.4.85–86; *2H4* 4.5.115–16; *H8* 4.2.126–27
24.13–17	*R2* 3.2.36–46
24.17	*1H6* 5.4.89
24.20	*1H4* 5.4.85–86; *H8* 4.2.126–27
28.3	*1H6* 5.4.89
29.10	*R2* 5.3.31
31.6	*2H6* 2.1.200–201
31.15	*R2* 1.2.22–24
31.19–21	*2H6* 4.10.22–23
33.6	*1H6* 2.5.14; *R2* 1.2.22–24; *2H4* 1.2.7; *H5* 3.2.22
34.19	*R3* 4.4.51
34.22	*1H6* 5.4.89
34.36	*2H4* 2.2.47
38.17	*1H6* 5.4.89
39.19–25 (39.22–28)	*H5* 3.7.11–40
39.27 (39.24)	*2H4* 1.1.47
40.4 (40.9)	*R3* 1.4.217
40.20 (41.1)	*H5* 3.3.26–27

Psalms

1.4. (1.3)	*R2* 1.2.20
2.2	*R3* 4.4.151
2.4	*2H4* 2.2.143
2.9	*R3* 5.3.110; *1H4* 3.2.10–11
3.8	*2H6* 3.2.140
6.2	*2H6* 1.3.215
7.8	*H8* 3.1.100–101
7.15–17 (7.14–16)	*2H6* 2.1.182–83
7.17 (7.16)	*R3* 5.1.23–24; *1H4* 5.2.20; 5.4.150; *H5* 1.2.97; *H5* 4.1.186–87; *H8* 2.1.137–39
8.2	*1H6* 3.1.196
9.8	*H8* 3.1.100–101
9.13	*2H6* 1.3.215
9.15–16	*R3* 5.1.23–24
11.7 (11.6)	*R2* 1.2.8
13.3	*2H4* 2.1.194
14.8 (14.4)	*2H6* 2.1.182–83
17.8	*Jn.* 2.1.14
17.12	*1H6* 1.2.27–28
18.1 (18.2)	*1H6* 2.1.26–27
18.3 (18.4)	*2H6* 3.3.24; *3H6* 2.3.17
18.4 (18.5)	*R2* 3.1.34; *Jn.* 4.3.138
18.18	*2H6* 2.3.24–25
18.28	*2H6* 2.1.64–65; *3H6* 2.6.1
19.5 (19.4–5)	*3H6* 2.1.21–24; *1H4* 1.3.33–34
19.8	*2H4* 2.1.194
20.5	*1H6* 2.1.26–27
20.7	*1H6* 2.1.26–27
23.4	*1H6* 5.4.89
24.7, 9	*2H6* 4.9.13
24.10	*1H6* 1.1.31
31.4 (31.3)	*1H6* 2.1.26–27; *2H6* 2.3.24–25
31.6 (31.5)	*Jn.* 4.3.10
34.7	*R2* 3.2.60–62; *2H4* 1.2.164
34.13 (34.14)	*H8* 3.2.445
36.7	*Jn.* 2.1.14
37.15	*R3* 5.1.23–24
39.6–7 (39.5–6)	*H8* 1.1.223–24
39.8 (39.7)	*2H6* 2.3.24–25; 4.4.55
42.11 (42.9)	*2H6* 2.3.24–25
44.3–4 (44.3)	*R3* 1.4.217; *H5* 4.8.106–8
44.15 (44.14)	*3H6* 1.1.42
44.23	*R3* 1.3.286–87
48.13 (48.14)	*2H6* 2.3.24–25
49.7–10, 14	*2H4* 3.2.37–38

50.6	*H8* 3.1.100–101
50.19	*H5* 5.2.117–18
51.1	*1H6* 1.4.70–71; *2H6* 1.3.215
51.5	*Jn.* 2.1.182
52.1	*H8* 2.1.66
57.1	*Jn.* 2.1.14
58.4–5	*2H6* 3.2.76–77; *H8* 2.1.128–30
58.6 (58.7)	*H8* 2.1.128–30
59.6, 14	*3H6* 1.4.56
59.8	*2H4* 2.2.143
61.3	*R3* 5.3.12; *R2* 1.3.101–2
61.4	*Jn.* 2.1.14
61.8	*Jn.* 3.1.265–66
62.9	*R2* 3.4.84–86
62.11	*2H6* 3.2.140
63.6 (63.5)	*1H6* 2.5.21
63.8 (63.7)	*Jn.* 2.1.14
68.5	*R2* 1.2.43; *Jn.* 3.1.108
69.21 (69.20)	*2H4* 4.5.8
69.29 (69.28)	*R2* 1.3.202
71.4 (71.5)	*2H6* 2.3.24–25; 4.4.55
71.5 (71.6)	*2H6* 2.3.24–25
71.8–9 (71.9–10)	*H8* 3.2.455–57
71.16 (71.18)	*H8* 3.2.455–57
73.23 (73.24)	*2H6* 2.3.24–25
74.15 (74.14)	*H5* 3.3.26–27
75.8 (75.7)	*3H6* 2.3.37
77.9	*H5* 3.3.10
78.66 (78.65)	*R3* 1.3.286–87
80.5	*3H6* 5.4.74–75
84.6	*2H6* 2.1.68
89.14 (89.13)	*R3* 1.4.217
89.22 (89.21)	*R3* 1.4.217
89.32	*1H4* 1.3.239; 3.2.10–11; *2H4* 4.1.213–14
89.47 (89.48)	*2H4* 3.2.37–38
90.9	*Jn.* 3.4.108
91.1, 4	*Jn.* 2.1.14
91.11	*R2* 3.2.60–62
92.11–12 (92.12–13)	*H8* 5.4.52–54
94.1	*2H6* 3.2.140
94.3	*1H6* 1.5.9
98.2 (98.1)	*H5* 4.8.106–8
100.2 (100.3)	*R3* 4.4.51
103.15–16	*H8* 3.1.151–53
104.4	*1H4* 3.3.35
104.15	*H5* 5.2.41
104.26	*H5* 3.3.26–27
106.17	*3H6* 1.1.161; *R3* 1.2.65

112.4	*2H6* 2.1.64–65
Psalm 114	*H5* 4.8.123
Psalm 115	*H5* 4.8.123
115.1	*H5* 4.1.292–94; 4.8.106–8
116.3	*R2* 3.1.34; *Jn.* 4.3.138
118.8–9	*1H6* 3.2.112
118.9	*H8* 3.2.366–67
118.19	*3H6* 1.4.177
119.73	*R3* 4.4.51
119.105	*2H6* 2.3.24–25
125.1	*1H6* 2.5.102–3
125.5	*2H4* 4.5.183–85
127.4 (127.3)	*1H6* 5.4.63; *2H4* 5.4.12–13
132.4	*3H6* 1.1.24; *H5* 3.2.114–15
133.3	*H8* 1.3.57; 4.2.133
137.5	*H5* 2.2.33–34
137.6	*R2* 5.3.31
139.6–7 (139.7–8)	*2H6* 5.2.73
139.6–9 (139.7–10)	*H5* 4.1.167–69
140.3	*3H6* 1.4.112
140.9	*2H6* 2.1.182–83
140.10	*2H6* 5.2.36; *R2* 1.2.8
141.2	*H8* 2.1.77–78
146.2 (146.3)	*1H6* 3.2.112; *H8* 3.2.366–67
146.2–3 (146.3–4)	*Jn.* 3.1.7–8
146.4 (146.5)	*2H6* 2.3.24–25
146.9	*2H6* 5.1.187–88; *R2* 1.2.43; *Jn.* 3.1.108

Proverbs

1.20, 24	*1H4* 1.2.88–89
2.15	*2H4* 4.5.183–85
3.20	*H8* 4.2.133
3.33	*2H4* 2.4.327–29
4.14	*2H4* 2.4.327–29
4.19	*2H4* 2.4.327–29
6.23	*2H6* 2.3.24–25
6.30	*1H6* 2.5.21
10.6	*2H4* 2.4.327–29
10.7	*2H4* 2.4.327–29
10.19	*H5* 3.2.36–37
10.20	*2H4* 2.4.327–29
10.27–28, 32	*2H4* 2.4.327–29
11.11, 23	*2H4* 2.4.327–29
12.5, 6, 10, 26	*2H4* 2.4.327–29
14.10	*R3* 1.3.178
14.11	*2H4* 2.4.327–29

14.20	*H8* 2.1.128–30; 3.2.412–13
16.18	*R2* 5.5.88
17.17–28	*H5* 3.2.36–37
18.10	*1H6* 2.1.26–27; *R3* 5.3.12; *R2* 1.3.101–2
19.4	*H8* 2.1.128–30
19.7	*H8* 2.1.128–30; 3.2.412–13
19.12	*1H4* 3.3.149; *H8* 4.2.133
20.2	*1H4* 3.3.149
21.19	*1H4* 3.1.157–62
22.15	*R2* 5.1.32–33
23.13	*R2* 5.1.32–33
23.24	*R3* 3.4.99–101
23.34	*2H4* 3.1.18–19
25.13	*R3* 1.4.241–42
25.16	*1H4* 3.2.71–73
25.24	*1H4* 3.1.157–62
26.1	*R3* 1.4.241–42
26.11	*2H4* 1.3.95–99
26.27	*H8* 5.2.139–40
27.7	*1H4* 3.2.71–73
27.15	*1H4* 3.1.157–62
28.1	*1H4* 3.1.165
29.13	*2H4* 2.1.194
29.23	*R2* 5.5.88
30.15	*H5* 2.3.55–56

Ecclesiastes

1.2	*1H4* 5.3.33
2.17	*1H6* 1.2.26
5.1 (5.2)	*H5* 3.2.36–37
5.3–4 (5.4–5)	*R3* 1.4.201–6
7.30 (7.28)	*R2* 4.1.170–71
10.16	*1H6* 4.1.191–92; *R3* 2.3.11
12.8	*1H4* 5.3.33

Song of Solomon

1.4–5 (1.5–6)	*1H6* 1.2.77, 84

Isaiah

1.17	*2H6* 5.1.187–88; *Jn.* 3.1.108
1.18	*H8* 3.2.254–55
1.24	*1H6* 1.1.31

1.30	*R2* 1.2.20
2.12	*1H6* 1.1.31
2.22	*Jn.* 3.1.7–8
3.4	*1H6* 4.1.191–92
5.14	*2H4* 5.5.53–54; *H5* 2.1.61
6.3, 5	*1H6* 1.1.31
6.5	*1H4* 2.2.86
10.20	*2H6* 2.3.24–25
11.3–4	*H8* 3.1.100–101
11.6	*2H6* 3.1.69–71
13.13	*1H6* 1.1.31
13.18	*1H6* 5.4.63; *2H4* 5.4.12–13
14.11	*H8* 4.2.126–27
14.12	*Jn.* 4.3.122; *1H4* 2.4.337; *2H4* 2.4.333; *H5* 4.7.137–38; *H8* 3.2.371–72
14.12–15	*H8* 3.2.440–41
14.13	*1H6* 5.3.6
23.9	*1H6* 1.1.31
27.1	*H5* 3.3.26–27
27.5	*R3* 1.4.249
29.6 (29.7)	*H5* 2.4.99–100
30.20	*R2* 3.1.21
35.6	*2H6* 2.1.158
36.16	*H8* 5.4.33–35
38.1	*H8* 4.2.1
38.15	*R3* 1.3.178
40.6–8	*H8* 3.2.352–58
40.10	*R3* 1.4.217
42.16	*2H6* 2.1.64–65
45.11	*R3* 4.4.51
48.2	*2H6* 2.3.24–25
49.26	*3H6* 2.3.23
50.10	*2H6* 2.3.24–25
51.8	*1H4* 5.4.85–86; *2H4* 4.5.115-16; *H8* 4.2.126–27
51.9	*R3* 1.4.217
52.12	*H5* 3.6.156
53.11	*1H6* 2.5.21
54.4–5	*Jn.* 3.1.108
56.10	*2H4* 2.4.88
58.11	*2H6* 2.3.24–25
59.8	*2H4* 4.5.183–85
61.10	*1H4* 1.3.33–34
62.8	*R3* 1.4.217
63.1–3	*1H4* 3.2.135–36
64.8	*R3* 4.4.51; *2H4* 1.2.7
65.21–22	*H8* 5.4.33–35
66.24	*R3* 1.3.221

Jeremiah

2.34	*1H6* 5.4.44
3.4	*2H6* 2.3.24–25
7.6	*2H6* 5.1.187–88
10.16	*1H6* 1.1.31
13.23	*R2* 1.1.174–75
14.8	*2H6* 4.4.55
17.5	*1H6* 3.2.112
17.5, 7	*H8* 3.2.366–67
17.7, 17	*2H6* 2.3.24–25
17.13	*2H6* 4.4.55
17.17	*2H6* 4.4.55
20.14	*Jn.* 3.1.87–88
22.3	*2H6* 5.1.187–88
23.19	*H5* 1.2.97
23.23–24	*H5* 4.1.167–69
23.24	*2H6* 5.2.73
31.29	*1H4* 3.1.131
31.35	*1H6* 1.1.31
46.10	*3H6* 2.3.23
46.18	*1H6* 1.1.31
48.15	*1H6* 1.1.31
50.19	*1H6* 2.5.21

Lamentations

3.1	*1H4* 3.2.10–11
4.20	*R3* 4.4.151
5.17	*1H6* 2.5.8–9

Ezekiel

3.26	*R2* 5.3.31
10.4–7	*H8* 1.1.23
11.19	*2H6* 5.2.50–51; *2H4* 4.5.107
17.3	*R3* 1.3.263
17.22	*R3* 1.3.263
17.22–23	*H8* 5.4.52–54
22.25	*1H6* 1.2.27–28
28.13	*R2* 2.1.42
31.3	*H8* 5.4.52–54
31.3–8	*3H6* 5.2.11–15
31.6–7	*H8* 5.4.52–54
36.26	*2H4* 4.5.107

37.7–8	*H5* 4.1.135–37
38.22	*R2* 1.2.8
39.19	*3H6* 2.3.23

Daniel

2.21	*3H6* 2.3.37
3.19, 22	*H8* 1.1.140–41; *H8* 5.2.148
3.22	*2H6* 5.1.159–60
4.34 (4.37)	*R2* 3.3.101
5.27	*R2* 3.4.84–86
9.3	*R2* 5.1.49; *Jn.* 4.1.110
9.7	*2H6* 3.2.140

Joel

3.4	*1H4* 5.2.20; 5.4.150
3.16	*2H6* 4.4.55

Amos

9.1–3	*2H6* 5.2.73
9.2–3	*H5* 4.1.167–69
9.9	*H8* 5.1.110–11

Jonah

3.6	*R2* 5.1.49; *Jn.* 4.1.110; *2H4* 1.2.197–98

Micah

4.4	*H8* 5.4.33–35
6.12	*H5* 5.2.117–18
7.8	*2H6* 2.1.64–65

Nahum

1.15	*Jn.* 3.1.265–66

Zechariah

1.13	*R2* 2.2.76

3.10	*H8* 5.4.33–35
13.7	*2H6* 2.2.73–74

The Apocrypha

2 Esdras

9.38	*Jn.* 4.1.110

Tobit

8.8 (8.6)	*H5* 3.2.22

Judith

6.4	*3H6* 2.3.23
9.4	*Jn.* 3.1.108
9.7	*2H4* 5.3.101; *H5* 4.7.61–62

Wisdom

2.1	*Jn.* 3.4.108
2.3	*Jn.* 3.1.344–45
5.18–20	*2H6* 3.2.232–33
15.7	*H8* 2.2.47–49

Ecclesiasticus

2.4–5	*3H6* 3.1.24–25
5.11 (5.12)	*H5* 4.1.267–70
7.10	*R2* 5.3.103
11.27	*2H4* 2.2.47
13.1	*2H6* 2.1.191–92; *1H4* 2.4.412–14
13.22	*H8* 2.1.128–30; *H8* 3.2.412–13
18.14	*R2* 2.2.76
19.24–25	*2H4* 2.1.109–11
20.18	*Jn.* 3.4.108
28.4	*H5* 2.2.79–81

28.12	*H8* 5.2.148
30.21, 22, 24	*R2* 2.2.3–4
30.23	*R2* 2.2.3–4
30.23–24	*1H4* 3.3.11–12
31.28	*H5* 5.2.41
38.18	*2H6* 2.1.179
38.18, 20	*R2* 2.2.3–4
41.1	*Jn.* 3.4.25, 28
41.2	*Jn.* 3.4.25–36
42.16	*H5* 4.chorus.43–44
46.4	*Jn.* 3.1.77–78

1 Maccabees

3.56	*H5* 4.3.34–36
5.49	*H5* 4.3.34–36
14.11–12	*H8* 5.4.33–35

2 Maccabees

14.18	*H5* 4.3.34–36

The New Testament

Matthew

2.6	*R2* 4.1.99–100
2.16, 18	*H5* 3.3.39–41
3.7	*R2* 3.2.129
3.8, 11	*1H4* 1.2.102
3.12	*H8* 5.1.110–11
4.1	*R3* 4.4.418
4.1–11	*R3* 1.3.337
4.10	*2H6* 1.4.40
4.16	*1H6* 5.4.89
5.4	*2H4* 5.3.137–38
5.6	*2H4* 5.3.137–38
5.9	*2H6* 2.1.34; *R3* 2.1.50–53; *H8* 3.1.166–67
5.10	*2H4* 5.3.137–38
5.16	*2H6* 2.1.72–73
5.33	*R3* 1.4.201–6
5.37	*2H4* 2.2.131

5.44	*2H6* 5.2.71; *R3* 1.2.69; 1.3.315–16; 1.3.334; *H8* 2.1.64–65; 3.2.443
5.45	*H5* 4.chorus.43–44
6.8	*H8* 1.2.12
6.10	*2H6* 3.1.86; *H8* 1.1.209–10, 215
6.14–15	*H8* 2.1.64–65; 2.1.82–83
6.20	*2H6* 2.1.17–18
6.21	*2H6* 2.1.20
6.28–29	*H8* 3.1.151–52
6.30	*H8* 3.1.151–53
7.1	*2H6* 3.3.31
7.2	*3H6* 2.6.55
7.3	*Jn.* 4.1.90–91
7.7	*H8* 1.2.12
7.15	*1H6* 1.3.55; *2H6* 3.1.77–78; *H8* 1.1.158–60
7.17–18	*3H6* 5.6.52
7.24–25	*H8* 3.2.197
7.26–27	*2H4* 1.3.89–90
8.12	*R3* 1.3.326; *1H4* 3.3.37
8.29	*R2* 4.1.270
9.12	*2H4* 2.2.101–5
9.33–34	*1H6* 5.4.47–48
9.34	*Jn.* 4.3.122; *H5* 3.3.16
10.16	*2H6* 3.1.69–71
10.28	*R3* 1.2.47–48
10.34	*2H6* 2.1.35–36
10.38	*3H6* 4.4.20; *R3* 3.1.4–5; *R2* 2.2.79; *2H4* 3.1.55
11.21	*Jn.* 4.1.110; *2H4* 1.2.197–98; 5.3.138
12.24	*Jn.* 4.3.122; *H5* 3.3.16; 4.7.137–38
12.25	*R2* 4.1.145–46
12.33	*1H4* 2.4.428–29
12.34	*R2* 3.2.129
13.22	*Jn.* 4.3.140–41
13.25–30	*2H4* 4.1.203–7
15.19	*H5* 4.8.46
16.2–3	*R2* 3.2.194–95
16.18	*1H6* 1.5.9
16.24	*3H6* 4.4.20; *R3* 3.1.4–5; *R2* 2.2.79; *2H4* 3.1.55
17.2	*R2* 4.1.283–84
18.8	*R2* 5.5.108
18.10	*R2* 3.2.60–62; *2H4* 1.2.164; 2.4.335
18.35	*R2* 5.3.131; *H8* 2.1.64–65; 2.1.82–83
19.6	*3H6* 4.1.21–23; *H5* 5.2.359–61
19.14, 24	*R2* 5.5.15–17
19.18	*R3* 1.4.197
19.21	*2H6* 2.1.17–18
20.28	*R2* 2.1.55–56

20.30	*1H6* 1.4.70–71
21.6	*1H6* 3.1.196
22.13	*R3* 1.3.326; *1H4* 3.3.37
22.37	*R2* 5.3.104
22.60–66	*R2* 2.1.55–56
23.13–29	*2H4* 5.3.137–38
23.33	*R2* 3.2.129
24.19–20	*Jn.* 3.1.89–90
25.8	*1H6* 2.5.8; 2.5.8–9
25.30	*1H4* 3.3.37
25.34	*2H4* 2.2.23–24
26.14–16	*R2* 3.2.132
26.28	*R3* 1.4.189–90
26.31	*2H6* 2.2.73–74; 3.1.191–92
26.38	*R3* 1.4.74
26.39, 42	*H8* 1.1.209–10, 215
26.40–41	*R3* 3.7.73–77
26.41	*1H4* 2.4.277; 3.3.166–68
26.43	*R3* 1.4.74
26.49	*3H6* 5.7.33–34; *R2* 4.1.169–70
26.53	*R2* 3.2.60–62
26.59–60	*H8* 5.1.135–38
26.67	*1H4* 1.3.239
27.24	*R3* 1.4.272–73; *R2* 3.1.5–6; 4.1.239–42
27.25	*3H6* 1.4.168
27.26	*R2* 4.1.239–42
27.29	*3H6* 1.4.90–95; *R3* 1.3.174
27.33	*R2* 4.1.143–44
28.1–8	*R2* 2.1.55–56
28.9	*3H6* 5.7.33–34

Mark

2.17	*2H4* 2.2.101–5
3.22	*Jn.* 4.3.122; *H5* 3.3.16; 4.7.137–38
3.25	*R2* 4.1.145–46
4.24	*3H6* 2.6.55
5.9	*1H6* 5.3.10–12; *R3* 1.4.58; *H5* 2.2.123–24
6.14–15	*R2* 5.3.131
6.22–23	*H8* 1.2.10–12
7.21	*H5* 4.8.46
8.34	*3H6* 4.4.20; *R3* 3.1.4–5; *R2* 2.2.79; *2H4* 3.1.55
9.43	*R2* 5.5.108
10.9	*3H6* 4.1.21–23
10.14	*R2* 5.5.15–17
10.21	*3H6* 4.4.20; *R3* 3.1.4–5; *R2* 2.2.79; *2H4* 3.1.55

10.24–25	*R2* 5.5.15–17
11.25	*R2* 5.3.131
12.30	*R2* 5.3.104; *H5* 3.6.7–9
13.33	*1H4* 2.4.277
14.38	*1H4* 2.4.277; 3.3.166–68
14.55–57	*H8* 5.1.135–38
14.65	*1H4* 1.3.239
15.15	*1H4* 1.3.239
15.22	*R2* 4.1.143–44

Luke

1.28	*H5* 1.1.22
1.42	*1H6* 5.4.63; *2H4* 5.4.12–13
1.79	*1H6* 5.4.89; *2H6* 2.1.64–65
2.29	*Jn.* 1.1.23
2.29–30	*1H6* 3.2.110–11
2.40	*2H6* 1.2.72
3.7	*R2* 3.2.129
3.9	*3H6* 2.2.163–65
4.1–13	*R3* 1.3.337
4.2	*R3* 4.4.418
4.23	*2H6* 2.1.51–52
6.27	*R3* 1.3.334
6.27–28	*2H6* 5.2.71; *H8* 3.2.443
6.28	*R3* 1.3.315–16
6.37	*H8* 2.1.82–83
6.38	*3H6* 2.6.55
6.41	*Jn.* 4.1.90–91
6.44	*1H4* 2.4.428–29
6.49	*2H4* 1.3.89–90
7.8	*2H4* 5.3.111–12
8.14	*Jn.* 4.3.140–41
8.30	*1H6* 5.3.10–12
9.23	*3H6* 4.4.20; *R3* 3.1.4–5; *R2* 2.2.79; *2H4* 1.2.225–26; 3.1.55
10.3	*2H6* 3.1.69–71
10.13	*R2* 5.1.49; *2H4* 1.2.197–98
10.18	*Jn.* 4.3.122; *H8* 3.2.371–72
10.27	*R2* 5.3.104; *H5* 3.6.7–9
11.2	*2H6* 3.1.86; *H8* 1.1.209–10, 215
11.9	*H8* 1.2.12
11.15	*H5* 4.7.137–38
11.17	*R2* 4.1.145–46
12.33	*2H6* 2.1.17–18

12.34	*2H6* 2.1.20
13.6–7	*3H6* 2.2.163–65
14.15	*H8* 4.2.87–90
14.27	*3H6* 4.4.20; *R3* 3.1.4–5; 3.1.126–27; *R2* 2.2.79; *2H4* 1.2.225–26; 3.1.55
14.28–30	*2H4* 1.3.41–61
14.31–32	*2H4* 1.3.15–17
15.7	*1H4* 1.2.102
15.11–31 (15.11–32)	*1H4* 3.3.79–80; *2H4* 2.1.144–45
15.15–16	*1H4* 4.2.33–35
16.3	*R2* 3.3.77–78
16.19–31	*1H4* 3.3.31–33; *2H4* 1.2.34–35
16.20	*H5* 1.1.15
16.20–21	*1H4* 4.2.25–26
16.22	*R3* 4.3.38; *R2* 4.1.103–4
16.22–23	*H5* 2.3.9–10
17.13	*1H6* 1.4.70–71
17.29	*R2* 1.2.8
18.7–8	*R3* 1.4.215–19
18.10–14	*R2* 5.3.107–10
18.13	*1H6* 1.4.70–71
18.16, 25	*R2* 5.5.15–17
21.25–26	*R3* 2.3.38–44
Chap 22	*1H4* 2.4.277
22.31	*H8* 5.1.110–11
22.44	*1H6* 4.4.18; *H8* 2.1.32–33
23.34	*2H6* 4.4.38
23.43	*2H6* 5.1.214
23.46	*Jn.* 4.3.10

John

1.14	*2H6* 3.2.154; *H5* 1.1.22
1.29	*2H6* 3.1.69–71
2.4	*1H6* 1.5.13
6.63	*2H4* 3.2.257–60
7.30	*1H6* 1.5.13
8.44	*1H4* 2.4.225–26
9.10	*2H6* 2.1.72–73
9.15	*2H6* 2.1.72–73
9.18–20	*2H6* 2.1.95–96
9.24	*2H6* 2.1.72–73
9.26	*2H6* 2.1.72–73
9.41	*2H6* 2.1.69
10.1–16	*2H6* 3.1.191–92

10.12	*R3* 4.2.22–23
10.12–13	*3H6* 5.6.7
12.36	*1H4* 2.4.172
13.1	*1H6* 1.5.13
13.10–11	*R2* 4.1.170–71
13.18	*R2* 4.1.170–71
15.4–6	*R3* 2.2.41–42
15.16	*H8* 1.2.12
19.16	*R2* 4.1.239–42
19.17	*R2* 4.1.143–44

Acts

1.18	*Jn.* 5.6.29–30
1.24	*H8* 3.1.145
2.38	*H5* 1.2.31–32
2.46	*H8* 5.2.73
3.19	*1H4* 1.2.102
5.28	*3H6* 1.4.168
7.30	*1H4* 3.3.35
7.60	*Jn.* 1.1.256
8.18–20	*H8* 4.2.36
10.2	*2H4* 4.2.27
11.23	*2H6* 1.2.72
12.15	*2H4* 1.2.164
13.43	*2H6* 1.2.72
14.26	*2H6* 1.2.72
15.40	*2H6* 1.2.72
16.40	*H8* 3.2.366
21.8–9	*1H6* 1.2.143
22.16	*R2* 4.1.239–42; *H5* 1.2.31–32
23.12	*R3* 3.4.76–77
26.20	*1H4* 1.2.102

Romans

1.9	*2H6* 1.3.188
1.29	*1H4* 1.1.78–79
2.11	*H8* 3.1.100–101
2.21	*1H6* 3.1.129–30
2.21–23	*R3* 1.4.209–10
3.13	*H5* 5.2.117–18
3.20, 28	*1H4* 1.2.107
3.23	*2H6* 3.3.31
5.1	*R3* 1.4.249

6.6	*H5* 1.1.29
9.21	*H8* 2.2.47–49
10.14	*1H4* 1.2.152–54
12.14	*R3* 1.2.69; *H8* 3.2.443
12.14, 21	*H8* 2.1.64–65
12.18	*H8* 3.2.445
12.19	*R3* 1.4.199–200; 1.4.215–19; *R2* 1.2.38–41[b]
12.21	*R3* 1.3.334
13.1–4	*2H6* 3.2.285–86
13.3–6	*2H4* 2.1.51; 4.2.28
13.4	*R3* 1.4.199–200; 5.3.108, 113; *R2* 1.2.38–41[b]; 2.3.104–105; *Jn.* 2.1.87
13.4, 6	*R3* 1.4.220
15.1	*2H4* 2.4.57–59

1 Corinthians

1.4	*2H6* 1.2.72
3.10	*2H6* 1.2.72
7.20	*2H6* 4.2.16; *1H4* 1.2.104–5
9.25	*R2* 5.1.24
10.13	*Jn.* 5.6.37–38
10.24	*H8* 3.2.443
11.25	*1H4* 1.3.239
12.6	*2H6* 2.1.7
12.9–10	*1H6* 1.2.55
12.28	*2H6* 1.3.57
13.5	*H8* 3.2.443
13.8	*H5* 1.1.67
14.20	*2H4* 1.2.191–92
15.10	*2H6* 1.2.72
15.52	*2H6* 5.2.43
16.6	*R2* 1.3.304

2 Corinthians

4.4	*2H4* 2.4.335–36
5.14–15	*2H6* 1.1.113
5.17	*R2* 5.3.146; *H5* 1.1.29
6.6	*3H6* 3.3.51
11.13–14	*R3* 1.3.337
11.14	*Jn.* 3.1.208–209; *2H4* 1.2.165–67
11.24–25	*1H4* 2.4.165–68

Galatians

3.13	*2H6* 3.2.155
5.4	*1H4* 2.4.446–47
5.22–23	*H8* 2.4.107–9

Ephesians

1.11	*2H6* 2.1.7
2.20	*2H6* 1.3.57
4.1	*2H6* 4.2.16; *1H4* 1.2.104–5
4.2	*H8* 2.4.107–9
4.22–24	*R2* 5.3.146; *2H4* 2.2.149–50; *H5* 1.1.29
4.32	*R2* 5.3.131; *H8* 2.1.182–83
5.3–4	*2H4* 2.2.149–50
5.7	*2H4* 2.2.149–50
5.8	*1H4* 2.4.172
5.15–16	*2H4* 2.2.142; 2.4.362
5.16	*1H4* 1.2.217
5.18	*2H4* 2.2.149–50
6.5	*2H4* 4.3.14; *H8* 5.2.73
6.14	*2H6* 3.2.232–33
6.17	*2H4* 4.2.10
6.18	*1H4* 2.4.277

Philippians

1.8	*H5* 2.4.102
1.21	*H5* 4.1.180
2.3	*H8* 3.2.443
2.7	*2H6* 3.2.154
2.13	*2H6* 2.1.7
2.16	*2H4* 4.2.10
2.26	*2H4* 4.5.8
2.27	*H8* 4.2.1
3.17	*H8* 1.3.62
4.3	*R2* 1.3.202

Colossians

3.5	*H5* 1.1.26–27
3.9–10	*R2* 5.3.146; *H5* 1.1.29
3.12	*H8* 2.4.107–9
3.13	*H8* 2.1.64–65

3.22	*H8* 5.2.73
4.2	*1H4* 2.4.277
4.5	*1H4* 1.2.217

1 Thessalonians

5.5	*1H4* 2.4.172
5.15	*R3* 1.2.69; 1.3.334
5.27	*H5* 1.2.23

2 Thessalonians

3.9	*H8* 1.3.62
3.10	*2H6* 4.2.16; *1H4* 1.2.104–5

1 Timothy

2.6	*R2* 2.1.55–56
3.2	*H8* 1.3.61
3.6	*H8* 3.2.440–41
4.12	*H8* 1.3.62
5.21	*H5* 1.2.23
6.11	*R3* 2.2.107–8
6.13	*H5* 1.2.23
6.15	*1H6* 1.1.28; *R3* 1.4.195

2 Timothy

2.3–4	*R2* 4.1.99–100; *1H4* 1.1.19–21
2.24–25	*H8* 2.4.107–9
4.1	*H5* 1.2.23
4.8	*R2* 5.1.24
4.16	*Jn.* 1.1.256

Titus

1.8	*H8* 1.3.61
3.3	*1H4* 1.1.78–79

Philemon

20   *H5* 2.4.102

Hebrews

1.7   *1H4* 3.3.35
1.14   *2H4* 1.2.164
2.10   *R2* 4.1.99–100
9.5   *H8* 1.1.23
10.22   *H5* 1.2.31–32
10.30   *2H6* 3.2.140
12.14   *H8* 3.2.445
13.21   *2H6* 2.1.7

James

1.12   *R2* 5.1.24
2.11   *R3* 1.4.209–10
2.13   *H5* 2.2.79–81
2.19   *2H6* 1.4.25–26
5.11   *2H4* 1.2.126–27

1 Peter

1.2   *2H6* 1.2.72–73
1.18–19   *R3* 1.4.189–90
1.19   *2H6* 3.1.69–71
1.24   *H8* 3.2.352–58
3.7   *2H4* 2.4.60
3.9   *R3* 1.2.69
4.3   *H5* 2.2.42
5.3   *H8* 1.3.62
5.4   *R2* 5.1.24
5.8   *1H4* 1.3.125; *H5* 2.2.121–22

2 Peter

2.4   *H5* 2.2.123; *H8* 3.2.440–41
2.22   *2H4* 1.3.95–99; *H5* 3.7.64–65
3.10   *2H6* 5.2.40–42
3.12   *2H6* 5.2.40–42

1 John

2.15–17   *H8* 3.2.365

Jude

6   *H8* 3.2.440–41
7   *2H6* 5.2.36; *R2* 1.2.8; *1H4* 3.2.10–11

Revelation

1.16	*R2* 4.1.283–84
2.10	*R2* 5.1.24
2.27	*R3* 5.3.110
3.5	*R2* 1.3.202; 4.1.236
3.20	*2H6* 5.1.214
5.8	*R3* 5.3.241–42
5.9	*R3* 1.4.189–90
6.9–10	*R3* 5.3.241–42
6.14–17	*1H6* 1.1.29–30
7.9	*H8* 4.2.82, s. d.
12.9	*1H4* 2.4.463; *H8* 3.2.371–72; 3.2.440–41
17.4	*H5* 2.3.38–39
17.5	*H5* 2.3.38–39
17.6	*3H6* 2.3.23
17.8	*R2* 1.3.202
17.14	*1H6* 1.1.28; *R3* 1.4.195
19.9	*2H6* 5.1.214; *H8* 4.2.87–90
19.10	*1H6* 1.2.55
19.13	*1H4* 3.2.135–36
19.16	*1H6* 1.1.28; *R3* 1.4.195
19.20	*2H6* 1.4.39
20.10	*2H6* 1.4.39
20.11–15	*1H6* 1.1.29–30
20.12	*R2* 4.1.274–75
20.12, 15	*R2* 1.3.202
21.2, 10	*3H6* 5.5.7–8
21.8	*R2* 5.5.108
21.27	*R2* 1.3.202

Appendix B
References to the
Book of Common Prayer

Morning Prayer: *2H6* 2.1.64–65; *1H4* 1.2.102; *H8* 4.1.92

Evening Prayer: *1H6* 3.2.110–11; *2H6* 2.1.64–65; *Jn.* 1.1.23; *1H4* 1.2.102; *2H4* 2.1.194

The Litany: *1H6* 1.4.70–71; 4.4.18; *R3* 1.4.189–90; *1H4* 1.1.78–79; 1.2.102; *H8* 2.1.32–33

Communion Service: *1H6* 1.4.70–71; 1.5.9; *2H6* 1.4.40; 2.1.17–18; 2.1.72–73; 3.2.154; *3H6* 3.3.51; 5.7.33–34; *R3* 1.4.197; 3.5.41; *R2* 1.2.38–41ᵇ; 2.2.76; *Jn* 2.1.177–82; *1H4* 1.1.25–27; 1.2.152–54; *2H4* 4.1.203–207; *H5* 1.1.22
  Exhortation: *1H4* 1.2.102
  General Confession: *Jn.* 4.3.135–36

Baptism: *R2* 4.1.99–100; 5.3.146; 5.5.15–17; *Jn.* 2.1.182; *H5* 1.1.29; 1.2.31–32; *H8* 3.2.365

Confirmation: *1H4* 3.3.166–68

The Catechism: *1H6* 3.1.25–26; *2H6* 4.2.16; *R3* 1.4.197; *Jn.* 1.1.251–52; 2.1.177–82; *1H4* 1.2.104–5; *H5* 4.1.131–33, 145–46

Matrimony: *1H6* 3.1.68; *3H6* 4.1.21–23; *1H4* 3.3.164–65; *H5* 5.2.359–61

Burial Service: *Jn.* 3.1.344–45; 4.3.10; *2H4* Epilogue.13–14

Commination Service: *2H6* 4.2.16; *R3* 1.4.136–37; *Jn.* 3.1.181–82; *1H4* 1.2.104–5

(Prayer Book Calendar): *Jn.* 3.1.83–86

Appendix C
References to the Homilies

Of the True, Liuely, and Christian Faith: *2H6* 1.4.25–26

Against Swearing and Periury: *2H6* 5.1.182–83; *3H6* 5.1.90–91; *Jn.* 3.1.283–87

Against the Feare of Death: *R2* 4.1.103–4

Concerning Good Order, and Obedience to Rulers and Magistrates: *2H6* 3.2.285–86; 4.2.16; *3H6* 1.1.61; *R3* 1.4.215–19; 5.3.108, 113; *R2* 1.2.38–41ᵇ; 3.3.77–78; *Jn.* 2.1.87; 3.1.153–60; *1H4* 1.2.104–5; *2H4* 2.1.51; 4.2.28; *H5* 1.2.183–90; 4.1.131–33, 145–46

Against Whoredome and Vncleannesse (Against Adultery): *2H6* 4.1.71–72

Of Fasting: *1H4* 1.2.107

Against Gluttony and Drunkennesse: *R3* 3.4.99–101; *2H4* 3.1.18–19; *H5* 4.7.34–39

Against Idlenesse: *2H6* 2.1.68; 4.2.16; *1H4* 1.2.104–5

Of Repentance: *1H4* 1.2.102

Against Disobedience and Wilfull Rebellion: *1H6* 4.1.141–42; 5.1.9; *2H6* 2.1.68; 3.2.285–86; 4.1.71–72; 4.1.74; 4.8.28–31; *R3* 2.3.11; 5.3.108, 113; *R2* 3.3.88; 4.1.136–41; 4.1.234–35; 4.1.322–23; *Jn.* 2.1.87; 3.1.172–79; *1H4* 1.3.125; 2.4.337; 3.3.164–65; 4.3.40; 5.1.72–80; *2H4* Induction.32; 2.1.51; 2.4.333; 4.5.107; *H5* 1.2.183–90; 1.2.287–88; *H8* 3.2.371–72; 3.2.440–41

Bibliography

Works actually consulted or cited. Titles listed in the introductory comments on each play that are not included in this bibliography are those sources used by Shakespeare that can be found in Geoffrey Bullough's *Narrative and Dramatic Sources of Shakespeare,* 8 vols.

Works by Shakespeare

The Riverside Shakespeare. Edited by G. Blakemore Evans, et al. Boston: Houghton Mifflin, 1974.

The First Part of King Henry IV. Edited by A. R. Humphreys. The Arden Shakespeare. London: Methuen, 1966.

The First Part of the History of Henry IV. Edited by John Dover Wilson. The New Shakespeare. Cambridge: Cambridge University Press, 1968.

The Second Part of King Henry IV. Edited by A. R. Humphreys. The Arden Shakespeare. London: Methuen, 1967.

The Second Part of the History of Henry IV. Edited by John Dover Wilson. The New Shakespeare. Cambridge: Cambridge University Press, 1968.

King Henry V. Edited by J. H. Walter. The Arden Shakespeare. London: Methuen, 1954.

King Henry V. Edited by John Dover Wilson. The New Shakespeare. Cambridge: Cambridge University Press, 1947.

Henry V. Edited by Gary Taylor. The Oxford Shakespeare. Oxford: Clarendon Press of Oxford University Press, 1982.

The First Part of King Henry VI. Edited by Andrew S. Cairncross. The Arden Shakespeare. London: Methuen, 1962.

The First Part of King Henry VI. Edited by John Dover Wilson. The New Shakespeare. Cambridge: Cambridge University Press, 1952.

The Second Part of King Henry VI. Edited by Andrew S. Cairncross. The Arden Shakespeare. London: Methuen, 1962.

The Second Part of King Henry VI. Edited by John Dover Wilson. The New Shakespeare. Cambridge: Cambridge University Press, 1952.

The Third Part of King Henry VI. Edited by Andrew S. Cairncross. The Arden Shakespeare. London: Methuen, 1964.

The Third Part of King Henry VI. Edited by John Dover Wilson. The New Shakespeare. Cambridge: Cambridge University Press, 1952.

King Henry VIII. Edited by R. A. Foakes. The Arden Shakespeare. London: Methuen, 1957.

King Henry the Eighth. Edited by J. C. Maxwell. The New Shakespeare. Cambridge: Cambridge University Press, 1962.

King John. Edited by E. A. J. Honigmann. The Arden Shakespeare. London: Methuen, 1967.

King John. Edited by John Dover Wilson. The New Shakespeare. Cambridge: Cambridge University Press, 1936.

King Richard II. Edited by Peter Ure. The Arden Shakespeare. London: Methuen, 1961.

King Richard II. Edited by Andrew Gurr. The New Cambridge Shakespeare. Cambridge: Cambridge University Press, 1984.

King Richard II. Edited by John Dover Wilson. The New Shakespeare. 1939. Reprint. Cambridge: Cambridge University Press, 1971.

King Richard III. Edited by Antony Hammond. The Arden Shakespeare. London: Methuen, 1981.

Richard III. Edited by John Dover Wilson. The New Shakespeare. Cambridge: Cambridge University Press, 1968.

The First Folio of Shakespeare. (The Norton Facsimile.) Edited by Charlton Hinman. New York: W. W. Norton & Co., 1968.

Shakespeare's Plays in Quarto: A Facsimile Edition of Copies Primarily from the Henry E. Huntington Library. Edited by Michael J. B. Allen and Kenneth Muir. Berkeley and Los Ángeles: University of California Press, 1981.

Other Works Cited

Ackermann, Carl. *The Bible in Shakespeare.* N.d. Reprint. Folcroft, Pa.: Folcroft Press, 1971.

The Agony and the Betrayal. In *York Plays.* Edited by Lucy Toulmin Smith. 1885. Reprint. New York: Russell & Russell, 1963.

Anders, Henry R. D. *Shakespeare's Books.* 1904. Reprint. New York: AMS Press, 1965.

Arden of Feversham. *The Tragedy of Master Arden of Faversham.* Edited by M. L. Wine. The Revels Plays. London: Methuen, 1973.

Arden of Feversham. 1592. Reprint. Menston, England: Scolar Press, 1971.

Baikie, James. *The English Bible and Its Story.* London: Seeley, Service & Co., 1928.

Baldwin, Thomas W. *William Shakspere's Small Latine & Lesse Greeke.* 2 vols. Urbana: University of Illinois Press, 1944.

Bale, John. *John Bale's King Johan.* Edited by Barry B. Adams. San Marino, Calif.: The Huntington Library, 1969.

Berry, Lloyd E. "Introduction to the Facsimile Edition." In *The Geneva Bible: A facsimile of the 1560 edition.* Madison: University of Wisconsin Press, 1969.

The Bible. (The Geneva Bible.) Geneva, 1560, 1562.

The Bible. (The Geneva Bible.) London, 1582. Many other editions were consulted printed between 1576 and 1616, including six of the spurious "1599" editions.

The holie Bible. (The Bishops' Bible.) London, 1568, 1572, 1577, 1584, 1585.

The Byble. (The Great Bible.) London, 1553.

The Byble. (Matthew's Bible.) London, August, 1549.

The whole Byble. (The Coverdale Bible.) London, 1553.

Biblia. The Byble. (The Coverdale Bible.) 1535. Reprint. Folkestone, England: Wm. Dawson & Sons, 1975.

The Holy Bible . . . Made from the Latin Vulgate by John Wycliffe and His Followers. Edited by Josiah Forshall and Sir Frederic Madden. 4 vols. Oxford: Oxford University Press, 1850.

The Holy Bible. (Authorized King James Bible.) London, 1612, 1613, 1648; Cambridge, 1630.

The Holie Bible. (Roman Catholic Douay Old Testament.) 2 vols. Doway, 1609–10.

The Bible. *The New Testament. Translated out of the Latin Vulgat by John Wiclif . . . about 1378.* London, 1731.

The Bible. *New Testament.* (Tyndale's New Testament.) 1526. Reprint. London: Paradine, 1976.

The Bible. *The New Testament translated by William Tyndale 1534.* Edited by N. Hardy Wallis. Cambridge: Cambridge University Press, 1938.

The Bible. *William Tyndale's Five Books of Moses called the Pentateuch: Being a verbatim reprint of the edition of M.CCCCC.XXX.* Edited by J. I. Mombert. Carbondale: Southern Illinois University Press, 1967.

The Bible. *The Nevv Testament.* (Roman Catholic Rheims New Testament.) Rhemes, 1582, 1600, 1633.

The Bible. *The Newe Testament.* (Tomson's New Testament.) London, 1583, 1596, 1597, 1599, 1601, 1607, 1610.

The Bible. *The Revelation of Saint Iohn the Apostle.* (Junius's edition of Revelation.) London, 1599, 1600, 1607.

The Bible. *The Whole Booke of Psalmes. Collected into English Meetre, by Thomas Sternhold, John Hopkins, and others.* London, 1583, 1591, 1599, 1600, 1604, 1607, 1609, 1613, 1615.

The Bible. *Biblia Sacra.* (Latin Vulgate Bible.) Rome: Vatican Press, 1598.

The Bible. *Biblia Sacra.* 2 vols. (Henry Middleton's 3d ed. of the Latin Bible of Tremellius and Junius.) London, 1585.

The Bible. New Testament. *Novvm Testamentvm. Omne, Tertio Iam Ac Diligentius ab Erasmo Roterdamo.* (Greek and Latin texts in parallel columns.) Basle, Switzerland: J. Froben, March, 1519; 1535.

Birch, William John. *An Inquiry into the Philosophy and Religion of Shakspere.* N.d. Reprint. New York: Haskell House, 1972.

The Booke of Common Prayer. London, June 16, 1549; 1577?, 1591, 1603?, 1605, 1607, 1613.

The Book of Common Prayer, 1559. Edited by John E. Booty. Charlottesville, Va.: University Press of Virginia, 1976.

Brooke, C. F. Tucker, ed. *The Shakespeare Apocrypha: Being a Collection of Fourteen Plays which have been Ascribed to Shakespeare.* Oxford: Clarendon Press, 1918.

Brown, James Buchan. *Bible Truths with Shakespearian Parallels.* 1886. Reprint. New York: AMS Press, 1975.

Bruce, Frederick F. *The English Bible: A History of Translations from the earliest English Versions to the New English Bible.* Rev. ed. New York: Oxford University Press, 1970.

Bullock, Charles. *Shakespeare's Debt to the Bible.* N.d. [1879?]. Reprint. Folcroft, Pa.: Folcroft Press, 1970.

Bullough, Geoffrey. *Narrative and Dramatic Sources of Shakespeare.* 8 vols. New York: Columbia University Press, 1957–75.

Burgess, William. *The Bible in Shakespeare.* 1903. Reprint. New York: Haskell House, 1968.

Butterworth, Charles C. *The Literary Lineage of the King James Bible 1340–1611.* Philadelphia: University of Pennsylvania Press, 1941.

The Cambridge History of the Bible. Edited by S. L. Greenslade. Cambridge: Cambridge University Press, 1963.

Carter, Thomas. *Shakespeare and Holy Scripture.* 1905. Reprint. New York: AMS Press, 1970.

Catullus Tibullus and Pervigilium Veneris: The Poems of Gaius Valerius Catullus. Translated by F. W. Cornish. Loeb Classical Library. Cambridge, Mass.: Harvard University Press, 1950.

Cavendish, George. *The Life and Death of Cardinal Wolsey.* Edited by Richard S. Sylvester. London: Early English Text Society, 1959.

Chambers, Edmund K. *The Elizabethan Stage.* 4 vols. 1923. Reprint. Oxford: Clarendon Press, 1965.

————. *William Shakespeare: A Study of Facts and Problems.* 2 vols. Oxford: Clarendon Press, 1930.

Chaucer, Geoffrey. *A Concordance to the Complete Works of Geoffrey Chaucer and to the Romaunt of the Rose.* Edited by John S. P. Tatlock and Arthur G. Kennedy. 1927. Reprint. Gloucester, Mass.: Peter Smith, 1963.

————. *The Works of Geoffrey Chaucer.* 2d ed. Edited by F. N. Robinson. Boston: Houghton Mifflin, 1957.

Chronicque de la Traïson et Mort de Richart Deux Roy Dengleterre. Edited by Benjamin Williams. London: English Historical Society, 1846.

Constitvtions and Canons Ecclesiasticall. 1604. Reprint. Oxford: Clarendon Press, 1923.

Cooper, Thomas. *Thesaurus Linguae Romanae et Britannicae 1565.* Reprint. Menston, England: Scolar Press, 1969.

Créton, Jean. *Histoire du Roy d'Angleterre Richard: Traictant particulierement la Rebellion de ses subiectz et prinse de sa personne. . . . 1399.* Edited and translated by the Rev. John Webb. In *Archaeologia: or, Miscellaneous Tracts relating to Antiquity,* 20 (1824), 1–442.

Daniel, Samuel. *The First Fowre Bookes of the Ciuile Warres betweene the Two Houses of Lancaster and Yorke.* London, 1595.

Darlow, T. H. and Moule, H. F. *Historical Catalogue of Printed Editions of the English Bible 1525–1961*. Revised by A. S. Herbert. London: British and Foreign Bible Society, 1968.

Dent, Robert William. *Shakespeare's Proverbial Language: An Index.* Berkeley and Los Angeles: University of California Press, 1981.

Eaton, Thomas Ray. *Shakespeare and the Bible*. 1860. Reprint. New York: AMS Press, 1972.

Elson, John James. "The Non-Shakespearian *Richard II* and Shakespeare's *Henry IV, Part I.*" *Studies in Philology* 32 (1935): 177–88.

Froissart, Jean. *The Chronicle of Froissart. Translated out of the French by Sir John Bourchier, Lord Berners. Annis 1523–25.* Edited by William P. Ker. Vol. 6. 1903. Reprint. New York: AMS Press, 1967.

Frye, Roland Mushat. *Shakespeare and Christian Doctrine*. Princeton: Princeton University Press, 1963.

Fulke, William. *The Text of the New Testament of Iesus Christ, Translated ovt of the vulgar Latine by the Papists of the traiterous Seminarie at Rhemes. . . . Whereunto is added the Translation out of the Original Greeke, commonly vsed in the Church of England, With a Confvtation Of all Svch Argvments . . . By William Fvlke.* London, 1589, 1617.

Greene, Robert. *Groats-Worth of Witte*. Edited by G. B. Harrison. 1592. Reprint. New York: Barnes & Noble, 1966.

Greenslade, S. L. "Introduction" to *The Coverdale Bible, 1535*. Folkestone, England: Wm. Dawson & Sons, 1975.

Greer, C. A. "A Lost Play the Source of Shakespeare's 'Henry IV' and 'Henry V.' " *Notes and Queries*, 199 (1954): 53–55.

Hall, Edward. *The Vnion of the Two Noble and Illustre Famelies of Lancastre and Yorke*. London, 1550.

———. *Hall's Chronicle . . . Carefully Collated with the Editions of 1548 and 1550*. Edited by Henry Ellis. 1809. Reprint. New York: AMS Press, 1965.

Hall, Joseph Bishop. *A Plaine and Familiar Explication . . . of All the Hard Texts of the whole Divine Scripture*. London, 1633.

Harding, John. *The Chronicle of Iohn Hardyng. . . . Together with the Continuation by Richard Grafton*. Edited by Henry Ellis. 1812. Reprint. New York: AMS Press, 1974.

Henslowe's Diary. Edited by R. A. Foakes and R. T. Rickert. Cambridge: Cambridge University Press, 1961.

Herbert, A. S. (See Darlow and Moule.)

Holinshed, Raphael. *The Third Volume of Chronicles . . . first compiled by Raphaell Holinshed, and by him extended to the yeare 1577. Now newlie . . . augmented . . . to the yeare 1586*. 2d ed., variant 2. N.p., n.d. [1587]. (STC 13569.)

———. *Holinshed's Chronicles of England, Scotland, and Ireland*. 6 vols. Edited by Henry Ellis. 1808. Reprint. New York: AMS Press, 1965.

Homilies. *Certaine Sermons Or Homilies appointed to be read in Chvrches, In the time of the late Queene Elizabeth of famous memory*. London, 1623, 1676; Oxford, 1683.

Homilies. *The Seconde Tome of Homelyes, . . . set out by the aucthoritie of the Quenes Maiestie.* London, 1563.

Jonson, Ben. *Sejanus.* In *Ben Jonson.* Edited by C. H. Herford and Percy Simpson. Vol. 4. Oxford: Clarendon Press, 1932.

Jorgensen, Paul A. "'Redeeming Time' in Shakespeare's *Henry IV.*" *Tennessee Studies in Literature,* 5 (1960): 101–9.

———. *Shakespeare's Military World.* Berkeley and Los Angeles: University of California Press, 1956.

Kendall, Paul Murray. *Richard the Third.* New York: W. W. Norton & Co., 1955.

Kyd, Thomas. *The Spanish Tragedy.* In *The First Part of Hieronimo* and *The Spanish Tragedy.* Edited by Andrew S. Cairncross. Regents Renaissance Drama Series. Lincoln: University of Nebraska Press, 1967.

Lancelot du Lac. *Lancelot of the Laik: A Scottish Metrical Romance.* Edited by W. W. Skeat. 1865. Reprint. London: Early English Text Society, 1965.

Lodge, Thomas. "Trvths Complaint Ouer England." In *An Alarum Against Vsurers.* London, 1584.

Lusty Juventus. In *A Select Collection of Old English Plays.* Vol. 2. Edited by Robert Dodsley. 4th ed. 1874–76. Reprint. New York: Benjamin Blom, Inc., 1964.

Lyly, John. *The Complete Works of John Lyly.* 2 vols. Edited by R. Warwick Bond. 1902. Reprint. Oxford: Oxford University Press, 1967.

Mancini, Dominic. *The Usurpation of Richard the Third.* 2d ed. Translated by C. A. J. Armstrong. Oxford: Clarendon Press, 1969.

A Manual of the Writings in Middle English. 6 vols. Edited by J. Burke Severs and Albert E. Hartung. New Haven: The Connecticut Academy of Arts and Sciences, 1967–80.

Marlowe, Christopher. *The Complete Works of Christopher Marlowe.* 2 vols. Edited by Fredson Bowers. Cambridge: Cambridge University Press, 1973.

Mendl, R. W. S. *Revelation in Shakespeare.* London: John Calder, 1964.

Middleton, Thomas. *The Family of Love.* In *The Works of Thomas Middleton.* Vol. 3. Edited by A. H. Bullen. [1885?] Reprint. New York: AMS Press, 1964.

Milton, John. *John Milton: Complete Poems and Major Prose.* Edited by Merritt Y. Hughes. New York: Odyssey Press, 1957.

The Mirror for Magistrates. Edited by Lily B. Campbell. Cambridge: Cambridge University Press, 1938.

Misogonus. In *Early Plays from the Italian.* Edited by Richard W. Bond. 1911. Reprint. New York: Benjamin Blom, 1967.

More, Thomas. *The History of King Richard the Third.* In *The Complete Works of St. Thomas More.* Vol. 2. Edited by Richard S. Sylvester. New Haven: Yale University Press, 1963.

———. *The History of King Richard III and Selections from the English and Latin Poems.* Edited by Richard S. Sylvester. New Haven and London: Yale University Press, 1976.

Muir, Kenneth. *The Sources of Shakespeare's Plays*. London: Methuen, 1977.

Nashe, Thomas. *The Works of Thomas Nashe*. 5 vols. Edited by Ronald B. McKerrow. Oxford: Basil Blackwell, 1958.

Noble, Richmond. *Shakespeare's Biblical Knowledge and Use of the Book of Common Prayer*. London: Society for Promoting Christian Knowledge, 1935.

Nowell, Alexander. *A Catechisme, or First Instruction and Learning of Christian Religion*. London, 1570.

Sir John Oldcastle. See C. F. Tucker Brooke, ed., *The Shakespeare Apocrypha*.

Ovid. *The.XV.Bookes of P. Ouidius Naso, Entituled, Metamorphosis. Translated out of Latine into English Meeter, by Arthur Golding, Gentle-man*. London, 1603.

————. *Metamorphoses: with an English Translation by Frank Justus Miller*. 2 vols. The Loeb Classical Library. New York: G. P. Putnam's Sons, 1933.

The Paradise of Dainty Devices 1576: With the Additional Poems from the Editions of 1578, 1580, and 1585. Edited by Richard Edwards. Menston, England: Scolar Press, 1972.

Peele, George. *The Love of King David and Fair Bethsabe*. In *The Life and Works of George Peele*. Vol. 3. Edited by Charles T. Prouty. New Haven and London: Yale University Press, 1970.

Pollard, Alfred W., ed. *Records of the English Bible: The Documents Relating to the Translation and Publication of the Bible in English, 1525–1611*. 1911. Reprint. Folkestone, England: Wm. Dawson & Sons, 1974.

Pope, Hugh. *English Versions of the Bible*. 1952. Reprint. Westport, Conn.: Greenwood Press, 1972.

Rees, James. *Shakespeare and the Bible*. 1876. Reprint. New York: AMS Press, 1972.

Rowley, Samuel. *When You See Me You Know Me*. Edited by John S. Farmer. Tudor Facsimile Texts. 1912. Reprint. New York: AMS Press, 1970.

Sackville, Thomas and Thomas Norton. *Gorbuduc or Ferrex and Porrex*. Edited by Irby B. Cauthen, Jr. Regents Renaissance Drama Series. Lincoln: University of Nebraska Press, 1970.

Schoenbaum, Samuel. *William Shakespeare: A Documentary Life*. New York: Oxford University Press, 1975.

Shaheen, Naseeb. *Biblical References in "The Faerie Queene."* Memphis: Memphis State University Press, 1976.

————. *Biblical References in Shakespeare's Tragedies*. Newark: University of Delaware Press, 1987.

A Short-Title Catalogue of Books Printed in England, Scotland, & Ireland . . . 1475–1640. Compiled by A. W. Pollard, G. R. Redgrave, et al. London: The Bibliographical Society, 1926.

A Short-Title Catalogue of Books Printed in England, Scotland & Ireland . . . 1475–1640. 2d ed. 2 vols. Revised by W. A. Jackson, F. S. Ferguson, and K. F. Pantzer. London: The Bibliographical Society, 1976–86.

Sims, James, H. *Dramatic Use of Biblical Allusion in Marlowe and Shakespeare.* University of Florida Monographs. Humanities–no. 24. Gainesville: University of Florida Press, 1966.

Spenser, Edmund. *The Works of Edmund Spenser: A Variorum Edition.* Edited by E. Greenlaw, C. G. Osgood, and F. M. Padelford. 11 vols. Baltimore: Johns Hopkins University Press, 1932–57.

Spevack, Marvin. *The Harvard Concordance to Shakespeare.* Cambridge, Mass.: Harvard University Press, 1973.

Stow, John. *A Summarie of the Chronicles of England . . . vnto this present yeare of Christ 1575.* London, 1575.

Thirty-Nine Articles. *Articles wherevpon it was agreed by the Archbishop and Byshops of both prouinces and the whole Cleargie, in the Conuocation holden at London in the yeare of our Lorde GOD 1562 . . . touching true Religion.* London, 1593. (STC 10046.)

Thomas of Woodstock. *The First Part of the Reign of King Richard the Second or Thomas of Woodstock.* Oxford: Malone Society, 1929.

Thompson, Craig R. *The Bible in English 1525–1611.* Charlottesville, Va.: Published for the Folger Shakespeare Library by The University Press of Virginia, 1958.

Tilley, Morris Palmer. *A Dictionary of the Proverbs in England in the Sixteenth and Seventeenth Centuries.* Ann Arbor: University of Michigan Press, 1950.

The Troublesome Reign of King John. Edited by F. J. Furnivall and John Munro. The Shakespeare Classics. 1913. Reprint. Folcroft, Pa.: Folcroft Press, 1971.

The True Tragedy of Richard the Third, 1594. Oxford: The Malone Society, 1929.

Virgil (Publius Vergilius Maro). *Virgil.* Translated by H. Rushton Fairclough. 2 vols. The Loeb Classical Library. London: William Heinemann, 1916.

Virgil (Publius Vergilius Maro). *The Aeneid of Virgil.* Translated by C. Day Lewis. Garden City, N.Y.: Doubleday, 1952.

Walker, Alice. "The Folio Text of *I Henry IV.*" *Studies in Bibliography* 6 (1954): 45–59.

West, Robert H. *Shakespeare and the Outer Mystery.* Lexington, Ky.: University of Kentucky Press, 1968.

Westcott, Brooke Foss. *A General View of the History of the English Bible.* 2d ed. London, Macmillan, 1872.

Wilson, John Dover. "Shakespeare's *Richard III* and The True Tragedy of Richard the Third, 1594." *Shakespeare Quarterly* 3 (1952): 299–306.

Wordsworth, Charles. *Shakespeare's Knowledge and Use of the Bible.* 1880. Reprint. New York: AMS Press, 1975.

Index